THE COMMUNIST BLUEPRINT
FOR THE FUTURE

THE COMMUNIST
BLUEPRINT
FOR THE FUTURE

The complete texts of all
four Communist manifestoes
1848–1961

A Dutton **dep** *Paperback*

Introduction by
THOMAS P. WHITNEY

NEW YORK
E. P. DUTTON & CO., INC.
1962

CONTENTS

INTRODUCTION

I. *Preliminary*

On July 30, 1961 there was published in Moscow the *draft* of the new "Program of the Communist Party of the Soviet Union." This event received great attention in the world press—both in Communist and non-Communist countries. Despite its length—running to nearly 50,000 words—it was printed complete not only in *Pravda,* official organ of the Soviet Communist Party, where it took up nine pages, but also in *The New York Times* where it took eight. Editorial writers all over the world commented on the document, and the opinions they expressed were varied.

Some fell over themselves with praise. *Pravda,* for instance, declared warmly:

The draft Program of the Communist Party of the Soviet Union is a great political and theoretical Marxist-Leninist document of our epoch. In it for the first time in all the history of humanity there is advanced *a scientifically-founded concrete plan for the building of a Communist society*. Before our country there open thrilling prospects.

The New York Times took a somewhat dimmer view:

It is a curious document indeed that the Soviet Communist Party has issued as its new draft program. The hardy reader who works his way through the text will find mythology and fact intermingled in disconcerting fashion, boundless Utopian optimism separated by only a few words from admissions of persistent scarcity. The fact that the world is now paying a great deal of attention to this strange document is more a tribute to the great power of the Soviet Union than to any real intrinsic merits of the program as a political and philosophical contribution.

The Soviet Communist Party and its leadership have always been verbose—documents, speeches, diplomatic notes, official declarations and the like. If this new document has aroused so much interest, it is not merely because it is so lengthy. There are other good reasons for this interest.

The first reason is that the basic program documents of the Communist movement have sometimes had great historical significance. The very beginning of the Marxist Communist movement is dated from the promulgation by Karl Marx and Frederick Engels of the Communist Manifesto of 1848, the first of Marxist program documents. It would be difficult to overestimate the importance of this particular document. Its slogans have entered the language, and the line of logic and plan of action it puts forward have influenced all history since.

In the second place it is of significance that the recently issued draft Program is the first formal program the Soviet Communist Party has issued since 1919. The program put out in 1919 reflected, of course, the early phases of the Bolshevik Revolution and the circumstances of civil war of that time. When it was adopted, the Soviet regime was not a year and a half old and had had little experience in the practical affairs of state administration in peacetime. Repeated calls for a new Party program remained for decades without result.

For example, a new Party program was promised for the Eighteenth Party Congress which was held in 1939—but none was delivered. Work on a new program continued after the war. At the meeting in Poland in 1947 which established the "Cominform" one of the Soviet representatives there, Georgi Malenkov, then a member of the Soviet Politburo, told the delegates that the Soviet Central Committee was preparing a new Party program. He declared: "The presently effective program of the Soviet Communist Party has clearly become obsolete and must be replaced."

However, no new program was presented for another fourteen years. The Nineteenth Soviet Party Congress was held in 1952, after a lapse of thirteen years since the previous Congress, and instead of discussing and adopting a new program it established a committee, with Premier Joseph Stalin as its Chairman, which was to draft the new program and present it to the next Party Congress to be held, presumably, another four years later.

The next—Twentieth—congress of the party was held in February 1956. Stalin had died in early 1953, and there had been many changes. The chief feature of the Twentieth Congress was, in fact, the denunciation by Premier Nikita Khrushchev of the Stalin "personality cult," and the only action taken about the Party program was the adoption of another decree calling for the presentation of a new program at the Twenty-first Congress. The Twenty-first Congress was held in January 1959—but again there was no Party program.

So now, at long last, the new program has appeared.

Men have always been fascinated by visions and versions of Utopia. Many a thinker, before and after Plato with his *Republic,* Sir Thomas More with his *Utopia,* and Sir Francis Bacon with his *New Atlantis,* has devoted himself to describing the image and outlines of a perfect society. How many daydreams have been devoted to this theme throughout the ages! As the poet has written:

> Every mind holds, half beyond conscious thoughts,
> The vision of an enchanted landscape,
> Islands of the blest, an Atlantis lost in time . . .

There is apparently deep in the consciousness of every human being both hope and faith in the perfectibility of society. Some people project this beyond life into a Kingdom of Heaven, while others look for it on this earth. Among the latter are many Socialists, including that branch of the Socialist movement which adheres to the teachings of Marx as interpreted by V. I. Lenin, in other words the Communists.

It is one of the particular traits of the Marxist-Leninists, that while looking toward and working for the coming of a sort of heaven on earth in the form of that future society they describe as *communism,* they have always been careful to avoid giving any detailed picture of this Communist society. Yet there have been some aspects of it about which they have always been precise. These are among the fundamental principles laid down by Marx and Engels.

Under *communism* there will be no private property in the means of production; there will be no "exploitation" of any man's labor by any other man; people will work not because they are forced to but because labor has become for them the first necessity of life; all will work according to their abilities and be compensated according to their needs; the distinction between physical and mental labor will disappear and likewise the difference between city and country; and ultimately the state will "wither away."

These are broad generalizations but they are as far as the Marxist-Leninists have been willing to go—up till now. Claim-

ing to hold the belief that social development is determined
not by the will of men imposing itself on the scheme of
things, but instead by objective laws of social development,
they have always held to the principle that it would be a
grievous error to draw up a blueprint in total detail and then
to force things into that mold. They have always condemned
socialists who attempted to visualize a future society in full
detail as "Utopian." The shape of things to come, they have
held, will reveal itself in good time if only the general framework of a "dictatorship of the proletariat" with abolition of
private property in the means of production is established
and allowed to seek its own path. The Marxist-Leninists may
also have been aware of the advantages of deliberately leaving
the image of the future vague so that it could not be picked
apart by critics, and anyone could thus project his own dreams
into it.

It has been possible for the Marxist-Leninists to take this
position till now. But no longer. The Soviet regime has now
been in power not quite half a century. Its leaders have long
since proclaimed the arrival of the Soviet Union in a state of
social development known as socialism, the immediate historical precursor, in Marxist-Leninist definition, of communism. Its leaders have also declared that the arrival of the
Soviet Union into the state of communism was not far distant. Accordingly, it has been pretty obvious for some while
that so far as the Soviet Union is concerned the time has come
to talk about communism no longer in vague generalities but
in actual practical details—time to get down to brass tacks, so
to speak.

This is the most important single point of significance in
the new Party program. If before it was "Utopian"—in
Marxist-Leninist terms—to spell out in detail the plan for the
Soviet Communist ideal society of the future, now it has become a practical necessity for the Soviet regime to do this
because the future is almost here.

So now we have, for the first time, in this new Program
a comprehensive picture of the society which the leadership
of the Soviet Communist Party is planning to build in the
Soviet Union over the next two decades. At last it can be
studied and analyzed—and admired or criticized.

Here is the Soviet Communist "Utopia" set down on paper.
The Soviet Communists would, of course, resent the use of
the term "Utopia" to describe it. In this they have a point in

their favor. It is, after all, very different from the Utopias of the philosophers, most of which never got beyond the covers of the books in which they were described.

This "Utopia" of the Soviet Communists is already more than half built. It is sponsored by a ruthless and determined government which has made Russia into one of the two super-powers in the world, a government which has guided the construction of a rapidly growing industry second only to that of the United States, a government which has made Russia pre-eminent in space exploration and hurled the first human being into the cosmos. Most significant is the fact that this "Utopia" has been specifically designed not just for the Soviet Union but for the rest of the world as well. The Soviet Communists have never made any secret of the fact that they expect communism eventually to defeat or "bury" capitalism.

This "Utopia," in short, is designed not just for the Russian people—*but for you too.* For this reason alone the new Soviet Party Program is worth reading.

II. *Historical Background*

To put the new Soviet Party Program into the proper perspective it is first necessary to describe its whole ancestry consisting of the important program documents of the Marxist-Leninist movement which have preceded it. It can hardly be overstressed that the new Program is merely the latest in a series, that in form and content it bears deeply the stamp of its predecessors, and that it cannot be fully understood without reference to them.

All the program documents of the Marxist-Leninist movement have one common characteristic. They combine propaganda with an actual plan.

Their function as propaganda was well described by V. I. Lenin, referring to the 1919 Russian Communist Party Program:

A simple translation of our program will best answer the question what the Russian Communist Party, which is a contingent of the world proletariat, has accomplished. Our program will be very forceful propaganda and agitation material. It will be a document which will entitle the workers to say: "Here we have our comrades, our brothers. It is here that our common cause is being realized."

But to dismiss these programs as mere propaganda would be to miss their other function. They do represent practical outlines for action, setting forth both immediate aims and ultimate goals.

The original Communist Manifesto of 1848 declared forcibly: "The Communists disdain to conceal their views and aims. They openly declare that their ends can be attained only by the forcible overthrow of all existing social conditions."

This dual purpose of combining propaganda with an actual plan is not the only respect in which the basic Communist program documents are double-edged. They all outline basic theories and principles plus immediate practical steps for political action. All of them put forward, specifically or by implication, both the ultimate long-range goal of the establishment of a true Communist society—a "maximum program" —and also the immediate particular goals arising out of the practical needs and possibilities of the given time and place— a "minimum program."

A. *The Communist Manifesto of 1848*

The most famous of all Communist program documents is certainly the original Communist Manifesto written by Marx and Engels. Engels himself has described the genesis of the document. It was, as Engels recounted, published as the platform of the Communist League, an underground German workingmen's association. Marx and Engels were instructed by a Congress of the League, held in London in 1847, to prepare the program to set forth theoretical and practical principles for the movement. It was written in German in January 1848 and sent to the printers a few weeks before the French Revolution of February 24, 1848, which was followed by a revolutionary wave throughout Europe. The Manifesto was thus sown in revolutionary soil. It was widely read and circulated in Europe. Not till 1850 did it appear in English, and not till 1863 in Russian.

Engels has summarized what he regards as the "fundamental proposition" of the Manifesto which he credits to Marx:

That proposition is: That in every historical epoch the prevailing mode of economic production and exchange, and the social organization necessarily following from it, form the basis upon which is built up and from which alone can be explained, the political and intellectual history of that epoch; that consequently the whole history of mankind (since the dissolution of primitive tribal society, holding land in common ownership) has been a history of class struggles, contests between exploiting and exploited, ruling and oppressed classes; that the history of these class struggles forms a development in which a stage has now been reached where the exploited and oppressed class—the proletariat—cannot attain its emancipation from the sway of the exploiting and ruling classes—the bourgeoisie—without at the same time and once and for all, emancipating society at large from all exploitation, oppression, class-distinction and class struggles.

On this basis the Manifesto called for the "formation of the proletariat into a class, overthrow of bourgeois supremacy, conquest of political power by the proletariat" with the "forcible overthrow of all existing social conditions."

"The proletariat," declared the Manifesto, "will use its political supremacy to wrest, by degrees, all capital from the bourgeoisie, to centralize all instruments of production in the hands of the state—that is, of the proletariat organized as a ruling class; and to increase the total productive forces as rapidly as possible. Of course, in the beginning, this cannot be effected except by means of despotic inroads on the right of property . . ."

The Manifesto then outlined some specific steps which might be taken toward implementation of this general plan. They included such items as abolition of property in land, a heavy graduated income tax, abolition of inheritance, centralization of credit in the hands of the state through a national bank, centralization of means of transport and communication in the hands of the state, extension of factories and means of production owned by the state, establishment of equal liability of all to labor and establishment of industrial armies, abolition of the distinction between town and country, free education for all children in public schools and abolition of child labor in factories.

Proclaimed the Manifesto: "When in the course of development, class distinctions have disappeared, and all production has been concentrated in the hands of a vast association of the whole nation, the public power will lose its political character."

And it went on to say: "In place of the old bourgeois society, with its classes and class antagonisms, we shall have an association in which the free development of each is the condition for the free development of all."

"The Communists turn their attention chiefly to Germany," wrote Marx and Engels, claiming that "the bourgeois revolution in Germany will be but the prelude to an immediately following proletarian revolution."

This hope pinned on Germany, of course, is one example of just how far wrong even these two brilliant men could be. A similarly mistaken prediction of even more colossal proportions was their ringing declaration that "national differences and antagonisms between peoples are daily more and more vanishing . . ." and that "working men have no country."

The Manifesto concluded with its famous call to arms:

The proletarians have nothing to lose but their chains. They have a world to win.
Working men of all countries, unite!

It is notable that Marx and Engels said everything they wished to say in this world-shaking little document in about 12,000 words.

B. *The Critique of the Gotha Program of 1875*

"The Critique of the Gotha Program" written by Karl Marx in 1875 was not of itself a program document. Instead, it was Marx's criticism of the draft Program of the German Workers' Party, a group later to be known as the Socialist Workers' Party of Germany. The criticism of Marx was given rather short shrift, incidentally, by the Congress of this party when adopting its program. Nevertheless, the formulations contained in Marx's critique of the Gotha Program are so important to the Marxist-Leninist movement that no essay on the historical background of the new Soviet Communist Party Program should omit mention of them.

In the Communist Manifesto of 1848 Marx and Engels outlined some of the characteristics of communism as a state of social development, as they saw them. But in that document they did not define any of the transition stages that might be necessary between a social revolution in which the "proletariat" seized power and the actual realization of a state of communism. From the Communist Manifesto the impression could well arise that it was only necessary for there to be a social revolution and then the Marxist Kingdom of Heaven—

i.e., communism—would automatically be established, ready-made and complete.

In his "Critique of the Gotha Program," however, Marx, despite his general unwillingness to discuss in detail the Communist future, was considerably more specific:

> Between capitalist and Communist society lies the period of the revolutionary transformation of the one into the other. There corresponds to this also a political transition period in which the state can be nothing but *the revolutionary dictatorship of the proletariat.*

Here Marx reaffirmed once again his fundamental belief that the destruction or withering away of the state is fundamental for human freedom:

> Freedom consists in converting the state from an organ standing above society into one completely subordinated to it, and today also the forms of the state are more free or less free to the extent that they restrict the "freedom of the state."

Frederick Engels, in a letter of March 1875 that also discusses the Gotha Program, spoke out forcefully on the key Marxist thesis of "the withering away of the state":

> ... it is pure nonsense to talk of a "free people's state"; so long as the proletariat still uses the state, it does not use it in the interests of freedom but in order to hold down its adversaries, and as soon as it becomes possible to speak of freedom, the state as such ceases to exist.

This doctrine of "the withering away of the state," forcefully stated by both Marx and Engels, is a point which still haunts the Soviet Communists, whose Soviet state has done anything but "wither away."

In the *Critique* Marx spelled out some of the characteristics of the transition between capitalism and communism as he envisioned them. Thus, during the period immediately following the revolution, he declared, the individual worker would receive back from society, after necessary deductions for essential social services and administration, "exactly what he gives to it." Marx wrote:

> He [the worker] receives a certificate from society that he has furnished such and such an amount of labor (after deducting his labor for the common fund), and with this certificate he draws from the social stock of means of consumption as much as the same amount of labor costs. The same

amount of labor which he has given to society in one form he
receives back in another.

It is from this definition, and its further elaboration by
Marx that the Soviet Communists have drawn what they
describe as the fundamental principle of the transition period
between capitalism and communism in which they still find
themselves—the period known as "socialism." They phrase this
principle thus: "From each according to his abilities, to each
according to his work."

This principle contrasts with that which is supposed to
prevail in the era of communism: "From each according to
his abilities, to each according to his needs."

This slogan, in exactly these words, was advanced by Marx
in the Critique of the Gotha Program:

> In a higher phase of Communist society, after the enslaving
> subordination of individuals under division of labor, and there-
> with also the antithesis between mental and physical labor, has
> vanished; after labor, from a mere means of life, has itself be-
> come the prime necessity of life; after the productive forces
> have also increased with the all-round development of the indi-
> vidual, and all the springs of co-operative wealth flow more
> abundantly—only then can the narrow horizon of bourgeois
> right be fully left behind and society inscribe on its banners:
> From each according to his ability, to each according to his
> needs!

It is difficult to overestimate the significance of Marx's new
elaboration of his political theories as stated in this document. They lie at the heart of Soviet Communist thinking
about the present and future organization of their society.

C. *The Russian Socialist Program of 1903*

Marxism did not gain much of a foothold in the Russian
Empire until the 1890's. Even then the Russian Marxists
were scattered and poorly organized. At Minsk in 1898 there
was held, in secret, the First Congress of "The Russian Social-
Democratic Labor Party." This first congress lasted only two
days and was attended by only nine delegates.

In the years immediately following, the Marxist movement
grew despite Czarist repressions. Outside Russia, there were
talented Russian revolutionaries in exile, including Vladimir
Ilyich Lenin, working in support of the Marxist movement
inside their country.

Lenin and others succeeded in getting most Russian Marxist groups together to hold a Second Congress in July and August 1903, in Brussels and in London. The principal business of this gathering included both the adoption of party statutes and the adoption of a formal party program.

The program actually adopted in August 1903 at this Second Congress of the Russian Social-Democratic Labor Party was written by several Russian Marxist leaders, in particular Georgi V. Plekhanov and Lenin. It was published long before the Congress in draft form in the party paper, *Iskra,* and was widely discussed by Russian Marxists. Its text, as finally adopted, reflected in some measure the conflict in Russian Marxist thinking which subsequently led, at this same Congress, to the never-healed split of the Party into the factions of the Bolsheviks ("the majority faction") and the Mensheviks ("minority faction") In some respects the program was a compromise formulation. For the most part, however, it appears to have been based largely on the more extreme—Bolshevik—thinking, and Lenin found it acceptable.

The document is short, amounting to about 2,000 words. It begins with a declaration that Russian social-democracy constitutes "one of the detachments of the universal army of the proletariat" pursuing the same ultimate goal as Social-Democrats of all countries—social revolution.

There is an extensive section of the program devoted to a restatement of basic Marxist revolutionary theory and a call for "the social revolution of the proletariat."

It declared: "A necessary condition for this social revolution is the dictatorship of the proletariat, i.e., the conquering by the proletariat of such political power as would enable it to crush any resistance offered by the exploiters."

The program went on to make the point that although in Russia "capitalism has already become the dominant mode of production," there still remained many vestiges of pre-capitalist ways which hinder economic progress in the greatest degree.

"The first and immediate task," said the program, "put before itself by the Russian Social-Democratic Labor Party is to overthrow the tsarist monarchy and to create a democratic republic whose constitution would guarantee the following": a unicameral parliament, concentrating all state power in its hands, elected every two years by universal, secret suffrage; local self-government; unlimited freedom of conscience, speech, press, assembly, strikes and trade unions; freedom of movement and crafts; destruction of class distinctions and equality of all before the law; the right of education, etc. in one's native language; the right of self-determination for all nations making up the state; the right to call officials to account through the system of justice; the replacement of a permanent army with a universal arming of the people; separation of church and state; free and obligatory education of all up to the age of sixteen and free food, clothing and educational aids for poor children.

It also called for the repeal of all direct taxes and establishment of a progressive tax on incomes and inheritances.

The program went on to demand a long list of measures, drastic and far-reaching for the Russia of those times, for the protection of workers. For the peasants it demanded both abolition of payments still being exacted from them as a result of the liberation from serfdom and other drastic measures which would have involved confiscation of the lands of the church, of the royal family, and perhaps of the nobility as well.

The program promised support to every opposition and revolutionary movement directed against the existing order, but at the same time it rejected "all reformist projects which look toward the widening or strengthening of the guardianship of the police and bureaucracy over the laboring classes."

It concluded: "On its own part, the Russian Social-Democratic Labor Party is firmly convinced that a full, consistent, and thorough realization of the indicated political and social changes can only be attained by the overthrow of autocracy and by the convocation of a Constituent Assembly freely elected by the entire people."

The 1903 Program remained the official program of the Russian Bolsheviks (who later renounced the name of Social-Democrats in favor of the term Communists) right up to and after the Bolshevik seizure of power in the October Revolution of 1917.

D. *The 1919 Russian Communist Party Program*

Even before the Bolshevik Revolution in late 1917 the 1903 Party Program had in part become obsolete. Therefore it was at the Eighth Congress of the Party in March 1919 that a new program was adopted. It is 6,000 words or so in length. Early

1919 was a period in which boundless revolutionary enthusiasm among Communists combined with a wave of revolutionary unrest on the continent after World War I. It was a time in Russia in which the most drastic measures aimed at destroying the old social order were mingled with anarchy and the brutality and hardship of civil war to produce that state of affairs known to history as "war communism." At that time, for Lenin and his followers, the world revolution, the coming of communism, and the withering away of the state were not remote goals but imminent events. The new program bore the imprint of this psychology. Its first paragraph declared: ". . . there had begun the era of world-wide, proletarian, Communist revolution."

The 1919 Program took over from the 1903 Program two pages of basic theoretical statements harking back to the Communist Manifesto. Following these, Lenin, who guided the composition of this document, introduced his thesis of "imperialism as the highest and last stage of capitalism"—imperialism which, he claimed, gives rise to imperialist wars which lead straight to world revolution.

The imperialist war, said the program, could not be ended with a stable peace; it is being transformed into a civil war of the exploited masses against the bourgeoisie.

There followed a bitter attack against Western European socialists who pursued non-violent and constitutional courses of action in efforts to achieve social gains through "opportunism and social-chauvinism."

The program took up the sharp limitations the new Soviet state had already imposed on the civil rights and freedoms won by Russians for the first time in the October Revolution of 1917 in which Czarism was overthrown.

The aim of the Party of the proletariat consists in . . . explaining that deprivation of political rights and any kind of limitation of freedom are necessary as temporary measures in order to defeat the attempts of the exploiters to retain or reestablish their privileges. With the disappearance of the possibility of the exploitation of one human being by another, the necessity for these measures will also gradually disappear, and the Party will aim to reduce and completely abolish them.

Said one of the program's platforms for women: "The Party's aim is not to limit itself to the formal proclamation of woman's equality, but to liberate woman from all burdens of antiquated methods of housekeeping, by replacing them by house-communes, public kitchens, central laundries, nurseries, etc."

It called for a struggle against bureaucracy and declared that systematic fulfillment of the proposed measures would lead to "the abolition of state authority."

The program called for the reform of justice to "change the character of punishment"—wider use of suspended sentences, public condemnations, obligatory labor under conditions of freedom, replacement of prisons with reform institutions.

In education the program demanded free and obligatory education for all to the age of seventeen with free food, clothes and textbooks. It called for the broadest organization of atheistic propaganda.

In the economic field it demanded the completion of the expropriation of the bourgeoisie.

"All possible increase of the productive forces of the country," said the program, "must be considered the fundamental and principal point upon which the economic policy of the Soviet Government is based."

Calling for maximum centralization of production, the program at the same time suggested turning over the entire management of the economy to the trade unions. It demanded as well the total mobilization of the population in order to carry out certain kinds of public works.

While striving toward equal remuneration of labor and to realize communism, the Soviet Government does not regard the immediate realization of such equality possible at the moment, when only the first steps are being taken toward replacing capitalism by communism.

In the agricultural field the program announced support for state-owned farms, for agricultural cooperatives, and for agricultural communes. The program said, however, that since small-scale peasant farms would continue long to exist in Russia measures must be taken to increase their foodstuff production.

The program announced the intent of the government to continue to replace trade with government distribution of products, to organize the population into consumer communes capable of distribution of all products. For the time being, the program admitted, the destruction of money was not possible, but the Party would carry out measures to prepare for the destruction of money.

In labor protection the program announced the putting into effect of the full 1903 labor program and its extension to include such additional benefits as full month vacations with pay. But, admitted the program, war needs had forced the government to make exceptions from its new labor laws. In public health the program called for the assurance of free medical aid to all.

The Russian Communist Party Program of 1919 was almost completely out of date in little less than a year after it was enacted. A long list of items in it were discarded or never realized. World revolution did not materialize. Russians never got back their temporarily restricted civil liberties. Russian women did not take to communal homes. The trade unions did not take over the administration of industry. The state did not disappear. The proposed reforms in criminal justice didn't last. Free and obligatory education for all children to the age of seventeen has probably not even yet been fully realized, and all Soviet workers do not get a full month's vacation with pay, even today. There is no equality of pay, and money has not been destroyed. Nor has a system of distribution through consumer communes replaced trade.

Nevertheless, the Soviet regime remained in power and developed the productive forces of the country—the item in this program called the "chief and basic thing"—on a grandiose scale. In these senses the program was fulfilled. It is interesting reading, revealing in its own way of the frequently vast differences between dreams and reality.

E. *The 1928 Program of the Communist International*

Although the Soviet Communist Party issued no new program for itself between 1919 and 1961, there was an official program issued for international Communism during this period which to some extent filled this gap. The Third International—often known as the Comintern—came into being under Soviet sponsorship in March 1919. At its Fifth Congress in 1924 it adopted a draft program and this program was officially adopted in final form at its Sixth Congress in 1928.

It is a lengthy document, taking up nearly eighty pages in one of its English editions. It restates international communism's theory, strategy and tactics in the light of the formal establishment of the Soviet regime in the Soviet Union, the absence of any world revolution following World War I, and the recession of the postwar revolutionary upsurge on the Continent and the other political circumstances of the mid-1920's.

This was the first among Marxist-Leninist program documents to direct major attention to the overseas colonies of European powers. In fact, it equates "the masses of the people in the colonies, marching under the leadership and the hegemony of the international revolutionary proletariat movement" with "the workers of the capitalist states" as the "two most revolutionary forces" in revolt against world capitalism.

Like all the Marxist-Leninist programs it foresaw the immediate destruction of capitalism and imperialism: "the capitalist system as a whole is approaching its final collapse."

Pinpointing the United States as the Communist movement's public enemy No. One, the Comintern program predicted "another world war, the destructiveness of which will increase proportionately to the progress achieved in the furiously developing technique of war." With great frankness it proclaimed the aim of the Communist movement to be a world "proletarian" dictatorship—"a World Union of Soviet Socialist Republics uniting the whole of mankind under the hegemony of the international proletariat organized as a State." It specifically denounced any idea that a bourgeois state could be taken over by the Communist movement through capturing a parliamentary majority.

It dealt at length and in great detail with specifiic programs of the Communist movement, both in states in which it should be able to seize power and in the Soviet Union where it was already in power. It declared that the world proletariat must view the U.S.S.R. as "a country that is really its own" and "facilitate the success of the work of Socialist construction in the U.S.S.R. and defend it against the attacks of the capitalist powers by all the means in its power."

With such phraseology the Comintern program revealed the chief characteristic of the international Communist movement in this new era—its domination by the newly established Soviet Union. It was therefore natural that this program should devote major attention to attacks on Social-Democrats of Western Europe and elsewhere who refused to subordinate their policies and activities to control by Moscow.

F. *The Statement of 81 Communist Parties of 1960*

In the post-Stalin era there were twice held under Soviet sponsorship large-scale meetings of Communist Party representatives from many different countries which adopted highly generalized declarations on the international situation. These cannot properly be called formal program documents, but they shared some of the characteristics of such formal programs.

The first of these two documents was a "Declaration and Peace Manifesto" adopted in 1957. The second of these was entitled: "Statement of 81 Communist and Workers' Parties Meeting in Moscow, U.S.S.R. in 1960."

In the background of these two documents was the continuing conflict within the international Communist movement between the relatively rigid and "dogmatic" approach of the Chinese Communist leadership toward both internal and international affairs and the relatively more flexible and pragmatic views of the post-Stalin leadership in the Soviet Union. In this sense the declarations of 1957 and 1960 both represent in some degree a compromise between these two views, although, generally speaking, it would appear that it was the Soviet attitude which generally prevailed despite considerable resistance to the Soviet views on the part of elements in the Communist movement which are often termed "Stalinist"—conservative and rigidly dogmatic elements which are evidently in complete control of the Chinese and Albanian Communist parties, and which are strongly influential in a number of Asian and African Communist organizations and still present in some force in the Soviet Union as well.

The basic question of principle at stake in this controversy is that of the "fatal inevitability of war" in the modern era and the concomitant question of how actively aggressive Communist countries should be in their policies toward non-Communist countries.

It is clear that the Soviet leadership, supported by many other parties, favors a tactically more flexible and "softer" line involving, as they claim, less risk of thermonuclear war. The more Stalinist elements, in particular the Chinese Communists, favor much more militant policies which take into account the real risk of a thermonuclear war.

Proclaimed the 1960 declaration: "It is the principal characteristic of our time that the world socialist system is becoming the decisive factor in the development of society." Citing the spread of Communist rule in the postwar period to numerous countries of Eastern Europe and Asia and also the economic and scientific triumphs of the Soviet Union, the declaration claimed that the spread of communism throughout the world cannot be stopped. Like all of the preceding program documents this declaration predicted "complete victory for socialists with the entire system."

But the proclamation announced in what was apparently its main point of emphasis: "War is not fatally inevitable . . . The time has come when the attempts of the imperialist aggressors to start a world war can be curbed . . . The important thing is to curb the aggressors in time to prevent war, and not to let it break out . . . The policy of peaceful co-existence meets the basic interests of all peoples, of all who want no cruel wars and seek durable peace."

It is thus worth noting that although the contemporary Soviet view that a new world war is not "fatally inevitable" has been adopted as the official international Communist line, there is no renunciation of the concept of worldwide socialist revolution and communism.

III. *The New 1961 Program: An Analysis*

The new 1961 Draft Program is not easy to comprehend and digest. It makes its own obstacles. It is unnecessarily verbose. The slow turgidity of its plodding prose is lacquered over with the gloss of high-flung pseudo-inspirational rhetoric.

As with all Communist documents it cannot be understood without some knowledge of both Soviet reality and the Communist jargon in which proper semantic meanings so often become reversed. Let us take one example.

The program says: "The October Revolution smashed the chains of national oppression; it proclaimed and put into effect the right of nations to self-determination, up to and including the right to secede."

Literally understood this means that any one of the nationalities making up the Soviet Union has at any time the right to secede from the Soviet Union—a "right" inscribed in these same terms in the Soviet Constitution. To understand what this "right to secede" actually means one has to keep in mind that any move toward secession from the U.S.S.R. on the part of any leader of any of the Soviet republics has always been equated with treason. Many individual members of minority nationalities in the Soviet Union were physically liquidated on suspicion of sponsoring a secession movement. There were even some entire nationalities that were deported *en masse* because they failed to show enthusiasm for the Soviet system. Another illustration of this "right to secede" is the infamous case of the abortive revolution in Hungary in 1956, which was crushed by the Soviets when the new government of that country, nominally an independent nation, showed a desire to leave the "Socialist camp" and become a "neutral."

However, in making an analysis of the program it is all too easy to get bogged down in that first section dealing with theory and international affairs and to become fascinated with the way in which many penetrating observations and clever outlines of tactics for international communism are commingled with outdated theories, half truths, misstatements, and distorted word pictures of reality.

For example, we find that one of the program's first paragraphs restates some fundamental theses of Marxism going back in part to the Communist Manifesto of 1848. Thus the program declares that under capitalism: "The exploitation of the working class and all working people is becoming more and more marked, the gulf between the haves and have-nots is widening, and the sufferings and privation of the millions are growing worse."

When you read this and compare it to what has actually happened in the United States and other economically developed democratic countries, one can only shrug in disbelief that such a statement could be published in all seriousness. It is beyond comment—rather, it constitutes its own commentary. And there is so much of this sort of thing in the new program!

Yet to concentrate on such misstatements in estimating what the program means in world politics would be to neglect its main point. If there is any one striking aspect of the Marxist-Leninist movement to the historian of current affairs, it is the fact that a movement which consistently has held so many outworn and grievously mistaken theories of social development has nevertheless had such great success in achieving and expanding its power. Obviously erroneous theory has not been a barrier to, and may even have assisted, practical success. Although it is useful to study the exposition of theory and of the international situation contained in this new program in order to find keys to Communist policy, it is irrelevant to dwell on the point that it is full of distortions, misstatements and upside-down versions of facts.

In attempting to determine the program's meaning and significance there are several points of departure. The first is that, like other Communist programs, this one also combines both propaganda and plan. If the Soviet government has by now had some forty-four years of experience in fulfilling its announced plans, the outside world has also had the same forty-four years to compare what has actually been accomplished to what has been projected in these plans. A second point of departure is the fact that a great deal is known about the Soviet Union today. The new Party Program looks ahead some twenty years and more—but it has to start from here. One can judge the program for tomorrow in part on the basis of what exists right now.

Beginning from these points we can now start a detailed examination of the program by asking several questions:

1. What does the new program promise, and how does it propose to fulfill those promises?

2. What does the new program fail to promise?

3. What sort of life seems to be indicated for Soviet citizens, in the light of what they have now and of the new program, two decades hence under communism?

4. What conclusions can one reach from this?

In the first place, the new Program promises peace.

Basic Soviet Communist theory has long held that so long as imperialism—defined as the last and highest stage of capitalism—continues to exist war is inevitable. One of the statements of this doctrine was made by Joseph Stalin in his last work, *Economic Problems of Socialism in the U.S.S.R.*, in which he declared in 1953: "To end the inevitability of wars, it is necessary to destroy imperialism."

More recently, the Soviet leadership has stated that a new world war is not necessarily "fatally inevitable" in the present epoch. Such was the position taken, under Soviet leadership, in the statement of 81 Communist Parties, as we have seen. Indeed this was apparently the main issue between the Chinese Communist leadership and that of the Soviet Union. Even though the Chinese Communists subscribed to the statement, they have continued to stress the inevitability of war and the necessity to pursue a consistently militant and hostile attitude toward capitalist powers.

The importance of this issue in the thermonuclear era can hardly be over-exaggerated. If, under contemporary conditions, even one of the world's two superpowers comes to believe that a new world war is really *inevitable* and should thus begin preparations for a surprise attack, war will certainly become *inevitable*.

It is therefore worth studying in considerable detail the Soviet position on peace and war expressed in this important document.

The program says:

The issue of war and peace is the principal issue of today.

The C.P.S.U. maintains that forces capable of preserving and promoting world peace have arisen and are growing in the world.

The important thing is to ward off a thermonuclear war, not to let it break out. This can be done by the present generation.

. . . socialism does not require war to spread its ideas.

To abolish war and establish everlasting peace on earth is a historical mission of communism.

Peaceful coexistence of the Socialist and capitalist countries is an objective necessity for the development of human society . . . Peaceful coexistence implies renunciation of war as a means of settling international disputes . . .

No one can doubt that peace is a desire closer to the hearts of the Soviet people, and of all others as well, than anything else. This emphasis on peace, repeated many times in the Party Program, does have meaning. The Soviet leadership has long tried to present itself to its own and other peoples as the main apostle of peace in the world. How then does the Soviet leadership intend to fulfill its promise of peace?

If one studies carefully the new program the conclusion is inescapable that peace will be insured by strengthening the might of the Soviet Union and the Socialist camp to such an extent that the "imperialist" powers will be too cowed to attack.

The growing superiority of the Socialist forces over the forces of imperialism, of the forces of peace over those of war, will make it actually possible to banish world war from the life of society even before the complete victory of socialism on earth, with capitalism surviving in a part of the world.

It is possible to avert a war by the combined efforts of the mighty Socialist camp, the peace-loving non-Socialist countries, the international working class and all the forces championing peace.

A vast peace zone has taken shape on earth. In addition to the Socialist countries it includes a large group of non-Socialist countries that for various reasons are not interested in starting a war.

The C.P.S.U. regards the defense of the socialist motherland and the strengthening of the defense potential of the U.S.S.R., of the might of the Soviet armed forces, as a sacred duty of the Party and the Soviet people as a whole, as a most important function of the Soviet state . . . The Soviet state will see to it that its armed forces are powerful, that they have the most up-to-date means of defending the country—atomic and thermonuclear weapons, rockets of every range, and that they keep all types of military equipment and all weapons up to standard.

Does this mean that the Soviet Union will be opposed to all wars? By no means, says the program: "The C.P.S.U. and the Soviet people as a whole will continue to oppose all wars of conquest, including wars between capitalist countries and local wars aimed at strangling peoples' emancipation movements, and consider it their duty to support the sacred struggle of the oppressed peoples and their just anti-imperialist wars of liberation."

In other words, the Soviet Union will support civil wars aimed against non-Communist states for the purpose of establishing a Communist revolutionary dictatorship or of establishing national independence vis-à-vis an imperialist power. Thus Soviet Communists declare that they consider it to be their "duty" to support such nationalist rebellions as that in Algiers against French rule or Angola against Portuguese rule. Under the same rule they would consider it their duty to support the pro-Communist regime of Fidel Castro in Cuba if the United States should attempt to intervene there to overthrow it.

So the Soviet position on peace is clear: A new world war is not inevitable and can be prevented. The means to peace is the strengthening of the Soviet Union and the forces of communism so that imperialist aggressors will fear to attack. While striving to avert thermonuclear war, the Soviet Union will nonetheless consider itself free to support forces engaged in local wars of Communist revolution or national liberation.

The only gesture in the program toward international agreement to secure peace is a platform favoring complete and universal disarmament, a proposal long since made by the Russians that has very little promise of success.

One can wrap up the whole thing in one sentence: The program promises peace—a peace apparently no different from the present peace except insofar as the promised shift in balance of power in favor of the U.S.S.R. and its allies might make it firmer.

As the *New Republic* commented editorially: "In a sense the Soviet commitment to peaceful coexistence may prove even more dangerous than the old doctrine of the inevitability of war. For it is the assumption of Western weakness—above all, weakness of will—that underpins the new line."

In the second place, the program promises the world-wide victory of socialism: "The Socialist world is expanding; the capitalist world is shrinking. Socialism will inevitably succeed capitalism everywhere."

This promise is not new. It has been made in every program document of the Marxist-Leninist movement since 1848. One might therefore be able to view it with skepticism were it not for the fact that in recent years Marxist-Leninist totalitarianism has expanded its realms to the point of ruling over a third of the world's people. In Cuba it has now even extended into the Western hemisphere.

The program sets no timetable for the world-wide victory of socialism. It declares that "socialist revolution is not necessarily connected with war" and that "the great objectives of the working class can be realized without war." In fact, declares the program, "peaceful coexistence affords more favorable opportunities for the struggle of the working class . . ."

The program makes several important points about revolutionary possibilities. One is that because of the strength of the Socialist camp newly independent countries can, if they wish, go over to socialism immediately, bypassing the capitalist stage of development. There is a promise of Soviet assistance: "In view of the present balance of world forces and the actual feasibility of powerful support on the part of the world Socialist system, the peoples of the former colonies can decide this question in their own interest."

Another suggestion is that in some countries it may be possible for the revolution to take place through Communist control over parliament. A few years ago this suggestion would have been rank heresy. Marx, Lenin, and Stalin all held that it was impossible to gain political power through parliamentary means. Another suggestion is that in some countries it may be possible for the revolutionary forces within a given country to "buy up" from the bourgeoisie and capitalists control over the means of production.

By suggesting these tactics, previously condemned as "reformist," the Russian Communists appear to be telling their Communist allies in non-Communist countries that flexibility is now the order of the day:

The success of the struggle which the working class wages for the victory of revolution will depend on how well the working class and its party master the use of all forms of struggles—peaceful and non-peaceful, parliamentary and extra-parliamentary—and how well they are prepared to replace one form of struggle with another as quickly and unexpectedly as possible.

But, no matter how reached, the program warns, the revolutionary goal *must* everywhere be the same—seizure of power by a dictatorship of the proletariat, the only means to achieve a transition from capitalism to socialism. Thus even if Communists win power in a country through parliamentary means, the parliamentary system must be destroyed and replaced with a dictatorship.

Basic to the promise of the world-wide victory of socialism, and to the promise of peace, is still another of the program's promises, the most important.

In the third place, the program promises to make the Soviet Union the world's most powerful industrial nation in a few years' time.

The details of the economic program are set forth clearly and precisely in Part Two of the program. By 1970, the Soviet industrial output will rise by 150 per cent over the present and be higher, it is claimed, than present per capita industrial output in the United States.[1] By 1980, it promises, the increase over present Soviet levels will be 500 per cent. Figures are also given for two specific items: Electric power output is

[1] It is not specified how over-all industrial output of the two countries is to be compared and by whom. And, as all experts on this subject have noted, it is notoriously difficult to compare over-all industrial output of two countries with radically different price systems and assortments of production items—such as the United States and the Soviet Union.

to reach the level of about 900 to 1,000 billion kilowatt hours by 1970, and the level of about 2,700 to 3,000 billion by 1980. (For comparison, Soviet power output was 292 billion kwh. in 1960, and American 840 billion.) Steel output is scheduled to rise to about 250 million metric tons in 1980. This would amount to nearly four times the 1960 Soviet steel output of 65 million metric tons and 2.8 times that of the United States (90 million metric tons) in the same year. (American steel *capacity,* rarely used in full these days, runs to 140 million tons a year right now.)

These targets are very ambitious. Their validity can he judged in part by the fact that the Soviet Union has in the period since World War II succeeded systematically in fulfilling its long-range targets for heavy industry. One illustration: In 1946 Stalin announced targets for the period 1960 to 1965: steel—60 million metric tons; coal—500 million; petroleum—60 million. At the time these were regarded as very ambitious by most experts. In 1960 the U.S.S.R. actually produced, for comparison, 65 million metric tons of steel, 513 million of coal, and 148 of petroleum. All the targets were overfulfilled.

The stated goal for increase of industrial production of 500 per cent over current levels by 1980 leaves one a little skeptical. It implies an annual average growth rate of 10 per cent, compared with the growth rate of 8.1 per cent for 1960 over 1959 claimed by the U.S.S.R. last year. Normally, as an economy matures and gets larger one can expect the growth rate to decline. It has also to be pointed out that to catch up with the United States *of today* is, of course, also not necessarily to catch up with it tomorrow. Presumably the United States will not be standing still either in electric power output or in total industrial output.[1]

Here is a sober, objective American commentary on the Soviet Party Program and the economic race between the United States and the Soviet Union.

According to authoritative current estimates, the Soviet national income and product have been growing at an average rate of about seven per cent a year in the Fifties and will, in

[1] For example, United States industrial production in 1960 was about three per cent higher than in 1959 which is typical of recent rates of increase in American industrial output. American electric power output in 1960 was about six per cent higher than in 1959, also a fairly representative rate of increase.

all likelihood, continue to grow at this rate . . . Thus Soviet national income and product may be expected to double in the next 10 years—that is, to increase about twofold rather than two and one-half fold as promised in the program. Should Soviet national income indeed be doubled within the decade it will then roughly equal the present national income level of the United States. And assuming that the performance of our economy in the Sixties is no better than in the Fifties, and that we continue to grow at an average rate no higher than three per cent per year while the Soviets grow at the seven per cent rate, then by 1970 the Soviet national product would be about three-quarters of the U.S. level rather than one-half. As a practical matter, however, this means that Soviet output would *exceed* United States production in a number of areas, most probably those directly related to military potential and to economic competition in the underdeveloped countries.

It would probably be reasonable to assume that one can discount something in the Soviet plan figures for propaganda and overenthusiasm—but not much.

The Soviet Union has set out to become a richer, wealthier, and more powerful country than the United States and has already been engaged for many years with great success in catching up with the United States. And now the era has come when the Soviet leadership can actually go all out in a race to leave the United States behind in the crucial race for industrial-technological superiority. Given the slowness of American industrial progress in the current era and the absence of any plan for maintaining a steady growth rate in the U.S. economy, the Russians can have good hope of success in the not-too-distant future in attaining their goal of surpassing America in many areas of production.

We have to take into account another facet of this question of economic superiority. It is clear that the Soviet Union has habitually devoted a much smaller proportion of its gross national product to supplying consumer needs than Western capitalist countries, especially the United States, and a larger proportion to state expenditures—defense, capital investment, research, education, etc. The question can well be raised whether even *at the present time* the Soviet state does not have more material resources available to spend for state purposes, despite a considerably lower gross national product than the United States. (Making allowance for differences in organization of industry and the economy.) In the future the resources that will become available to the Soviet state are going to grow rapidly.

One important clause of the new program provides that wages of Soviet workers will rise at a slower rate than their labor productivity. Says the program, discussing technical progress: "This implies a higher rate of increase in labor productivity as compared with remuneration . . ."

This is a key point. How will it work? Let us suppose that a Soviet worker doubles his production as a result of better equipment, greater efficiency, etc. His wages, however, will not double, but will rise, under this rule, by only about fifty per cent.

Obviously, the result will be either lower prices of the goods produced, which would possibly benefit both individual consumers and the state (which as both a heavy-spending government and as proprietor of the entire economy is by far the biggest customer in the Soviet Union), or in higher profits which would benefit the state that collects all the profits. One cannot foresee exactly how this will work out, but it will possibly result in the state's getting a continually larger share of the total national product. Even if the Soviet state continues to take only the proportion of Soviet production it appropriates right now, the material resources at its disposal for government spending will grow enormously as the total national product increases.

The state can effectively use these funds coming to it through tax revenues and profits. It will spend them for improvement of public health services and education, for rent-free apartments and free public transportation, for more modern industrial plants, for more nuclear submarines, weapons and intercontinental missiles. It will use them for increasing the Soviet lead in the space race and for all phases of Soviet espionage and propaganda abroad.

It is quite possible that in the not-too-distant future the Soviet Union may dispose of more wealth than the United States, and that it will probably use this wealth in ways which contribute more directly and effectively to national strength. Most Americans realize such wealth used effectively is *power*, and such power may prove the undoing of the United States. The Soviet Union has always been frank in its intent "to bury" the West.

It is fashionable among some economists and political leaders to belittle the danger to the non-Communist world arising from the possibility of the Soviet Union's forging ahead of America in the production race. This seems short-sighted. Right now, while any over-all Soviet economic superiority is still a long way off, the serious consequences of the growth of Soviet power in the world are alarmingly visible.

Of course, it is obvious that America could, if it wished to, do much to prevent Russia's winning such a production race. The Soviet Party Program is clearly basing its calculations on the concept that the United States and its leaders will do little or nothing to prevent such economic conquest. The Soviet position is that a capitalist country like the United States cannot plan for or force a steady increase in national productivity, that America is powerless under its present social system to do anything about the Soviet economic challenge. Is this correct? Time will tell.

In the fourth place the progam promises a big increase in the Soviet standard of living and the transition, by 1980, to full communism, in which remuneration will be on the basis of need.

The sections outlining plans for increased living standards for Soviet people are among the most impressive in the new Party Program. It is necessary to give only the briefest summary of what they promise. Among the more significant items on the list are: an increase in real income per capita of 250 per cent in 20 years—to 3.5 times the present levels; doubling, or more than doubling, of real income per capita over the shorter ten-year period by 1970; trebling of the real income of the lowest-paid categories of factory and office workers by 1970; greatly improved public services for all, with many of them becoming (or remaining) free, such as housing, some utilities and public transport, education, public health care and medicines, etc.; reduction of working hours by 1970 to a thirty-four- or thirty-six-hour workweek; vacations for factory and office workers increased to three weeks a year as the minimum; free room and board for children at boarding schools; partially free rest homes; pensions and camping facilities for vacationers; increased provision of scholarships for students; and broadly increased social-security provisions and benefits.

At the same time that these improvements are being made, states the program, the disparity between lower-paid groups and higher-paid groups of the population will be reduced systematically, mainly, apparently, by raising compensation for lower-paid groups faster than for the rest and by increased provisions of free or cheap public services such as those already mentioned.

The increase in real income per capita which is planned, says the program, will be achieved by means of raising wages and lowering prices—along with increasing free services.

This plan for raising Soviet living standards is undoubtedly the most ambitious, the broadest and most fascinating program ever seriously advanced in any country for the improved well-being of the people.

However, it seems certain that under any objective system of measurement of real income that Soviet income in goods and services will not by 1970 be close to the present level of average per capita income in the United States. More than that, even if the plan is successfully and fully executed by 1980, the Soviet Union will probably still not have caught up with the American standard of living. Soviet statisticians will no doubt be able to "prove" that it has, but that is beside the point. Living standards are, after all, made up of imponderables as well as ponderables. But what is not imponderable is the clear fact that the economy of the United States is based on the stimulation and satisfaction of consumer wants —not necessarily a merit—while the Soviet economy is based on the increase in the might and power of the state.

Thus, although the Russians have come a long way in a short time, they still have a long way to go to catch up with America and surpass her in living standards. It will take longer than the next twenty years to do this.

One of the mainstays of the American system is the fact that anything from almost anywhere is "available" to the American consumer, available in the sense that if he wants it, and can pay for it, he can have it. There is always someone who will get it for him. Two elements are important here. One is that American money is freely convertible, and the other is that American foreign trade is relatively unrestricted. This is not so in the Soviet Union—not today and not tomorrow. The new program, at any rate, does *not* promise complete freedom of choice to the Soviet consumer, since the Soviet government will decide what is to be produced for sale to the public now and in the future, since the program does *not* promise to abolish the state's monopoly on foreign trade which controls all imports, and finally, since the new Party Program does *not* propose to make the Soviet ruble freely convertible. This is more important than it may at first sound. It involves more than fashions from Dior and caviar from Iran. It involves the right of the consumer in the capitalist world to pick and choose, to be capricious and fickle, to get what he (or she) wants when he wants it.

Let's take one concrete example—automobiles. America has an automobile economy because millions and millions of Americans consider the automobile essential to the "good life." It has been a matter of free choice which Americans have been able to indulge since the days when Henry Ford produced his first cars.

The new Party Program promises Soviet citizens "more automobiles." And this is probably just one of those Soviet promises—easy to make, not so easy to forget, but easier to put aside than to fulfill. In the Soviet Union the consumer does not have the power to make a choice. If Soviet industry does not make enough private cars for sale to the ordinary citizen, and if the Soviet monopoly of foreign trade does not import them, then there just won't be enough to go around. A policy decision on a high level is involved, and up till now the decision has been, so far as converting to an automobile economy is concerned, a firm "no." There are good reasons on the part of the government for this decision. Perhaps it *is* more efficient to develop public transport facilities than to have an automobile economy. But the Soviet consumer doesn't do the deciding. It's done for him. One can certainly say that the full freedom to choose is a part of a "standard of living," and that our "American standard of living" is inseparable from this freedom of choice.

Another element in American life that is inseparable from our "American standard of living" is the right to own private land. This is forbidden in the Soviet Union. The best a Soviet citizen can do who wishes to build himself a house is to get with difficulty a small lot allocated to him by local authorities. He does not own this as property but pays a small rental for it. He gets little help in building his house and private home ownership is not being encouraged. It is notable that the Party Program has nothing to say about expanding the building of private homes for Russians. Instead, the emphasis is entirely on apartments which are going to be furnished rent-free and, according to the plan, be available to all, including newlyweds, by 1980. Many Russians, just as many Americans, no doubt prefer apartments to owning a home of their own. But there is every indication that if they had the choice, many, many Russians would wish to own their own homes on comfortable lots. Once again, however, they will apparently be permitted no freedom of choice. They can't buy land, and the state is not going to make provisions for their buying or building their own houses.

The provision for rent-free apartments sounds wonderful, however. In actuality, since even at the present time rents are very, very low in the Soviet Union, this part of the program is not a big change from the present. The really significant promise is a sufficient supply of housing by 1980 so that each family can have an apartment of its own.

Even in 1980, however, it will doubtless be true that all housing will still be allocated—i.e., there will be then, as is certainly true now, no free choice of apartment space such as we usually enjoy in America. Russians take whatever they can get and are glad for it. Their housing is assigned to them either by local authorities or by their employing organizations, and they find it difficult to do any changing around.

There are a lot of other comments one should make on the Soviet plans for an improved standard of living. One of them is that free services are only nominally free since they all have to be paid for somehow. If Soviet citizens get free housing it is because there is included in the prices of the other things they do pay for, such as food, a hidden tax or a hidden profit (both the same in the socialist Soviet Union) which the government collects and which it uses to pay for construction and maintenance of housing facilities. In other words, Soviet housing will be "free" in exactly the same sense as American primary and secondary public education is "free"—paid for indirectly by taxpayers.

The Soviet Party Program proposes in one of its clauses to abolish taxes. What, of course, is meant here is direct taxes deducted from salary—the income tax which never has amounted to much in the Soviet Union anyway. Soviet citizens pay their indirect taxes—in heavy proportions too—as a part of the retail prices for things they buy. This practice will continue even after Soviet "taxes" have been "abolished" in the new millennium.

It should be noted that while in the past Soviet economic plans for increasing the output of heavy industry have usually been fulfilled, this has not been true of similar plans for the improvement of living standards. These have generally been underfulfilled. The reason obviously has been that plans for development of heavy industry, also the needs of the state for defense, etc., have had an absolute priority over plans for improving living conditions. This will still, no doubt, be true in the years to come.

However, as the Soviet economy grows and prospers, it would seem possible that this would be less of a negative factor than it has been up till now. It must also be admitted that under the new Party Program a real increase in the material well-being of Soviet citizens seems probable. If accomplished, this new prosperity will represent a tremendous triumph for the Soviet regime. Its accomplishment may at last justify the many cruel sacrifices which Russians have made in this century for the sake of a better life.

Now, what are some of the things that the new program does not promise?

As we have seen, the program does not promise every Soviet citizen a private car nor a private home to all that want one.

The new program also excludes anything that involves ownership of the "means of production." Thus Soviet citizens will not be able to own a few acres of their own. Soviet farmers will not be able to own farms. They will not even have left the little orchard and garden plots which they still possess. And, of course, Soviet citizens will not even be able to own small enterprises of their own such as a store, a gas station, a bar, a restaurant, a repair shop, a shoeshine stand, etc.

These are material things, but they are also political matters, for behind them lies Communist policy. Indeed, it is to the political field that we should essentially look to construct a list of things the program does not promise. The best approach is by examination of one very important promise in the new program—the promise to end "dictatorship." The promise is specific—but also vague as to when and how. If it means anything, it means that dictatorship as a system of rule of the Soviet Union will come to an end in 1980 or thereabouts when communism has been built: "The Party holds that the dictatorship of the proletariat will cease to be necessary before the state withers away."

In discussing this, the program describes different measures to be taken aimed at "extension and perfection of socialist democracy": a forced turnover in membership in local and national government and Party organs of rule, nationwide and local discussions and referendums on important draft laws, amplification of powers of local self-government and the like. However, all this leaves one unsatisfied. If there is no longer to be a dictatorship, there must be some kind of rule of law and "constitution" which provides orderly ways of settling public issues and selection of national leaders.

Does this mean the Soviet Union intends to go over to a multiparty system and parliamentary democracy, with elections in which more than one candidate is presented for a given office? There is no indication in the program that this will be true. Does an end to the "dictatorship of the proletariat" mean there will finally be established genuine freedom of speech, freedom of the press, freedom of assembly, and freedom to organize parties or groups to advance a political program? None of these freedoms is mentioned in the program. It is made very clear that any manifestations of "factionalism and group activity incompatible with Marxist-Leninist principles" will not be tolerated by the Communist Party which is described as "the brain, the honor and the conscience of our epoch . . ." Yet civil liberties are essential if there is no longer to be a dictatorship. And what of such things as the direct and indirect censorship on the flow into the Soviet Union from the outside world of ideas, publications, works of art and culture, such as there is today? The program does not say whether or not censorship will be lifted. Will there be any kind of censorship or attempts of the political authority toward limiting the freedom of creative artists or influencing their work? On this question the program says that "the Communist Party shows solicitude for the proper development of literature and art . . ." What kind of solicitude? And what is proper? The question is open. When the "dictatorship of the proletariat" is abolished will all Soviet citizens have an unrestricted right to travel abroad where, when and for as long as they please, to reside abroad if they wish, and even to emigrate if they wish? The program gives no hints. These are only a few of the important questions the new program leaves unanswered.

What sort of life seems probable for Soviet citizens twenty years hence under communism?

In considering this question, let us suppose that Khrushchev's new program will be fulfilled on schedule:

By 1980 in the U.S.S.R. everyone will have plenty to eat, together with adequate clothing and supplies of all the other necessities and amenities of life. Every urban family will have its own apartment. In the country, there will probably be many peasants still living in individual homes. However, the process of "urbanization" of the peasantry will nevertheless have advanced far, with provision for them in new and modern settlements with all kinds of service and cultural facilities. They will no longer be peasants, but workers. For regardless of where they live, all Soviet citizens will be employed as workers in one or another Soviet enterprise, mostly big enterprises, and receive wages or salaries. No one will be self-employed and no one will be his own boss. There will supposedly be a general social equality of all, and living standards will be generally similar everywhere in the country. When true communism is actually put into effect all will receive remuneration on the basis of their "needs," rather than on the basis of the relative quality and quantity of their work. Who will define what "needs" are is not spelled out.

All will get at least a complete secondary education of eleven years in which will be included participation in "socially useful labor." For all who want it there will be facilities, particularly in night schools and correspondence schools, to receive higher education and specialized technical education.

There will be all kinds of free public services and full cradle-to-grave social security and medical protection for all. At all enterprises there will be free lunches.

Women will be encouraged to have jobs. There will be free nurseries and boarding schools to take care of children. Many people will eat most of their meals in restaurants, it would appear.

Everyone will be required to work on the basis of the Communist principle of "He who does not work shall not eat." [1] The workweek will run from thirty-four to thirty-six hours with a weekend and paid annual vacation of three weeks' minimum, during which many will take advantage of free or low-priced vacation facilities.

All this makes quite an attractive picture—particularly to those millions of people in Asia, Africa, Latin America, and other countries who live in abject poverty.

One side of life in the coming Utopia might be elaborated. This is the matter of the family. What kind of family life will there be? It looks as if the concept behind the program is one

---

[1] It would be interesting to speculate just what the Communists would have to say if some non-Communist country were to adopt this as a slogan for its people.

in which the family will be weaker than it is now: wives encouraged to work; children often off at boarding schools for most of the time; dining out in restaurants widespread; few private homes, etc.

It will be a *collective* life with people existing close to each other, always in large numbers in all probability, and not off by themselves. In it there will be no place for the American dream of the rose-covered cottage with happy little tots playing in the yard with the family puppy and a loving and attractive husband and wife watching them affectionately —with a new car in the garage behind the house, and a dishwasher, an electric refrigerator, an automatic laundry, a home freezer, a TV set, a home movie set and an electric can opener and a score of other hallmarks of the American way of life all ensconced in their proper place inside the cottage. Russians under communism may have many of these things too, but not the cottage, not the car and particularly not "a world of their own." The very idea of a personal, intimate family happiness in a private little closed paradise belonging only to oneself and one's own, so dear to the hearts and imaginations of Americans and Western Europeans, is alien to this new Communist society.

In Russia it is to be "one for all and all for one," and the center of life is to be all of Communist society rather than the family.

In the Russian language there is, significantly, no word for *privacy*. This is a fact, and it doesn't look as if such a word is going to be invented. It probably won't be needed. But there will, at least, be more privacy for Russians in the future than there is now. At the present time many still live in communal apartments in which several families share together the kitchen, toilet and bath facilities—and often quarrel bitterly about who will keep them clean. That will presumably be a thing of the past by 1980, and so will poverty, if the Party makes good on all these promises.

IV. *Conclusions*

There are many things to be said about the new Party Program, and many have already been said by writers in the press of the free world.

It is important to note the current political significance of this document. In the internal Communist Party politics of the Soviet Union the program certainly represents a resounding salvo by Soviet Communist Party boss, Nikita Khrushchev, and his supporters against all in his own country who may disapprove of his politics, and who look back at the "good old days" of the Stalin era.

Not once is Stalin's name mentioned in this document—this man who ruled the Soviet Union with an iron fist for nearly thirty years! In addition, many of Stalin's projects are credited to Lenin by the program.

Another obvious point is that the program represents a major effort by the Soviet Communist Party to keep the Soviet Union in its position as leader of international communism. In this respect it represents a carefully prepared attack on the Chinese Communists led by Mao Tze-tung. These, with some other smaller Communist parties of Africa and Asia, are the "dogmatists and sectarians," spoken of so trenchantly in the declaration. The new program damns the Chinese Communists with faint praise. There are only eleven words devoted to them in the entire document.

Perhaps most significant is that the new program is clearly directed toward the people of underdeveloped countries, many of them newly independent. To such people, looking for a way to enter the main currents of modern life and pull their nations out of the swamp of problems in which they find themselves, this plan, standing for what a relatively underdeveloped nation did by itself and plans to do in the future, lifting itself up by its own bootstraps into a position as contender for world leadership, is a dramatic document. It will have real impact.

Any such document as this, constituting as it does a blueprint for the future of one enormous country (and by implication for the entire world), immediately touches on such central questions as the meaning of human life, the function and shape of society, the extent to which human beings can consciously plan for their own social future and realize those plans, and the possible goals of such plans. The new Party Program even tries to give a brief outline of the moral attributes of the new Soviet man. It is probably not the last word on that subject. But it shows that the authors of this document realized how basic were the problems they were called upon to face.

One of these problems I have already suggested previously. Should the social organism, as Western parliamentary systems assume it should, merely try to establish a framework of organization and operation of society in which the individual seeks his *own* happiness? Or should society determine, according to the Soviet pattern, the way in which the individual should seek his happiness or self-realization in the greater power, grandeur and development of the society of which he is a member, and then force the individual into that pattern? Can a society based on the worth of the individual survive in competition with one based on the "greater good" of the mass? Can a society oriented to the stimulation and satisfaction of consumer needs survive in competition with one oriented to the aggrandizement of state power? Can a society in which individuals and organizations alike are free to choose their own goals and govern their own activities within a framework of law compete with a totalitarian society in which one organization—the Party—maintains a monopoly on the right of organization and actively directs all other organizations within its realm in the pursuit of its goals? So far, the answers to these questions are not encouraging to all those who have faith in the value—and survival value—of human freedom as it is known in the West.

What is it all for, this new society? Let's go back for a moment to the picture of Soviet society in 1980 which I gave earlier: Everyone enjoys almost the same material standard; everyone lives in almost the same way; everyone has almost the same kind of education; everyone wears, no doubt, almost the same kind of clothes and sees the same motion pictures, TV network shows and reads the same kind of books; everyone gets the same this and that free; everyone smokes more or less the same kind of cigarettes. Everyone is almost equal.

What does this remind us of? Does it perhaps remind us of America, the country of uniformity and conformity in which a town in Iowa so often looks just like one in Washington or Michigan or New York or any other state in the Union? In America there is uniformity and conformity on a scale perhaps never seen before in history. Yet in America there is also real hope for non-conformity: non-conformity through the ability to own private property in land or enterprises and thereby to live a life "of one's own"; non-conformity through total freedom in the creative arts; non-conformity through freedom to eat even if one doesn't work, freedom to be a parasite, a beatnik, a Bowery bum, a beggar, a prostitute, a would-be author living on unemployment insurance in a loft and writing the "great American novel," freedom to be a loafing millionaire or a beach bum.

Machine culture with its big organizations, both in the Soviet Union and in America, seems to try to cut and trim human beings to fit a machine mold, to make people into automatons for the sake of its needs and convenience. If there are "organization men" and "organization wives" running the corporations of America there are the exact counterparts of them in the Soviet Union. All up and down the social ladder in both countries the same sort of "standardization" of human beings seems to take place in much the same way. How much more true this will be in the Soviet Union twenty years hence under this blueprint, as presented here! How much society loses, by the sacrifice of diversity, of social, cultural, national, and all sorts of other differences between individuals and societies and countries, for the sake of the greater economic efficiency of machines and organizations!

When one stops to think about it, just why should one have to work in order to eat? If, as has already happened in America and as is promised in Russia, all the wellsprings of economic productivity are to gush forth in a mighty never-ending torrent of the good things of life, why then should every citizen be obliged to go on laboring like a little beaver every day, dutifully upping his labor productivity every month—in order to feed the yawning maw of a voracious, insatiable state which is hellbent on achieving world revolution and world domination?

If there is going to be plenty for everybody in 1980 why should everyone work, even a thirty-six-hour week, to keep producing more and more and more? Isn't the Soviet Union going to make precisely the same mistake as the United States —confusing the good life with the "goods" life? And is conspicuous consumption by the state any more meritorious than consumption by individuals?

Should not the real slogan of genuine communism be: "Free food and work when you feel like it"?

The whole principle of the proposed Soviet Communist order as expressed in the slogan "he who does not work shall not eat" is really very Puritan and even Calvinist. Isn't it the natural vestige of a scarcity economy through the ages, and even now, which is seeking to impose itself on a scheme of things in which it will be irrelevant?

Yet those are just questions, and perhaps unnecessary ones. History, after all, often plays cruel tricks on the great men who have influenced its course. Marx and Engels had nightmares about the oppressive might of the state and directed their thinking toward a scheme for doing away with the state, thereby liberating mankind from its evils, and so they started a movement which has created the mightiest and most ruthless state of all. Lenin dreamed of freeing his country from police repression and guided the creation of a regime which under his successor, Stalin, imposed on the country a police repression far more brutal than that of the Czar whom Lenin had worked to overthrow.

Who knows what tricks the future may play on the authors of this new Party Program of 1961?

One thing is clear: Marx, Engels and Lenin let loose in this world a revolution by thought and deed which is indeed remaking history. It will not be easy for the Soviet leaders or anyone else to control that force or even to tell in which way it will move as it surges forward in a mighty tidal wave. It is, after all, a revolution which has not yet ended.

THE COMMUNIST BLUEPRINT
FOR THE FUTURE

MANIFESTO OF THE COMMUNIST PARTY, 1848

PREFACE TO THE ENGLISH EDITION OF 1888

Friedrich Engels

The Manifesto was published as the platform of the "Communist League," a workingmen's association, first exclusively German, later on international, and, under the political conditions of the Continent before 1848, unavoidably a secret society. At a Congress of the League, held in London in November, 1847, Marx and Engels were commissioned to prepare for publication a complete theoretical and practical party program. Drawn up in German, in January, 1848, the manuscript was sent to the printer in London a few weeks before the French revolution of February 24th. A French translation was brought out in Paris, shortly before the insurrection of June, 1848. The first English translation, by Miss Helen Macfarlane, appeared in George Julian Harney's *Red Republican,* London, 1850. A Danish and a Polish edition had also been published.

The defeat of the Parisian insurrection of June, 1848 —the first great battle between Proletariat and Bourgeoisie—drove again into the background, for a time, the social and political aspirations of the European working class. Thenceforth, the struggle for supremacy was again, as it had been before the revolution of February, solely between different sections of the propertied class; the working class was reduced to a fight for political elbow room, and to the position of extreme wing of the middle-class Radicals. Wherever independent proletarian movements continued to show signs of life, they were ruthlessly hunted down. Thus the Prussian police hunted out the Central Board of the Communist League, then located in Cologne. The members were arrested, and, after eighteen months' imprisonment, they were tried in October, 1852. This celebrated "Cologne Communist trial" lasted from October 4th till November 12th; seven of the prisoners were sentenced to terms of imprisonment in a fortress, varying from three to six years. Immediately after the sentence, the League was formally dissolved by the remaining members. As to the Manifesto, it seemed thenceforth to be doomed to oblivion.

When the European working class had recovered sufficient strength for another attack on the ruling classes, the International Workingmen's Association sprang up. But this association, formed with the express aim of welding into one body the whole militant proletariat of Europe and America, could not at once proclaim the principles laid down in the Manifesto. The International was bound to have a program broad enough to be acceptable to the English Trades' Unions, to the followers of Proudhon in France, Belgium, Italy, and Spain, and to the Lassalleans [1] in Germany. Marx, who drew up this program to the satisfaction of all parties, entirely trusted to the intellectual development of the working class, which was sure to result from combined action and mutual discussion. The very events and vicissitudes of the struggle against Capital, the defeats even more than the victories, could not help bringing home to men's minds the insufficiency of their various favorite nostrums, and preparing the way for a more complete insight into the true conditions of working-class emancipation. And Marx was right. The International, on its breaking up in 1874, left the workers quite different men from what it had found them in 1864. Proudhonism in France, Lassalleanism in Germany were dying out, and even the Conservative English Trades' Unions, though most of them had long since severed their connection with the International,

[1] Lassalle personally, to us, always acknowledged himself to be a disciple of Marx, and, as such, stood on the ground of the Manifesto. But in his public agitation, 1862-64, he did not go beyond demanding co-operative workshops supported by State credit. [*Note by Engels.*]

were gradually advancing toward that point at which, last year at Swansea, their President could say in their name: "Continental Socialism has lost its terrors for us." In fact, the principles of the Manifesto had made considerable headway among the working men of all countries.

The Manifesto itself thus came to the front again. The German text had been, since 1850, reprinted several times in Switzerland, England, and America. In 1872, it was translated into English in New York, where the translation was published in *Woodhull and Claflin's Weekly*. From this English version, a French one was made in *Le Socialiste* of New York. Since then at least two more English translations, more or less mutilated, have been brought out in America, and one of them has been reprinted in England. The first Russian translation, made by Bakunin, was published at Herzen's *Kolokol* office in Geneva about 1863; a second one, by the heroic Vera Zasulich, also in Geneva, 1882. A new Danish edition is to be found in *Social-democratisk Bibliothek*, Copenhagen, 1885; a fresh French translation in *Le Socialiste,* Paris, 1885. From this latter a Spanish version was prepared and published in Madrid, 1886. The German reprints are not to be counted; there have been twelve altogether at the least. An Armenian translation, which was to be published in Constantinople some months ago, did not see the light, I am told, because the publisher was afraid of bringing out a book with the name of Marx on it, while the translator declined to call it his own production. Of further translations into other languages I have heard, but have not seen them. Thus the history of the Manifesto reflects, to a great extent, the history of the modern working-class movement; at present it is undoubtedly the most widespread, the most international production of all Socialist literature, the common platform acknowledged by millions of working men from Siberia to California.

Yet, when it was written, we could not have called it a *Socialist* Manifesto. By Socialists, in 1847, were understood, on the one hand, the adherents of the various Utopian systems: Owenites in England, Fourierists in France, both of them already reduced to the position of mere sects, and gradually dying out; on the other hand, the most multifarious social quacks, who, by all manners of tinkering, professed to redress, without any danger to capital and profit, all sorts of social grievances, in both cases men outside the working-class movement, and looking rather to the "educated" classes for support. Whatever portion of the working class had become convinced of the insufficiency of mere political revolutions, and had proclaimed the necessity of a total social change, that portion then called itself Communist. It was a crude, rough-hewn, purely instinctive sort of communism; still, it touched the cardinal point and was powerful enough among the working class to produce the Utopian communism, in France, of Cabet, and in Germany, of Weitling. Thus socialism was, in 1847, a middle-class movement, communism, a working-class movement. Socialism was, on the Continent at least, "respectable"; communism was the very opposite. And as our notion, from the very beginning, was that "the emancipation of the working class must be the act of the working class itself," there could be no doubt as to which of the two names we must take. Moreover, we have, ever since, been far from repudiating it.

The Manifesto being our joint production, I consider myself bound to state that the fundamental proposition, which forms its nucleus, belongs to Marx. That proposition is: that in every historical epoch, the prevailing mode of economic production and exchange, and the social organization necessarily following from it, form the basis upon which is built up, and from which alone can be explained, the political and intellectual history of that epoch; that consequently the whole history of mankind (since the dissolution of primitive tribal society, holding land in common ownership) has been a history of class struggles, contests between exploiting and exploited, ruling and oppressed classes; that the history of these class struggles forms a series of evolutions in which, nowadays, a stage has been reached where the exploited and oppressed class—the proletariat —cannot attain its emancipation from the sway of the exploiting and ruling class—the bourgeoisie—without, at the same time, and once and for all, emancipating society at large from all exploitation, oppression, class distinctions, and class struggles.

This proposition which, in my opinion, is destined to do for history what Darwin's theory has done for biology, we, both of us, had been gradually approaching for some years before 1845. How far I had independently progressed toward it is best shown by my *Condition of the Working Class in England*. But when I again met Marx at Brussels, in spring, 1845, he had it ready worked out, and put it before me, in terms almost as clear as those in which I have stated it here.

From our joint preface to the German edition of 1872, I quote the following:

However much the state of things may have altered during the last twenty-five years, the general principles laid down in this Manifesto are, on the whole, as correct today as ever. Here and there some detail might be improved. The practical application of the principles will depend, as the Manifesto itself states, everywhere and at all times, on the historical conditions for the time being existing, and, for that reason, no special stress is laid on the revolutionary measures proposed at the end of Section II. That passage would, in many respects, be very differently worded today. In view of the gigantic strides of Modern Industry since 1848, and of the accompanying improved and extended organization of the working class, in view of the practical experience gained, first in the February Revolution, and then, still more, in the Paris Commune, where the proletariat for the first time held political power for two whole months, this program has in some details become antiquated. One thing especially was proved by the Commune, *viz.*, that "the working class cannot simply lay hold of the ready-made State machinery, and wield it for its own purposes." (See *The Civil War in France; Address of the General Council of the International Working Men's Association* [London: Truelove, 1871], p. 15, where this point is further developed.) Further, it is self-evident that the criticism of Socialist literature is deficient in relation to the present time, because it comes down only to 1847; also, that the remarks on the relation of the Communists to the various opposition parties (Section IV), although in principle still correct, yet in practice are antiquated, because the political situation has been entirely changed, and the progress of history has swept from off the earth the greater portion of the political parties there enumerated.

But then, the Manifesto has become a historical document which we have no longer any right to alter.

The present translation is by Mr. Samuel Moore, the translator of the greater portion of Marx's *Capital*. We have revised it in common, and I have added a few notes explanatory of historical allusions.

Manifesto of the Communist Party

A specter is haunting Europe—the specter of communism. All the Powers of old Europe have entered into a holy alliance to exorcise this specter: Pope and Czar, Metternich and Guizot, French Radicals and German police-spies.

Where is the party in opposition that has not been decried as Communistic by its opponents in power? Where the Opposition that has not hurled back the branding reproach of communism, against the more advanced opposition parties, as well as against its reactionary adversaries?

Two things result from this fact.

I. Communism is already acknowledged by all European Powers to be itself a Power.

II. It is high time that Communists should openly, in the face of the whole world, publish their views, their aims, their tendencies, and meet this nursery tale of the specter of communism with a Manifesto of the party itself.

To this end, Communists of various nationalities have assembled in London, and sketched the following Manifesto, to be published in the English, French, German, Italian, Flemish, and Danish languages.

I. Bourgeoisie and Proletariat [1]

The history of all hitherto existing society [2] is the history of class struggles.

Freeman and slave, patrician and plebeian, lord and

[1] By bourgeoisie is meant the class of modern capitalists, owners of the means of social production and employers of wage labor. By proletariat, the class of modern wage-laborers who, having no means of production of their own, are reduced to selling their labor power in order to live. [*Note by Engels to the English edition of 1888.*]

[2] That is, all *written* history. In 1847, the pre-history of society, the social organization existing previous to recorded history, was

9

serf, guild-master [1] and journeyman, in a word, oppressor and oppressed, stood in constant opposition to one
another, carried on an uninterrupted, now hidden, now
open fight, a fight that each time ended, either in a revolutionary reconstruction of society at large, or in the
common ruin of the contending classes.

In the earlier epochs of history, we find almost everywhere a complicated arrangement of society into various
orders, a manifold gradation of social rank. In ancient
Rome we have patricians, knights, plebeians, slaves; in
the Middle Ages feudal lords, vassals, guild-masters,
journeymen, apprentices, serfs; in almost all of these
classes, again, subordinate gradations.

The modern bourgeois society that has sprouted from
the ruins of feudal society has not done away with class
antagonisms. It has but established new classes, new
conditions of oppression, new forms of struggle in place
of the old ones.

Our epoch, the epoch of the bourgeoisie, possesses,
however, this distinctive feature: it has simplified the
class antagonisms. Society as a whole is more and more
splitting up into two great hostile camps, into two great
classes directly facing each other: Bourgeoisie and Proletariat.

From the serfs of the Middle Ages sprang the chartered burghers of the earliest towns. From these bur-

---

all but unknown. Since then, Haxthausen discovered common
ownership of land in Russia, Maurer proved it to be the social
foundation from which all Teutonic races started in history, and
by and by village communities were found to be, or to have been
the primitive form of society everywhere from India to Ireland.
The inner organization of this primitive Communistic society was
laid bare, in its typical form, by Morgan's crowning discovery of
the true nature of the *gens* and its relation to the *tribe*. With the
dissolution of these primeval communities society begins to be dif-
ferentiated into separate and finally antagonistic classes. I have
attempted to retrace this process of dissolution in: *Der Ursprung
der Familie, des Privateigenthums und des Staats* (*The Origin of
the Family, Private Property and the State*), 2nd edition, Stuttgart,
1886. [*Note by Engels to the English edition of 1888.*]

[1] Guild-master, that is, a full member of a guild, a master within,
not a head of a guild. [*Note by Engels to the English edition of
1888.*]

gesses the first elements of the bourgeoisie were developed.

The discovery of America, the rounding of the Cape, opened up fresh ground for the rising bourgeoisie. The East Indian and Chinese markets, the colonization of America, trade with the colonies, the increase in the means of exchange and in commodities generally, gave to commerce, to navigation, to industry, an impulse never before known, and thereby, to the revolutionary element in the tottering feudal society, a rapid development.

The feudal system of industry, under which industrial production was monopolized by closed guilds, now no longer sufficed for the growing wants of the new markets. The manufacturing system took its place. The guild-masters were pushed on one side by the manufacturing middle class; division of labor between the different corporate guilds vanished in the face of division of labor in each single workshop.

Meantime the markets kept ever growing, the demand ever rising. Even manufacture no longer sufficed. Thereupon, steam and machinery revolutionized industrial production. The place of manufacture was taken by the giant, Modern Industry, the place of the industrial middle class, by industrial millionaires, the leaders of whole industrial armies, the modern bourgeois.

Modern industry has established the world market, for which the discovery of America paved the way. This market has given an immense development to commerce, to navigation, to communication by land. This development has, in its turn, reacted on the extension of industry; and in proportion as industry, commerce, navigation, railways extended, in the same proportion the bourgeoisie developed, increased its capital, and pushed into the background every class handed down from the Middle Ages.

We see, therefore, how the modern bourgeoisie is itself the product of a long course of development, of a series of revolutions in the modes of production and of exchange.

Each step in the development of the bourgeoisie was accompanied by a corresponding political advance of that class. An oppressed class under the sway of the feudal nobility, an armed and self-governing association in the medieval commune; [1] here independent urban republic (as in Italy and Germany), there taxable "third estate" of the monarchy (as in France), afterward, in the period of manufacture proper, serving either the semi-feudal or the absolute monarchy as a counterpoise against the nobility, and, in fact, cornerstone of the great monarchies in general, the bourgeoisie has at last, since the establishment of Modern Industry and of the world market, conquered for itself, in the modern representative State, exclusive political sway. The executive of the modern State is but a committee for managing the common affairs of the whole bourgeoisie.

The bourgeoisie, historically, has played a most revolutionary part.

The bourgeoisie, wherever it has got the upper hand, has put an end to all feudal, patriarchal, idyllic relations. It has pitilessly torn asunder the motley feudal ties that bound man to his "natural superiors," and has left remaining no other nexus between man and man than naked self-interest, than callous "cash payment." It has drowned the most heavenly ecstasies of religious fervor, of chivalrous enthusiasm, of philistine sentiment-alism, in the icy water of egotistical calculation. It has resolved personal worth into exchange value, and in place of the numberless indefeasible chartered freedoms, has set up that single, unconscionable freedom—Free Trade. In one word, for exploitation, veiled by religious and political illusions, it has substituted naked, shameless, direct, brutal exploitation.

The bourgeoisie has stripped of its halo every occupation hitherto honored and looked up to with reverent

---

[1] "Commune" was the name taken, in France, by the nascent towns even before they had conquered from their feudal lords and masters local self-government and political rights of the "Third Estate." Generally speaking, for the economical development of the bourgeoisie, England is here taken as the typical country; for its political development, France. [*Note by Engels to the English edition of 1888.*]

This was the name given their urban communities by the townsmen of Italy and France, after they had purchased or wrested their initial rights of self-government from their feudal lords. [*Note by Engels to the German edition of 1890.*]

awe. It has converted the physician, the lawyer, the priest, the poet, the man of science, into its paid wage-laborers.

The bourgeoisie has torn away from the family its sentimental veil, and has reduced the family relation to a mere money relation.

The bourgeoisie has disclosed how it came to pass that the brutal display of vigor in the Middle Ages, which Reactionists so much admire, found its fitting complement in the most slothful indolence. It has been the first to show what man's activity can bring about. It has accomplished wonders far surpassing Egyptian pyramids, Roman aqueducts, and Gothic cathedrals; it has conducted expeditions that put in the shade all former Exoduses of nations and crusades.

The bourgeoisie cannot exist without constantly revolutionizing the instruments of production, and thereby the relations of production, and with them the whole relations of society. Conservation of the old modes of production in unaltered form was, on the contrary, the first condition of existence for all earlier industrial classes. Constant revolutionizing of production, uninterrupted disturbance of all social conditions, everlasting uncertainty and agitation distinguish the bourgeois epoch from all earlier ones. All fixed, fast-frozen relations, with their train of ancient and venerable prejudices and opinions, are swept away, all new-formed ones become antiquated before they can ossify. All that is solid melts into air, all that is holy is profaned, and man is at last compelled to face with sober senses his real conditions of life and his relations with his kind.

The need of a constantly expanding market for its products chases the bourgeoisie over the whole surface of the globe. It must nestle everywhere, settle everywhere, establish connections everywhere.

The bourgeoisie has through its exploitation of the world market given a cosmopolitan character to production and consumption in every country. To the great chagrin of Reactionists, it has drawn from under the feet of industry the national ground on which it stood. All old-established national industries have been destroyed or are daily being destroyed. They are dislodged by new industries, whose introduction becomes a life and death question for all civilized nations, by industries that no longer work up indigenous raw material, but raw material drawn from the remotest zones; industries whose products are consumed, not only at home, but in every quarter of the globe. In place of the old wants, satisfied by the productions of the country, we find new wants, requiring for their satisfaction the products of distant lands and climes. In place of the old local and national seclusion and self-sufficiency, we have intercourse in every direction, universal interdependence of nations. And as in material, so also in intellectual production. The intellectual creations of individual nations become common property. National one-sidedness and narrow-mindedness become more and more impossible, and from the numerous national and local literatures, there arises a world literature.

The bourgeoisie, by the rapid improvement of all instruments of production, by the immensely facilitated means of communication, draws all, even the most barbarian, nations into civilization. The cheap prices of its commodities are the heavy artillery with which it batters down all Chinese walls, with which it forces the barbarians' intensely obstinate hatred of foreigners to capitulate. It compels all nations, on pain of extinction, to adopt the bourgeois mode of production: it compels them to introduce what it calls civilization into their midst, *i.e.*, to become bourgeois themselves. In one word, it creates a world after its own image.

The bourgeoisie has subjected the country to the rule of the towns. It has created enormous cities, has greatly increased the urban population as compared with the rural, and has thus rescued a considerable part of the population from the idiocy of rural life. Just as it has made the country dependent on the towns, so it has made barbarian and semi-barbarian countries dependent on the civilized ones, nations of peasants on nations of bourgeois, the East on the West.

The bourgeoisie keeps more and more doing away with the scattered state of the population, of the means of production, and of property. It has agglomerated population, centralized means of production, and has concentrated property in a few hands. The necessary consequence of this was political centralization. Independent, or but loosely connected, provinces with separate interests, laws, governments, and systems of taxation, became lumped together into one nation, with one government, one code of laws, one national class-interest, one frontier, and one customs-tariff.

The bourgeoisie, during its rule of scarce one hundred years, has created more massive and more colossal productive forces than have all preceding generations together. Subjection of Nature's forces to man, machinery, application of chemistry to industry and agriculture, steam navigation, railways, electric telegraphs, clearing of whole continents for cultivation, canalization of rivers, whole populations conjured out of the ground—what earlier century had even a presentiment that such productive forces slumbered in the lap of social labor?

We see then: the means of production and of exchange, on whose foundation the bourgeoisie built itself up, were generated in feudal society. At a certain stage in the development of these means of production and of exchange, the conditions under which feudal society produced and exchanged, the feudal organization of agriculture and manufacturing industry, in one word, the feudal relations of property became no longer compatible with the already developed productive forces; they became so many fetters. They had to be burst asunder; they were burst asunder.

Into their place stepped free competition, accompanied by a social and political constitution adapted to it, and by the economical and political sway of the bourgeois class.

A similar movement is going on before our own eyes. Modern bourgeois society with its relations of production, of exchange and of property, a society that has conjured up such gigantic means of production and of exchange, is like the sorcerer, who is no longer able to control the powers of the nether world whom he has called up by his spells. For many a decade past the history of industry and commerce is but the history of the revolt of modern productive forces against modern conditions of production, against the property relations that are the conditions for the existence of the bourgeoisie and of its rule. It is enough to mention the commercial crises that by their periodical return put on its trial, each time more threateningly, the existence of the entire bourgeois society. In these crises a great part not only of the existing products, but also of the previously created productive forces, are periodically destroyed. In these crises there breaks out an epidemic that, in all earlier epochs, would have seemed an absurdity—the epidemic of overproduction. Society suddenly finds itself put back into a state of momentary barbarism; it appears as if a famine, a universal war of devastation had cut off the supply of every means of subsistence; industry and commerce seem to be destroyed; and why? Because there is too much civilization, too much means of subsistence, too much industry, too much commerce. The productive forces at the disposal of society no longer tend to further the development of the conditions of bourgeois property; on the contrary, they have become too powerful for these conditions, by which they are fettered, and so soon as they overcome these fetters, they bring disorder into the whole of bourgeois society, endanger the existence of bourgeois property. The conditions of bourgeois society are too narrow to comprise the wealth created by them. And how does the bourgeoisie get over these crises? On the one hand, by enforced destruction of a mass of productive forces; on the other, by the conquest of new markets, and by the more thorough exploitation of the old ones. That is to say, by paving the way for more extensive and more destructive crises, and by diminishing the means whereby crises are prevented.

The weapons with which the bourgeoisie felled feudalism to the ground are now turned against the bourgeoisie itself.

But not only has the bourgeoisie forged the weapons that bring death to itself; it has also called into existence the men who are to wield those weapons—the modern working class—the proletarians.

In proportion as the bourgeoisie, *i.e.*, capital, is developed, in the same proportion is the proletariat, the modern working class, developed—a class of laborers, who live only so long as they find work, and who find work only so long as their labor increases capital. These laborers, who must sell themselves piecemeal, are a commodity, like every other article of commerce, and are consequently exposed to all the vicissitudes of competition, to all the fluctuations of the market.

Owing to the extensive use of machinery and to division of labor, the work of the proletarians has lost all individual character, and, consequently, all charm for the workman. He becomes an appendage of the machine, and it is only the most simple, most monotonous, and most easily acquired knack that is required of him. Hence, the cost of production of a workman is restricted, almost entirely, to the means of subsistence that he requires for his maintenance, and for the propagation of his race. But the price of a commodity, and therefore also of labor, is equal to its cost of production. In proportion, therefore, as the repulsiveness of the work increases, the wage decreases. Nay more, in proportion as the use of machinery and division of labor increases, in the same proportion the burden of toil also increases, whether by prolongation of the working hours, by increase of the work exacted in a given time, or by increased speed of the machinery, etc.

Modern industry has converted the little workshop of the patriarchal master into the great factory of the industrial capitalist. Masses of laborers, crowded into the factory, are organized like soldiers. As privates of the industrial army they are placed under the command of a perfect hierarchy of officers and sergeants. Not only are they slaves of the bourgeois class, and of the bourgeois State; they are daily and hourly enslaved by the machine, by the overlooker, and, above all, by the individual bourgeois manufacturer himself. The more openly this despotism proclaims gain to be its end and aim, the more petty, the more hateful, and the more embittering it is.

The less the skill and exertion of strength implied in manual labor, in other words, the more modern industry becomes developed, the more is the labor of men superseded by that of women. Differences of age and sex have no longer any distinctive social validity for the working class. All are instruments of labor, more or less expensive to use, according to their age and sex.

No sooner is the exploitation of the laborer by the manufacturer, so far, at an end, that he receives his wages in cash, than he is set upon by the other portions of the bourgeoisie, the landlord, the shopkeeper, the pawnbroker, etc.

The lower strata of the middle class—the small trades-people, shopkeepers, and retired tradesmen generally, the handicraftsmen and peasants—all these sink grad-ually into the proletariat, partly because their diminu-tive capital does not suffice for the scale on which Mod-ern Industry is carried on, and is swamped in the com-petition with the large capitalists, partly because their specialized skill is rendered worthless by new methods of production. Thus the proletariat is recruited from all classes of the population.

The proletariat goes through various stages of devel-opment. With its birth begins its struggle with the bour-geoisie. At first the contest is carried on by individual laborers, then by the workpeople of a factory, then by the operatives of one trade, in one locality, against the individual bourgeois who directly exploits them. They direct their attacks not against the bourgeois conditions of production, but against the instruments of produc-tion themselves; they destroy imported wares that com-pete with their labor, they smash to pieces machinery, they set factories ablaze, they seek to restore by force the vanished status of the workman of the Middle Ages.

At this stage the laborers still form an incoherent mass scattered over the whole country, and broken up by their mutual competition. If anywhere they unite to form more compact bodies, this is not yet the conse-quence of their own active union, but of the union of the bourgeoisie, which class, in order to attain its own political ends, is compelled to set the whole proletariat in motion, and is moreover yet, for a time, able to do so. At this stage, therefore, the proletarians do not fight their enemies, but the enemies of their enemies, the remnants of absolute monarchy, the landowners, the non-industrial bourgeois, the petty bourgeoisie. Thus the whole historical movement is concentrated in the hands of the bourgeoisie; every victory so obtained is a victory for the bourgeoisie.

But with the development of industry the proletariat not only increases in number; it becomes concentrated in greater masses, its strength grows, and it feels that strength more. The various interests and conditions of life within the ranks of the proletariat are more and more equalized in proportion as machinery obliterates all distinctions of labor, and nearly everywhere reduces wages to the same low level. The growing competition among the bourgeois, and the resulting commercial crises, make the wages of the workers ever more fluctuating. The unceasing improvement of machinery, ever more rapidly developing, makes their livelihood more and more precarious; the collisions between individual workmen and individual bourgeois take more and more the character of collisions between two classes. Thereupon the workers begin to form combinations (Trades' Unions) against the bourgeois; they club together in order to keep up the rate of wages; they found permanent associations in order to make provision beforehand for these occasional revolts. Here and there the contest breaks out into riots.

Now and then the workers are victorious, but only for a time. The real fruit of their battles lies, not in the immediate result, but in the ever-expanding union of the workers. This union is helped on by the improved means of communication that are created by Modern Industry and that place the workers of different localities in contact with one another. It was just this contact that was needed to centralize the numerous local struggles, all of the same character, into one national struggle between classes. But every class struggle is a political struggle. And that union, to attain which the burghers of the Middle Ages, with their miserable highways, required centuries, the modern proletarians, thanks to railways, achieve in a few years.

This organization of the proletarians into a class, and consequently into a political party, is continually being upset again by the competition between the workers themselves. But it ever rises up again, stronger, firmer, mightier. It compels legislative recognition of particular interests of the workers, by taking advantage of the divisions among the bourgeoisie itself. Thus the ten-hours' bill in England was carried.

Altogether collisions between the classes of the old society further, in many ways, the course of development of the proletariat. The bourgeoisie finds itself involved in a constant battle—at first with the aristocracy; later on, with those portions of the bourgeoisie itself whose interests have become antagonistic to the progress of industry; at all times, with the bourgeoisie of foreign countries. In all these battles it sees itself compelled to appeal to the proletariat, to ask for its help, and thus, to drag it into the political arena. The bourgeoisie itself, therefore, supplies the proletariat with its own elements of political and general education; in other words, it furnishes the proletariat with weapons for fighting the bourgeoisie.

Further, as we have already seen, entire sections of the ruling classes are, by the advance of industry, precipitated into the proletariat, or are at least threatened in their conditions of existence. These also supply the proletariat with fresh elements of enlightenment and progress.

Finally, in times when the class struggle nears the decisive hour, the process of dissolution going on within the ruling class, in fact within the whole range of old society, assumes such a violent, glaring character, that a small section of the ruling class cuts itself adrift, and joins the revolutionary class, the class that holds the future in its hands. Just as, therefore, at an earlier period, a section of the nobility went over to the bourgeoisie, so now a portion of the bourgeoisie goes over to the proletariat, and in particular, a portion of the bourgeois ideologists, who have raised themselves to the level of comprehending theoretically the historical movement as a whole.

Of all the classes that stand face to face with the bourgeoisie today, the proletariat alone is a really revolutionary class. The other classes decay and finally disappear in the face of modern industry; the proletariat is its special and essential product.

The lower middle class, the small manufacturer, the shopkeeper, the artisan, the peasant, all these fight against the bourgeoisie, to save from extinction their existence as fractions of the middle class. They are therefore not revolutionary, but conservative. Nay more, they are reactionary, for they try to roll back the wheel of history. If by chance they are revolutionary, they are so only in view of their impending transfer into the proletariat; they thus defend not their present, but their future interests; they desert their own standpoint to place themselves at that of the proletariat.

The "dangerous class," the social scum, that passively rotting mass thrown off by the lowest layers of old society, may, here and there, be swept into the movement by a proletarian revolution; its conditions of life, however, prepare it far more for the part of a bribed tool of reactionary intrigue.

In the conditions of the proletariat, those of old society at large are already virtually swamped. The proletarian is without property; his relation to his wife and children has no longer anything in common with the bourgeois family relations; modern industrial labor, modern subjection to capital, the same in England as in France, in America as in Germany, has stripped him of every trace of national character. Law, morality, religion, are to him so many bourgeois prejudices, behind which lurk in ambush just as many bourgeois interests.

All the preceding classes that got the upper hand, sought to fortify their already acquired status by subjecting society at large to their conditions of appropriation. The proletarians cannot become masters of the productive forces of society except by abolishing their own previous mode of appropriation, and thereby also every other previous mode of appropriation. They have nothing of their own to secure and to fortify; their mission is to destroy all previous securities for, and insurances of, individual property.

All previous historical movements were movements of minorities, or in the interest of minorities. The proletarian movement is the self-conscious, independent movement of the immense majority, in the interest of the immense majority. The proletariat, the lowest stratum of our present society, cannot stir, cannot raise itself up, without the whole super-incumbent strata of official society being sprung into the air.

Though not in substance, yet in form, the struggle of the proletariat with the bourgeoisie is at first a national struggle. The proletariat of each country must, of course, first of all settle matters with its own bourgeoisie.

In depicting the most general phases of the development of the proletariat, we traced the more or less veiled civil war, raging within existing society, up to the point where that war breaks out into open revolution, and where the violent overthrow of the bourgeoisie lays the foundation for the sway of the proletariat.

Hitherto, every form of society has been based, as we have already seen, on the antagonism of oppressing and oppressed classes. But in order to oppress a class, certain conditions must be assured to it under which it can, at least, continue its slavish existence. The serf, in the period of serfdom, raised himself to membership in the commune, just as the petty bourgeois, under the yoke of feudal absolutism, managed to develop into a bourgeois. The modern laborer, on the contrary, instead of rising with the progress of industry, sinks deeper and deeper below the conditions of existence of his own class. He becomes a pauper, and pauperism develops more rapidly than population and wealth. And here it becomes evident that the bourgeoisie is unfit any longer to be the ruling class in society, and to impose its conditions of existence upon society as an overriding law. It is unfit to rule because it is incompetent to assure an existence to its slave within his slavery, because it cannot help letting him sink into such a state, that it has to feed him, instead of being fed by him. Society can no longer live under this bourgeoisie; in other words, its existence is no longer compatible with society.

The essential condition for the existence, and for the sway of the bourgeois class, is the formation and augmentation of capital; the condition for capital is wage labor. Wage labor rests exclusively on competition between the laborers. The advance of industry, whose involuntary promoter is the bourgeoisie, replaces the isolation of the laborers, due to competition, by their revolutionary combination, due to association. The development of Modern Industry, therefore, cuts from under its feet the very foundation on which the bourgeoisie produces and appropriates products. What the bourgeoisie, therefore, produces, above all, is its own gravediggers. Its fall and the victory of the proletariat are equally inevitable.

II. PROLETARIANS AND COMMUNISTS

In what relation do the Communists stand to the proletarians as a whole?

The Communists do not form a separate party opposed to other working-class parties.

They have no interests separate and apart from those of the proletariat as a whole.

They do not set up any sectarian principles of their own, by which to shape and mold the proletarian movement.

The Communists are distinguished from the other working-class parties by this only: 1. In the national struggles of the proletarians of the different countries, they point out and bring to the front the common interests of the entire proletariat, independently of all nationality. 2. In the various stages of development which the struggle of the working class against the bourgeoisie has to pass through, they always and everywhere represent the interests of the movement as a whole.

The Communists, therefore, are on the one hand, practically, the most advanced and resolute section of the working-class parties of every country, that section which pushes forward all others; on the other hand, theoretically, they have over the great mass of the proletariat the advantage of clearly understanding the line of march, the conditions, and the ultimate general results of the proletarian movement.

The immediate aim of the Communists is the same as that of all the other proletarian parties: formation of the proletariat into a class, overthrow of the bourgeois supremacy, conquest of political power by the proletariat.

The theoretical conclusions of the Communists are in no way based on ideas or principles that have been invented, or discovered, by this or that would-be universal reformer.

They merely express, in general terms, actual relations springing from an existing class struggle, from a historical movement going on under our very eyes. The abolition of existing property relations is not at all a distinctive feature of communism.

All property relations in the past have continually been subject to historical change consequent upon the change in historical conditions.

The French Revolution, for example, abolished feudal property in favor of bourgeois property.

The distinguishing feature of communism is not the abolition of property generally, but the abolition of bourgeois property. But modern bourgeois private property is the final and most complete expression of the system of producing and appropriating products that is based on class antagonisms, on the exploitation of the many by the few.

In this sense, the theory of the Communists may be summed up in the single sentence: Abolition of private property.

We Communists have been reproached with the desire of abolishing the right of personally acquiring property as the fruit of a man's own labor, which property is alleged to be the groundwork of all personal freedom, activity, and independence.

Hard-won, self-acquired, self-earned property! Do you mean the property of the petty artisan and of the small peasant, a form of property that preceded the bourgeois form? There is no need to abolish that; the development of industry has to a great extent already destroyed it, and is still destroying it daily.

Or do you mean modern bourgeois private property?

But does wage labor create any property for the laborer? Not a bit. It creates capital, *i.e.,* that kind of property which exploits wage labor, and which cannot increase except upon condition of begetting a new supply of wage labor for fresh exploitation. Property, in its present form, is based on the antagonism of capital and wage labor. Let us examine both sides of this antagonism.

To be a capitalist is to have not only a purely personal, but a social *status* in production. Capital is a collective product, and only by the united action of many members, nay, in the last resort, only by the united action of all members of society, can it be set in motion.

Capital is, therefore, not a personal, it is a social power.

When, therefore, capital is converted into common property, into the property of all members of society, personal property is not thereby transformed into social property. It is only the social character of the property that is changed. It loses its class character.

Let us now take wage labor.

The average price of wage labor is the minimum wage, *i.e.*, that quantum of the means of subsistence, which is absolutely requisite to keep the laborer in bare existence as a laborer. What, therefore, the wage-laborer appropriates by means of his labor merely suffices to prolong and reproduce a bare existence. We by no means intend to abolish this personal appropriation of the products of labor, an appropriation that is made for the maintenance and reproduction of human life, and that leaves no surplus wherewith to command the labor of others. All that we want to do away with is the miserable character of this appropriation, under which the laborer lives merely to increase capital, and is allowed to live only in so far as the interest of the ruling class requires it.

In bourgeois society, living labor is but a means to increase accumulated labor. In Communist society, accumulated labor is but a means to widen, to enrich, to promote the existence of the laborer.

In bourgeois society, therefore, the past dominates the present; in Communist society, the present dominates the past. In bourgeois society capital is independent and has individuality, while the living person is dependent and has no individuality.

And the abolition of this stage of things is called by the bourgeois, abolition of individuality and freedom! And rightly so. The abolition of bourgeois individuality, bourgeois independence, and bourgeois freedom is undoubtedly aimed at.

By freedom is meant, under the present bourgeois conditions of production, free trade, free selling and buying.

But if selling and buying disappears, free selling and buying disappears also. This talk about free selling and buying, and all the other "brave words" of our bourgeoisie about freedom in general, have a meaning, if any, only in contrast with restricted selling and buying, with the fettered traders of the Middle Ages, but have no meaning when opposed to the Communistic abolition of buying and selling, of the bourgeois conditions of production, and of the bourgeoisie itself.

You are horrified at our intending to do away with private property. But in your existing society, private property is already done away with for nine-tenths of the population; its existence for the few is solely due to its non-existence in the hands of those nine-tenths. You reproach us, therefore, with intending to do away with a form of property, the necessary condition for whose existence is the non-existence of any property for the immense majority of society.

In one word, you reproach us with intending to do away with your property. Precisely so; that is just what we intend.

From the moment when labor can no longer be converted into capital, money, or rent, into a social power capable of being monopolized, *i.e.*, from the moment when individual property can no longer be transformed into bourgeois property, into capital, from that moment, you say, individuality vanishes.

You must, therefore, confess that by "individual" you mean no other person than the bourgeois, than the middle-class owner of property. This person must, indeed, be swept out of the way, and made impossible.

Communism deprives no man of the power to appropriate the products of society; all that it does is to deprive him of the power to subjugate the labor of others by means of such appropriation.

It has been objected that upon the abolition of private property all work will cease, and universal laziness will overtake us.

According to this, bourgeois society ought long ago to have gone to the dogs through sheer idleness; for those of its members who work acquire nothing, and those who acquire anything do not work. The whole of this objection is but another expression of the tautology: that there can no longer be any wage labor when there is no longer any capital.

All objections urged against the Communistic mode of producing and appropriating material products have, in the same way, been urged against the Communistic modes of producing and appropriating intellectual products. Just as, to the bourgeois, the disappearance of class property is the disappearance of production itself, so the disappearance of class culture is to him identical with the disappearance of all culture.

That culture, the loss of which he laments, is, for the enormous majority, a mere training to act as a machine.

But don't wrangle with us so long as you apply, to our intended abolition of bourgeois property, the standard of your bourgeois notions of freedom, culture, law, etc. Your very ideas are but the outgrowth of the conditions of your bourgeois production and bourgeois property, just as your jurisprudence is but the will of your class made into a law for all, a will whose essential character and direction are determined by the economical conditions of existence of your class.

The selfish misconception that induces you to transform into eternal laws of nature and of reason the social forms springing from your present mode of production and form of property—historical relations that rise and disappear in the progress of production—this misconception you share with every ruling class that has preceded you. What you see clearly in the case of ancient property, what you admit in the case of feudal property, you are of course forbidden to admit in the case of your own bourgeois form of property.

Abolition of the family! Even the most radical flare up at this infamous proposal of the Communists.

On what foundation is the present family, the bourgeois family, based? On capital, on private gain. In its completely developed form this family exists only among the bourgeoisie. But this state of things finds its complement in the practical absence of the family among the proletarians, and in public prostitution.

The bourgeois family will vanish as a matter of course when its complement vanishes, and both will vanish with the vanishing of capital.

Do you charge us with wanting to stop the exploitation of children by their parents? To this crime we plead guilty.

But, you will say, we destroy the most hallowed of relations, when we replace home education by social.

And your education! Is not that also social, and determined by the social conditions under which you educate, by the intervention, direct or indirect, of society, by means of schools, etc.? The Communists have not invented the intervention of society in education; they do but seek to alter the character of that intervention, and to rescue education from the influence of the ruling class.

The bourgeois claptrap about the family and education, about the hallowed co-relation of parent and child, becomes all the more disgusting, the more, by the action of Modern Industry, all family ties among the proletarians are torn asunder, and their children transformed into simple articles of commerce and instruments of labor.

But you Communists would introduce community of women, screams the whole bourgeoisie in chorus.

The bourgeoisie sees in his wife a mere instrument of production. He hears that the instruments of production are to be exploited in common, and, naturally, can come to no other conclusion than that the lot of being common to all will likewise fall to the women.

He has not even a suspicion that the real point aimed at is to do away with the status of women as mere instruments of production.

For the rest, nothing is more ridiculous than the virtuous indignation of our bourgeois at the community of women which, they pretend, is to be openly and officially established by the Communists. The Communists have no need to introduce community of women; it has existed almost from time immemorial.

Our bourgeois, not content with having the wives and daughters of their proletarians at their disposal, not to speak of common prostitutes, take the greatest pleasure in seducing each other's wives.

Bourgeois marriage is in reality a system of wives in common and thus, at the most, what the Communists might possibly be reproached with is that they desire to introduce, in substitution for a hypocritically concealed, an openly legalized community of women. For the rest, it is self-evident that the abolition of the present system of production must bring with it the abolition of the community of women springing from that system, *i.e.*, of prostitution both public and private.

The Communists are further reproached with desiring to abolish countries and nationality.

The workingmen have no country. We cannot take from them what they have not got. Since the proletariat must first of all acquire political supremacy, must rise to be the leading class of the nation, must constitute itself *the* nation, it is, so far, itself national, though not in the bourgeois sense of the word.

National differences and antagonisms between peoples are daily more and more vanishing, owing to the development of the bourgeoisie, to freedom of commerce, to the world market, to uniformity in the mode of production and in the conditions of life corresponding thereto.

The supremacy of the proletariat will cause them to vanish still faster. United action, of the leading civilized countries at least, is one of the first conditions for the emancipation of the proletariat.

In proportion as the exploitation of one individual by another is put an end to, the exploitation of one nation by another will also be put an end to. In proportion as the antagonism between classes within the nation vanishes, the hostility of one nation to another will come to an end.

The charges against communism made from a religious, a philosophical, and, generally, from an ideological standpoint, are not deserving of serious examination.

Does it require deep intuition to comprehend that man's ideas, views, and conceptions, in one word, man's consciousness, changes with every change in the conditions of his material existence, in his social relations and his social life?

What else does the history of ideas prove than that intellectual production changes its character in proportion as material production is changed? The ruling ideas of each age have ever been the ideas of its ruling class.

When people speak of ideas that revolutionize society, they do but express the fact that within the old society, the elements of a new one have been created, and that the dissolution of the old ideas keeps even pace with the dissolution of the old conditions of existence.

When the ancient world was in its last throes, the ancient religions were overcome by Christianity. When Christian ideas succumbed in the eighteenth century to rationalist ideas, feudal society fought its death battle with the then revolutionary bourgeoisie. The ideas of religious liberty and freedom of conscience merely gave expression to the sway of free competition within the domain of knowledge.

"Undoubtedly," it will be said, "religious, moral, philosophical, and juridical ideas have been modified in the course of historical development. But religion, morality, philosophy, political science, and law constantly survived this change.

"There are, besides, eternal truths, such as Freedom, Justice, etc., that are common to all states of society. But communism abolishes eternal truths, it abolishes all religion, and all morality, instead of constituting them on a new basis; it therefore acts in contradiction to all past historical experience."

What does this accusation reduce itself to? The history of all past society has consisted in the development of class antagonisms, antagonisms that assumed different forms at different epochs.

But whatever form they may have taken, one fact is common to all past ages, *viz.*, the exploitation of one part of society by the other. No wonder, then, that the social consciousness of past ages, despite all the multiplicity and variety it displays, moves within certain common forms, or general ideas, which cannot completely vanish except with the total disappearance of class antagonism.

The Communist revolution is the most radical rupture with traditional property relations. No wonder that its development involves the most radical rupture with traditional ideas.

But let us have done with the bourgeois objections to communism.

We have seen above that the first step in the revolution by the working class is to raise the proletariat to the position of ruling class, to win the battle of democracy.

The proletariat will use its political supremacy to wrest, by degrees, all capital from the bourgeoisie, to centralize all instruments of production in the hands of the State, *i.e.,* of the proletariat organized as the ruling class; and to increase the total of productive forces as rapidly as possible.

Of course, in the beginning, this cannot be effected except by means of despotic inroads on the rights of property, and on the conditions of bourgeois production; by means of measures, therefore, which appear economically insufficient and untenable, but which, in the course of the movement, outstrip themselves, necessitate further inroads upon the old social order, and are unavoidable as a means of entirely revolutionizing the mode of production.

These measures will of course be different in different countries.

Nevertheless in the most advanced countries, the following will be pretty generally applicable:

1. Abolition of property in land and application of all rents of land to public purposes.

2. A heavy progressive or graduated income tax.

3. Abolition of all right of inheritance.

4. Confiscation of the property of all emigrants and rebels.

5. Centralization of credit in the hands of the State, by means of a national bank with State capital and an exclusive monopoly.

6. Centralization of the means of communication and transport in the hands of the State.

7. Extension of factories and instruments of production owned by the State; the bringing into cultivation of wastelands, and the improvement of the soil generally in accordance with a common plan.

8. Equal liability of all to labor. Establishment of industrial armies, especially for agriculture.

9. Combination of agriculture with manufacturing industries; gradual abolition of the distinction between town and country, by a more equable distribution of the population over the country.

10. Free education for all children in public schools. Abolition of children's factory labor in its present form.

Combination of education with industrial production, etc., etc.

When, in the course of development, class distinctions have disappeared, and all production has been concentrated in the hands of a vast association of the whole nation, the public power will lose its political character. Political power, properly so called, is merely the organized power of one class for oppressing another. If the proletariat during its contest with the bourgeoisie is compelled, by the force of circumstances, to organize itself as a class, if, by means of a revolution, it makes itself the ruling class and, as such, sweeps away by force the old conditions of production, then it will, along with these conditions, have swept away the conditions for the existence of class antagonisms and of classes generally, and will thereby have abolished its own supremacy as a class.

In place of the old bourgeois society, with its classes and class antagonisms, we shall have an association in which the free development of each is the condition for the free development of all.

III. SOCIALIST AND COMMUNIST LITERATURE

1. Reactionary Socialism

a. Feudal Socialism

Owing to their historical position, it became the vocation of the aristocracies of France and England to write pamphlets against modern bourgeois society. In the French revolution of July, 1830, and in the English reform agitation, these aristocracies again succumbed to the hateful upstart. Thenceforth, a serious political contest was altogether out of question. A literary battle alone remained possible. But even in the domain of literature the old cries of the restoration period [1] had become impossible.

[1] Not the English Restoration 1660 to 1689, but the French Restoration 1814 to 1830. [*Note by Engels to the English edition of 1888.*]

In order to arouse sympathy, the aristocracy were obliged to lose sight, apparently, of their own interests, and to formulate their indictment against the bourgeoisie in the interest of the exploited working class alone. Thus the aristocracy took their revenge by singing lampoons on their new master, and whispering in his ears sinister prophecies of coming catastrophe.

In this way arose feudal socialism: half lamentation, half lampoon; half echo of the past, half menace of the future; at times, by its bitter, witty, and incisive criticism, striking the bourgeoisie to the very heart's core; but always ludicrous in its effect, through total incapacity to comprehend the march of modern history.

The aristocracy, in order to rally the people to them, waved the proletarian alms-bag in front for a banner. But the people, so often as it joined them, saw on their hindquarters the old feudal coats of arms, and deserted with loud and irreverent laughter.

One section of the French Legitimists [1] and "Young England" [2] exhibited this spectacle.

In pointing out that their mode of exploitation was different to that of the bourgeoisie, the feudalists forget that they exploited under circumstances and conditions that were quite different, and that are now antiquated. In showing that, under their rule, the modern proletariat never existed, they forget that the modern bourgeoisie is the necessary offspring of their own form of society.

For the rest, so little do they conceal the reactionary character of their criticism that their chief accusation against the bourgeoisie amounts to this, that under the bourgeois *régime* a class is being developed, which is destined to cut up root and branch the old order of society.

What they upbraid the bourgeoisie with is not so much that it creates a proletariat, as that it creates a *revolutionary* proletariat.

In political practice, therefore, they join in all coercive

---

[1] *The Legitimists:* The party of the noble landowners, who advocated the restoration of the Bourbon dynasty.—*Ed.*

[2] *"Young England":* A group of British Conservatives—aristocrats and men of politics and literature—formed about 1842. Prominent among them were Disraeli, Thomas Carlyle, and others.—*Ed.*

measures against the working class; and in ordinary life, despite their highfalutin phrases, they stoop to pick up the golden apples dropped from the tree of industry, and to barter truth, love, and honor for traffic in wool, beetroot sugar, and potato spirits.[1]

As the parson has ever gone hand in hand with the landlord, so has clerical socialism with feudal socialism.

Nothing is easier than to give Christian asceticism a Socialist tinge. Has not Christianity declaimed against private property, against marriage, against the State? Has it not preached, in the place of these, charity and poverty, celibacy and mortification of the flesh, monastic life and Mother Church? Christian socialism is but the holy water with which the priest consecrates the heart-burnings of the aristocrat.

b. Petty-Bourgeois Socialism

The feudal aristocracy was not the only class that was ruined by the bourgeoisie, not the only class whose conditions of existence pined and perished in the atmosphere of modern bourgeois society. The medieval burgesses and the small peasant proprietors were the precursors of the modern bourgeoisie. In those countries which are but little developed, industrially and commercially, these two classes still vegetate side by side with the rising bourgeoisie.

In countries where modern civilization has become fully developed, a new class of petty bourgeois has been formed, fluctuating between proletariat and bourgeoisie and ever renewing itself as a supplementary part of bourgeois society. The individual members of this class, however, are being constantly hurled down into the proletariat by the action of competition, and, as modern industry develops, they even see the moment approach-

[1] This applies chiefly to Germany where the landed aristocracy and squirearchy have large portions of their estates cultivated for their own account by stewards, and are, moreover, extensive beetroot-sugar manufacturers and distillers of potato spirits. The wealthier British aristocracy are, as yet, rather above that; but they, too, know how to make up for declining rents by lending their names to floaters of more or less shady jointstock companies. [*Note by Engels to the English edition of 1888.*]

ing when they will completely disappear as an independent section of modern society, to be replaced, in manufactures, agriculture, and commerce, by overlookers, bailiffs, and shopmen.

In countries like France, where the peasants constitute far more than half of the population, it was natural that writers who sided with the proletariat against the bourgeoisie should use, in their criticism of the bourgeois *régime,* the standard of the peasant and petty bourgeois, and from the standpoint of these intermediate classes should take up the cudgels for the working class. Thus arose petty-bourgeois socialism. Sismondi was the head of this school, not only in France but also in England.

This school of socialism dissected with great acuteness the contradictions in the conditions of modern production. It laid bare the hypocritical apologies of economists. It proved, incontrovertibly, the disastrous effects of machinery and division of labor; the concentration of capital and land in a few hands; overproduction and crises; it pointed out the inevitable ruin of the petty bourgeois and peasant, the misery of the proletariat, the anarchy in production, the crying inequalities in the distribution of wealth, the industrial war of extermination between nations, the dissolution of old moral bonds, of the old family relations, of the old nationalities.

In its positive aims, however, this form of socialism aspires either to restoring the old means of production and of exchange, and with them the old property relations, and the old society, or to cramping the modern means of production and of exchange within the framework of the old property relations that have been, and were bound to be, exploded by those means. In either case, it is both reactionary and Utopian.

Its last words are: corporate guilds for manufacture; patriarchal relations in agriculture.

Ultimately, when stubborn historical facts had dispersed all intoxicating effects of self-deception, this form of socialism ended in a miserable fit of the blues.

c. German, or "True," Socialism

The Socialist and Communist literature of France, a literature that originated under the pressure of a bourgeoisie in power, and that was the expression of the struggle against this power, was introduced into Germany at a time when the bourgeoisie, in that country, had just begun its contest with feudal absolutism.

German philosophers, would-be philosophers, and *beaux esprits* eagerly seized on this literature, only forgetting that when these writings immigrated from France into Germany, French social conditions had not immigrated along with them. In contact with German social conditions, this French literature lost all its immediate practical significance, and assumed a purely literary aspect. Thus, to the German philosophers of the eighteenth century, the demands of the first French Revolution were nothing more than the demands of "Practical Reason" in general, and the utterance of the will of the revolutionary French bourgeoisie signified in their eyes the laws of pure Will, of Will as it was bound to be, of true human Will generally.

The work of the German *literati* consisted solely in bringing the new French ideas into harmony with their ancient philosophical conscience, or rather, in annexing the French ideas without deserting their own philosophic point of view.

This annexation took place in the same way in which a foreign language is appropriated, namely, by translation.

It is well known how the monks wrote silly lives of Catholic saints *over* the manuscripts on which the classical works of ancient heathendom had been written. The German *literati* reversed this process with the profane French literature. They wrote their philosophical nonsense beneath the French original. For instance, beneath the French criticism of the economic functions of money, they wrote, "Alienation of Humanity," and beneath the French criticism of the bourgeois State they wrote, "Dethronement of the Category of the General," and so forth.

The introduction of these philosophical phrases at the back of the French historical criticisms they dubbed "Philosophy of Action," "True Socialism," "German Science of Socialism," "Philosophical Foundation of Socialism," and so on.

The French Socialist and Communist literature was thus completely emasculated. And, since it ceased in the hands of the German to express the struggle of one class with the other, he felt conscious of having overcome "French one-sidedness" and of representing, not true requirements, but the requirements of Truth; not the interests of the proletariat, but the interests of Human Nature, of Man in general, who belongs to no class, has no reality, who exists only in the misty realm of philosophical fantasy.

This German socialism, which took its schoolboy task so seriously and solemnly, and extolled its poor stock-in-trade in such mountebank fashion, meanwhile gradually lost its pedantic innocence.

The fight of the German, and, especially, of the Prussian bourgeoisie, against feudal aristocracy and absolute monarchy, in other words, the liberal movement, became more earnest.

By this, the long-wished-for opportunity was offered to "True" socialism of confronting the political movement with the Socialist demands, of hurling the traditional anathemas against liberalism, against representative government, against bourgeois competition, bourgeois freedom of the press, bourgeois legislation, bourgeois liberty and equality, and of preaching to the masses that they had nothing to gain, and everything to lose, by this bourgeois movement. German socialism forgot, in the nick of time, that the French criticism, whose silly echo it was, presupposed the existence of modern bourgeois society, with its corresponding economic conditions of existence, and the political constitution adapted thereto, the very things whose attainment was the object of the pending struggle in Germany.

To the absolute governments, with their following of parsons, professors, country squires, and officials, it served as a welcome scarecrow against the threatening bourgeoisie.

It was a sweet finish after the bitter pills of floggings

and bullets with which these same governments, just at
that time, dosed the German working-class risings.

While this "True" socialism thus served the governments as a weapon for fighting the German bourgeoisie,
it, at the same time, directly represented a reactionary
interest, the interest of the German Philistines. In Germany the *petty-bourgeois* class, a relic of the sixteenth
century, and since then constantly cropping up again
under various forms, is the real social basis of the existing state of things.

To preserve this class is to preserve the existing state
of things in Germany. The industrial and political supremacy of the bourgeoisie threatens it with certain
destruction: on the one hand, from the concentration
of capital; on the other, from the rise of a revolutionary
proletariat. "True" socialism appeared to kill these two
birds with one stone. It spread like an epidemic.

The robe of speculative cobwebs, embroidered with
flowers of rhetoric, steeped in the dew of sickly senti-
ment, this transcendental robe in which the German
Socialists wrapped their sorry "eternal truths," all skin
and bone, served to wonderfully increase the sale of their
goods amongst such a public.

And on its part, German socialism recognized, more
and more, its own calling as the bombastic representative of the petty-bourgeois Philistine.

It proclaimed the German nation to be the model
nation, and the German petty Philistine to be the typical
man. To every villainous meanness of this model man
it gave a hidden, higher, Socialistic interpretation, the
exact contrary of its real character. It went to the extreme length of directly opposing the "brutally destructive" tendency of communism, and of proclaiming its
supreme and impartial contempt of all class struggles.
With very few exceptions, all the so-called Socialist and
Communist publications that now (1847) circulate in
Germany belong to the domain of this foul and ener-
vating literature.[1]

---

[1] The revolutionary storm of 1848 swept away this whole shabby
tendency and cured its protagonists of the desire to dabble further
in socialism. The chief representative and classical type of this
tendency is Herr Karl Grün. [*Note by Engels to the German edition of 1890.*]

2. Conservative, or Bourgeois, Socialism

A part of the bourgeoisie is desirous of redressing social grievances, in order to secure the continued existence of bourgeois society.

To this section belong economists, philanthropists, humanitarians, improvers of the condition of the working class, organizers of charity, members of societies for the prevention of cruelty to animals, temperance fanatics, hole-and-corner reformers of every imaginable kind. This form of socialism has, moreover, been worked out into complete systems.

We may cite Proudhon's *Philosophie de la Misère* as an example of this form.

The Socialistic bourgeois want all the advantages of modern social conditions without the struggles and dangers necessarily resulting therefrom. They desire the existing state of society minus its revolutionary and disintegrating elements. They wish for a bourgeoisie without a proletariat. The bourgeoisie naturally conceives the world in which it is supreme to be the best; and bourgeois socialism develops this comfortable conception into various more or less complete systems. In requiring the proletariat to carry out such a system, and thereby to march straightway into the social New Jerusalem, it but requires in reality that the proletariat should remain within the bounds of existing society, but should cast away all its hateful ideas concerning the bourgeoisie.

A second and more practical, but less systematic, form of this socialism sought to depreciate every revolutionary movement in the eyes of the working class by showing that no mere political reform, but only a change in the material conditions of existence, in economical relations, could be of any advantage to them. By changes in the material conditions of existence, this form of socialism, however, by no means understands abolition of the bourgeois relations of production, an abolition that can be effected only by a revolution, but administrative reforms, based on the continued existence of these relations; reforms, therefore, that in no respect affect the relations between capital and labor, but, at the best, lessen the cost, and simplify the administrative work, of bourgeois government.

Bourgeois socialism attains adequate expression when, and only when, it becomes a mere figure of speech.

Free trade: for the benefit of the working class. Protective duties: for the benefit of the working class. Prison reform: for the benefit of the working class. This is the last word and the only seriously meant word of bourgeois socialism.

It is summed up in the phrase: the bourgeois is a bourgeois—for the benefit of the working class.

3. Critical-Utopian Socialism and Communism

We do not here refer to that literature which, in every great modern revolution, has always given voice to the demands of the proletariat, such as the writings of Babeuf and others.

The first direct attempts of the proletariat to attain its own ends, made in times of universal excitement, when feudal society was being overthrown, these attempts necessarily failed, owing to the then undeveloped state of the proletariat, as well as to the absence of the economic conditions for its emancipation, conditions that had yet to be produced, and could be produced by the impending bourgeois epoch alone. The revolutionary literature that accompanied these first movements of the proletariat had necessarily a reactionary character. It inculcated universal asceticism and social leveling in its crudest form.

The Socialist and Communist systems properly so called, those of St. Simon, Fourier, Owen, and others, spring into existence in the early undeveloped period, described above, of the struggle between proletariat and bourgeoisie (see Section I: Bourgeoisie and Proletariat).

The founders of these systems see, indeed, the class antagonisms, as well as the action of the decomposing elements in the prevailing form of society. But the proletariat, as yet in its infancy, offers to them the spectacle of a class without any historical initiative or any independent political movement.

Since the development of class antagonism keeps even pace with the development of industry, the economic situation, as they find it, does not as yet offer to them the material conditions for the emancipation of the proletariat. They therefore search after a new social science, after new social laws, that are to create these conditions.

Historical action is to yield to their personal inventive action, historically created conditions of emancipation to fantastic ones, and the gradual, spontaneous class organization of the proletariat to an organization of society specially contrived by these inventors. Future history resolves itself, in their eyes, into the propaganda and the practical carrying out of their social plans.

In the formation of their plans they are conscious of caring chiefly for the interests of the working class, as being the most suffering class. Only from the point of view of being the most suffering class does the proletariat exist for them.

The undeveloped state of the class struggle, as well as their own surroundings, causes Socialists of this kind to consider themselves far superior to all class antagonisms. They want to improve the condition of every member of society, even that of the most favored. Hence, they habitually appeal to society at large, without distinction of class; nay, by preference, to the ruling class. For how can people, when once they understand their system, fail to see in it the best possible plan of the best possible state of society?

Hence, they reject all political, and especially all revolutionary, action; they wish to attain their ends by peaceful means, and endeavor, by small experiments, necessarily doomed to failure, and by the force of example, to pave the way for the new social Gospel.

Such fantastic pictures of future society, painted at a time when the proletariat is still in a very undeveloped state and has but a fantastic conception of its own position, correspond with the first instinctive yearnings of that class for a general reconstruction of society.

But these Socialist and Communist publications contain also a critical element. They attack every principle of existing society. Hence they are full of the most valuable materials for the enlightenment of the working class. The practical measures proposed in them—such as the abolition of the distinction between town and country, of the family, of the carrying on of industries for the account of private individuals, and of the wage system, the proclamation of social harmony, the conversion of the functions of the State into a mere superintendence of production, all these proposals point solely to the disappearance of class antagonisms which were, at that time, only just cropping up, and which, in these publications, are recognized in their earliest indistinct and undefined forms only. These proposals, therefore, are of a purely Utopian character.

The significance of Critical-Utopian socialism and communism bears an inverse relation to historical development. In proportion as the modern class struggle develops and takes definite shape, this fantastic standing apart from the contest, these fantastic attacks on it, lose all practical value and all theoretical justification. Therefore, although the originators of these systems were, in many respects, revolutionary, their disciples have, in every case, formed mere reactionary sects. They hold fast by the original views of their masters, in opposition to the progressive historical development of the proletariat. They, therefore, endeavor, and that consistently, to deaden the class struggle and to reconcile the class antagonisms. They still dream of experimental realization of their social Utopias, of founding isolated *"phalanstères,"* of establishing "Home Colonies," of setting up a "Little Icaria" [1]—duodecimo editions of the New Jerusalem—and to realize all these castles in the air, they are compelled to appeal to the feelings and purses of the bourgeois. By degrees they sink into the category of the reactionary conservative Socialists depicted above, differing from these only by more systematic pedantry, and by their fanatical and superstitious belief in the miraculous effects of their social science.

[1] *Phalanstères* were Socialist colonies on the plan of Charles Fourier; *Icaria* was the name given by Cabet to his Utopia and, later on, to his American Communist colony. [*Note by Engels to the English edition of 1888.*]

"Home Colonies" were what Owen called his Communist model societies. *Phalanstères* was the name of the public palaces planned by Fourier. *Icaria* was the name given to the Utopian land of fancy, whose Communist institutions Cabet portrayed. [*Note by Engels to the German edition of 1890.*]

They, therefore, violently oppose all political action on the part of the working class; such action, according to them, can only result from blind unbelief in the new Gospel.

The Owenites in England, and the Fourierists in France, respectively oppose the Chartists and the *Réformistes*.[1]

iv. Position of the Communists in Relation to the Various Existing Opposition Parties

Section II has made clear the relations of the Communists to the existing working-class parties, such as the Chartists in England and the Agrarian Reformers in America.

The Communists fight for the attainment of the immediate aims, for the enforcement of the momentary interests of the working class; but in the movement of the present, they also represent and take care of the future of that movement. In France the Communists ally themselves with the Social-Democrats,[2] against the conservative and radical bourgeoisie, reserving, however, the right to take up a critical position in regard to phrases and illusions traditionally handed down from the great Revolution.

In Switzerland they support the Radicals, without losing sight of the fact that this party consists of antagonistic elements, partly of Democratic Socialists, in the French sense, partly of radical bourgeois.

In Poland they support the party that insists on an

---

[1] This refers to the adherents of the newspaper *La Réforme*, which was published in Paris from 1843 to 1850.—*Ed.*

[2] The party then represented in Parliament by Ledru-Rollin, in literature by Louis Blanc, in the daily press by the *Réforme*. The name of Social-Democracy signified, with these its inventors, a section of the Democratic or Republican party more or less tinged with Socialism. [*Note by Engels to the English edition of 1888.*]

The party in France which at that time called itself Socialist-Democratic was represented in political life by Ledru-Rollin and in literature by Louis Blanc; thus it differed immeasurably from present-day German Social-Democracy. [*Note by Engels to the German edition of 1890.*]

agrarian revolution as the prime condition for national emancipation, that party which fomented the insurrection of Cracow in 1846.

In Germany they fight with the bourgeoisie whenever it acts in a revolutionary way, against the absolute monarchy, the feudal squirearchy, and the petty bourgeoisie.

But they never cease, for a single instant, to instill into the working class the clearest possible recognition of the hostile antagonism between bourgeoisie and proletariat, in order that the German workers may straightway use, as so many weapons against the bourgeoisie, the social and political conditions that the bourgeoisie must necessarily introduce along with its supremacy, and in order that, after the fall of the reactionary classes in Germany, the fight against the bourgeoisie itself may immediately begin.

The Communists turn their attention chiefly to Germany, because that country is on the eve of a bourgeois revolution that is bound to be carried out under more advanced conditions of European civilization, and with a much more developed proletariat, than that of England was in the seventeenth, and of France in the eighteenth century, and because the bourgeois revolution in Germany will be but the prelude to an immediately following proletarian revolution.

In short, the Communists everywhere support every revolutionary movement against the existing social and political order of things.

In all these movements they bring to the front, as the leading question in each, the property question, no matter what its degree of development at the time.

Finally, they labor everywhere for the union and agreement of the democratic parties of all countries.

The Communists disdain to conceal their views and claims. They openly declare that their ends can be attained only by the forcible overthrow of all existing social conditions. Let the ruling classes tremble at a Communistic revolution. The proletarians have nothing to lose but their chains. They have a world to win.

WORKING MEN OF ALL COUNTRIES, UNITE!

CRITIQUE OF THE GOTHA
PROGRAM, 1875

Marginal Notes to the Program of the German Workers' Party

I.

1. "Labor is the source of all wealth and all culture *and since* useful labor is only possible in society and through society, the proceeds of labor belong undiminished with equal right to all members of society."

First Part of the Paragraph: "Labor is the source of all wealth and all culture."

Labor is *not the source* of all wealth. *Nature* is just as much the source of use values (and it is surely of such that material wealth consists!) as is labor, which itself is only the manifestation of a natural force, human labor power. That phrase is to be found in all children's primers and is correct in so far as it is *implied* that labor proceeds with the appropriate subjects and instruments. But a socialist program cannot allow such bourgeois phrases to cause the *conditions* to be ignored that alone give them meaning. And in so far as man from the beginning behaves toward nature, the primary source of all instruments and subjects of labor, as her owner, treats her as belonging to him, his labor becomes the source of use values, therefore also of wealth. The bourgeois have very good grounds for fancifully ascribing *supernatural creative power* to labor, since it follows precisely from the fact that labor depends on nature, that the man who possesses no other property than his labor power must, in all conditions of society and culture, be the slave of other men who have made themselves the owners of the material conditions of labor. He can only work

45

with their permission, and hence only live with their permission.

Let us now leave the sentence as it stands, or rather limps. What would one have expected as conclusion? Obviously this:

"Since labor is the source of all wealth, in society also no one can appropriate wealth except as the product of labor. Therefore, if he himself does not work, he lives by the labor of others and also acquires his culture at the expense of the labor of others."

Instead of this, by means of the words *"and since"* a second proposition is added in order to draw a conclusion from this and not from the first one.

Second Part of the Paragraph: "Useful labor is only possible in society and through society."

According to the first proposition, labor was the source of all wealth and all culture, therefore also no society is possible without labor. Now we learn, conversely, that no "useful" labor is possible without society.

One could just as well have said that only in society can useless and even generally harmful labor become a branch of gainful occupation, that only in society can one live by being idle, etc., etc.—in short, one could just as well have copied the whole of Rousseau.

And what is "useful" labor? Surely only labor which produces the intended useful effect. A savage—and man was a savage after he had ceased to be an ape—who has killed an animal with a stone, who collects fruits, etc., performs "useful" labor.

Thirdly: The Conclusion: "And since useful labor is only possible in society and through society—the proceeds of labor belong undiminished with equal right to all members of society."

A fine conclusion! If useful labor is only possible in society and through society, the proceeds of labor belong to society—and only so much therefrom accrues to the individual worker as is not required to maintain the "condition" of labor, society.

In fact, also, this proposition has at all times been made use of by the champions of the *prevailing state of society*. First come the claims of the government and everything connected with it, since it is the social organ for the maintenance of the social order; then come the claims of the various kinds of private property, for the various kinds of private property are the foundations of society, etc. One sees that such hollow phrases can be twisted and turned as desired.

The first and second parts of the paragraph have some intelligible connection only in the following wording: "Labor only becomes the source of wealth and culture as social labor," or, what is the same thing, "in and through society."

This proposition is incontestably correct, for although isolated labor (its material conditions presupposed) can also create use values, it can create neither wealth nor culture.

But equally incontestable is this other proposition:

"In proportion as labor develops socially, and becomes thereby a source of wealth and culture, poverty and neglect develop among the workers, and wealth and culture among the non-workers."

This is the law of all history hitherto. What, therefore, had to be done here, instead of making general phrases about "labor" and "society," was to prove concretely how in present capitalist society the material, etc., conditions have at last been created which will enable and compel the workers to lift this social curse.

In fact, however, the whole paragraph, incorrect in style and content, is only there in order to inscribe the Lassallean catchword of the "undiminished proceeds of labor" as a slogan at the top of the party banner. I shall return to the "proceeds of labor," "equal right," etc., later on, since the same thing recurs in a somewhat different form.

2. "In present-day society, the instruments of labor are the monopoly of the capitalist class; the resulting dependence of the working class is the cause of misery and servitude in all its forms."

This sentence, borrowed from the Statutes of the International, is incorrect in this "improved" edition.

In present-day society the instruments of labor are the monopoly of the landowners (the monopoly of property in land is even the basis of the monopoly of capital) *and* the capitalists. In the passage in question, the Statutes of the International do not mention by name either the one or the other class of monopolists. They speak of the *"monopoly of the means of labor, that is, the sources of life."* The addition, *"sources of life"* makes it sufficiently clear that land is included in the instruments of labor.

The correction was introduced because Lassalle, for reasons now generally known, attacked *only* the capitalist class and not the landowners. In England, the capitalist is usually not even the owner of the land on which his factory stands.

3. "The emancipation of labor demands the promotion of the instruments of labor to the common property of society, and the co-operative regulation of the total labor with equitable distribution of the proceeds of labor."

"Promotion of the instruments of labor to the common property" ought obviously to read, their "conversion into the common property," but this only in passing.

What are the "proceeds of labor"? The product of labor or its value? And in the latter case, is it the total value of the product or only that part of the value which labor has newly added to the value of the means of production consumed?

The "proceeds of labor" is a loose notion which Lassalle has put in the place of definite economic conceptions.

What is "equitable distribution"?

Do not the bourgeois assert that the present-day distribution is "equitable"? And is it not, in fact, the only "equitable" distribution on the basis of the present-day mode of production? Are economic relations regulated by legal conceptions or do not, on the contrary, legal relations arise from economic ones? Have not also the socialist sectarians the most varied notions about "equitable" distribution?

To understand what idea is meant in this connection by the phrase "equitable distribution," we must take the first paragraph and this one together. The latter implies a society wherein "the instruments of labor are common property, and the total labor is co-operatively regulated," and from the first paragraph we learn that "the proceeds of labor belong undiminished with equal right to all members of society."

"To all members of society"? To those who do not work as well? What remains then of the "undiminished proceeds of labor"? Only to those members of society who work? What remains then of the "equal right" of all members of society?

But "all members of society" and "equal right" are obviously mere phrases. The kernel consists in this, that in this Communist society every worker must receive the "undiminished" Lassallean "proceeds of labor."

Let us take first of all the words "proceeds of labor" in the sense of the product of labor; then the co-operative proceeds of labor are the *total social product*.

From this is then to be deducted:

First, cover for replacement of the means of production used up.

Secondly, additional portion for expansion of production.

Thirdly, reserve or insurance fund to provide against misadventures, disturbances through natural events, etc. These deductions from the "undiminished proceeds of labor" are an economic necessity and their magnitude is to be determined by available means and forces, and partly by calculation of probabilities, but they are in no way calculable by equity.

There remains the other part of the total product, destined to serve as means of consumption.

Before this is divided among the individuals, there has to be deducted from it:

First, the general costs of administration not belonging to production.

This part will, from the outset, be very considerably restricted in comparison with present-day society and it diminishes in proportion as the new society develops.

Secondly, that which is destined for the communal satisfaction of needs, such as schools, health services, etc.

From the outset this part is considerably increased in comparison with present-day society and it increases in proportion as the new society develops.

Thirdly, funds for those unable to work, etc., in short, what is included under so-called official poor relief to-day.

Only now do we come to the "distribution" which the program, under Lassallean influence, alone has in view in its narrow fashion, namely, that part of the means of consumption which is divided among the individual producers of the co-operative society.

The "undiminished proceeds of labor" have already quietly become converted into the "diminished" proceeds, although what the producer is deprived of in his capacity as a private individual benefits him directly or indirectly in his capacity as a member of society.

Just as the phrase "undiminished proceeds of labor" has disappeared, so now does the phrase "proceeds of labor" disappear altogether.

Within the co-operative society based on common ownership of the means of production, the producers do not exchange their products; just as little does the labor employed on the products appear here *as the value* of these products, as a material quality possessed by them, since now, in contrast to capitalist society, individual labor no longer exists in an indirect fashion but directly as a component part of the total labor. The phrase "proceeds of labor," objectionable even today on account of its ambiguity, thus loses all meaning.

What we have to deal with here is a Communist society, not as it has *developed* on its own foundations, but, on the contrary, as it *emerges* from capitalist society; which is thus in every respect, economically, morally, and intellectually, still stamped with the birthmarks of the old society from whose womb it emerges. Accordingly the individual producer receives back from society —after the deductions have been made—exactly what he gives to it. What he has given to it is his individual amount of labor. For example, the social working day consists of the sum of the individual labor hours; the individual labor time of the individual producer is the part of the social labor day contributed by him, his share in it. He receives a certificate from society that he has furnished such and such an amount of labor (after deducting his labor for the common fund), and with this certificate he draws from the social stock of means of consumption as much as the same amount of labor costs. The same amount of labor which he has given to society in one form, he receives back in another.

Here obviously the same principle prevails as that which regulates the exchange of commodities, as far as this is exchange of equal values. Content and form are changed, because under the altered circumstances no one can give anything except his labor, and because, on the other hand, nothing can pass into the ownership of individuals except individual means of consumption. But, as far as the distribution of the latter among the individual producer is concerned, the same principle prevails as in the exchange of commodity-equivalents, so much labor in one form is exchanged for an equal amount of labor in another form.

Hence, *equal right* here is still in principle—*bourgeois right,* although principle and practice are no longer in conflict, while the exchange of equivalents in commodity exchange only exists on the *average* and not in the individual case.

In spite of this advance, this *equal right* is still stigmatized by a bourgeois limitation. The right of the producers is *proportional* to the labor they supply; the equality consists in the fact that measurement is made with an *equal standard,* labor.

But one man is superior to another physically or mentally and so supplies more labor in the same time, or can labor for a longer time; and labor, to serve as a measure, must be defined by its duration or intensity; otherwise it ceases to be a standard of measurement. This *equal right* is an unequal right for unequal labor. It recognizes no class differences, because everyone is only a worker like everyone else; but it tacitly recognizes unequal individual endowment and thus productive capacity as natural privileges. *It is therefore a right of inequality in its content, like every right.* Right by its very nature can only consist in the application of an equal standard; but unequal individuals (and they would not be different individuals if they were not unequal) are only measurable by an equal standard in so far as they are brought under an equal point of view, are taken from one *definite* side only, *e.g.,* in the present case are regarded *only as workers,* and nothing more seen in them, everything else being ignored. Further, one worker is married, another not; one has more children than another and so on and so forth. Thus with an equal output, and hence an equal share in the social consumption fund, one will in fact receive more than another, one will be richer than another, and so on. To avoid all these defects, right, instead of being equal, would have to be unequal.

But these defects are inevitable in the first phase of Communist society as it is when it has just emerged after prolonged birth pangs from capitalist society. Right can never be higher than the economic structure of society and the cultural development thereby determined.

In a higher phase of Communist society, after the enslaving subordination of individuals under division of labor, and therewith also the antithesis between mental and physical labor, has vanished; after labor, from a mere means of life, has itself become the prime necessity of life; after the productive forces have also increased with the all-round development of the individual, and all the springs of co-operative wealth flow more abundantly—only then can the narrow horizon of bourgeois right be fully left behind and society inscribe on its banners: from each according to his ability, to each according to his needs!

I have dealt more at length with the "undiminished proceeds of labor" on the one hand, and with "equal right" and "equitable distribution" on the other, in order to show what a crime it is to attempt, on the one hand, to force on our party again, as dogmas, ideas which in a certain period had some meaning but have now become obsolete rubbishy phrases, while on the other, perverting the realistic outlook, which has cost so much effort to instill into the party, but which has now taken root in it, by means of ideological nonsense about "right" and other trash common among the democrats and French Socialists.

Quite apart from the analysis so far given, it was in general incorrect to make a fuss about so-called *"distribution"* and put the principal stress on it.

The distribution of the means of consumption at any time is only a consequence of the distribution of the conditions of production themselves. The latter distribution, however, is a feature of the mode of production itself. The capitalist mode of production, for example, rests on the fact that the material conditions of production are in the hands of non-workers in the form of property in capital and land, while the masses are only owners of the personal condition of production, *viz.*, labor power. Once the elements of production are so distributed, then the present-day distribution of the means of consumption results automatically. If the material conditions of production are the co-operative property of the workers themselves, then this likewise results in a different distribution of the means of consumption from the present one. Vulgar socialism (and from it in turn a section of democracy) has taken over from the bourgeois economists the consideration and treatment of distribution as independent of the mode of production and hence the presentation of socialism as turning principally on distribution. After the real position has long been made clear, why go back again?

4. "The emancipation of labor must be the work of the working class, in contrast to which all other classes are *only one reactionary mass.*"

The first strophe is taken from the introductory words of the Statutes of the International, but "improved." There it is said: "The emancipation of the working class must be the act of the workers themselves." Here, on the contrary, the "working class" has to emancipate—what? "Labor." Let him who can, understand.

In compensation, the antistrophe on the other hand is a Lassallean quotation of the first water: "in contrast to which (the working class) all other classes *form only one reactionary mass.*"

In *The Communist Manifesto* it is said: "Of all the classes that stand face to face with the bourgeoisie today, the proletariat alone is a *really revolutionary class.* The other classes decay and finally disappear in the face of modern industry; the proletariat is its special and essential product."

The bourgeoisie is here conceived as a revolutionary class—as the bearer of large-scale industry—in contrast to the feudal lords and middle estates, who desire to maintain all social positions that are the creation of obsolete modes of production. Thus they do not form *together* with the *bourgeoisie* only one reactionary mass.

On the other hand, the proletariat is revolutionary in contrast to the bourgeoisie because, having itself grown up on the basis of large-scale industry, it strives to strip off from production the capitalist character that the bourgeoisie seeks to perpetuate. But the *Manifesto* adds that the "middle class . . . if by chance they are revolutionary, they are so only in view of their impending transfer into the proletariat."

From this point of view, therefore, it is again nonsense to say that they, together with the bourgeoisie, and with the feudal lords into the bargain, "form only one reactionary mass" in relation to the working class.

Did we proclaim to the artisans, small industrialists, etc., and *peasants* during the last elections: In contrast to us you, with the bourgeois and feudal lords, form only one reactionary mass?

Lassalle knew *The Communist Manifesto* by heart, as his faithful followers know the gospels written by him. If, therefore, he has falsified it so grossly, this has occurred only to put a good color on his alliance with absolutist and feudal opponents against the bourgeoisie.

In the above paragraph, moreover, his oracular saying is dragged in by force without any connection with the botched quotation from the Statutes of the International. Thus it is here simply an impertinence and indeed not at all displeasing to Herr Bismarck, one of those cheap pieces of insolence in which the Marat of Berlin deals.

5. "The working class strives for its emancipation first of all *within the framework of the present-day national state,* conscious that the necessary result of its efforts, which are common to the workers of all civilized countries, will be the international brotherhood of peoples."

Lassalle, in opposition to *The Communist Manifesto* and to all earlier socialism, conceived the workers' movement from the narrowest national standpoint. He is being followed in this—and that after the work of the International!

It is altogether self-evident that, to be able to fight at all, the working class must organize itself at home *as a class* and that its own country is the immediate arena of struggle. So far its class struggle is national, not in content, but, as *The Communist Manifesto* says, "in form." But the "framework of the present-day national state," *e.g.*, the German empire, is itself in its turn economically "within the framework" of the world market, politically "within the framework" of the system of states. Every businessman knows that German trade is at the same time foreign trade, and the greatness of Herr Bismarck consists, to be sure, precisely in a kind of *international* policy.

And to what does the German Workers' Party reduce its internationalism? To the consciousness that the result of its efforts will be *"the international brotherhood of peoples"*—a phrase borrowed from the bourgeois League of Peace and Freedom, which is intended to pass as equivalent to the international brotherhood of the working classes in the joint struggle against the ruling classes and their governments. Not a word, therefore, *about the international functions* of the German working class! And it is in this way it is to challenge its own bourgeoisie, which is already linked up in brotherhood against it with the bourgeois of all other countries, and Herr Bismarck's international policy of conspiracy!

In fact, the international consciousness expressed in the program stands *even infinitely below* that of the Free Trade Party. The latter also asserts that the result of its efforts will be "the international brotherhood of peoples." But it also *does* something to make trade international and by no means contents itself with the consciousness—that all peoples are carrying on trade at home.

The international activity of the working classes does not in any way depend on the existence of the International Workingmen's Association. This was only the first attempt to create a central organ for that activity, an attempt which was of lasting success on account of the impulse which it gave but which was no longer realizable in its *first historical form* after the fall of the Paris Commune.

Bismarck's *Norddeutsche* was absolutely correct when it announced for the satisfaction of its master that the German Workers' Party had repudiated internationalism in the new program.

II.

"Starting from these basic principles, the German Workers' Party strives by all legal means for the *free state—and—*socialist society; the abolition of the wage system *together with the iron law of wages—*and—exploitation in every form; the removal of all social and political inequality."

I shall return to the "free" state later.

Thus, in future, the German Workers' Party has got to believe in Lassalle's "iron law of wages!" That this shall not be lost, the nonsense is perpetrated of speaking of the "abolition of the wage system" (it should read: system of wage labor) *together with* the "iron law of wages." If I abolish wage labor, then naturally I abolish its laws also, whether they are of "iron" or sponge. But Lassalle's attack on wage labor turns almost solely on this so-called law. In order, therefore, to prove that Lassalle's sect has conquered, the "wage system" must be abolished *"together* with the iron law of wages" and not without it.

It is well known that nothing of the "iron law of wages" belongs to Lassalle except the word "iron" borrowed from Goethe's "great, eternal, iron laws." The word *iron* is a label by which the true believers recognize one another. But if I take the law with Lassalle's stamp on it and consequently in his sense, then I must also take it with his basis for it. And what is that? As Lange already showed, shortly after Lassalle's death, it is the Malthusian theory of population (preached by Lange himself). But if this theory is correct, then again I can *not* abolish the law even if I abolish wage labor a hundred times over, because the law then governs not only the system of wage labor but *every* social system. Basing themselves directly on this, the economists have proved for fifty years and more that socialism cannot abolish poverty, *which has its basis in nature,* but can only *generalize* it, distribute it simultaneously over the whole surface of society!

But all this is not the main thing. Quite *apart* from this *false* Lassallean formulation of the law, the truly infuriating retrograde step consists in the following:

Since Lassalle's death the scientific understanding has made progress in *our* party that wages are not what they *appear* to be, namely, the *value,* or *price, of labor,* but only a masked form for the *value,* or *price, of labor power.* Thereby the whole bourgeois conception of wages hitherto, as well as all the criticism hitherto directed against this conception, was thrown overboard once for all and it was made clear that the wage worker has permission to work for his own life, *i.e., to live,* only in so far as he works for a certain time gratis for the capitalist (and hence also for the latter's fellow consumers of surplus value); that the whole capitalist system of production turns on the prolongation of this gratis labor by extending the working day or by developing the productivity, *i.e.,* the greater intensity of labor power, etc., that, consequently, the system of wage labor is a system of slavery, and indeed a slavery which becomes more severe in proportion as the social productive forces of labor develop, whether the worker receives better or worse payment. And after this understanding has more and more made progress in our party, one returns to Lassalle's dogmas, although one must have known that Lassalle *did not know* what wages are, but following in the wake of the bourgeois economists took the appearance for the essence of the matter.

It is as if, among slaves who have at last got behind the secret of slavery and broken out in rebellion, a slave still in thrall to obsolete notions were to inscribe on the program of the rebellion: Slavery must be abolished because the upkeep of slaves in the system of slavery cannot exceed a certain low maximum!

Does not the mere fact that the representatives of our party were capable of perpetrating such a monstrous attack on the understanding that has spread among the mass of our party prove by itself with what criminal levity and with what lack of conscience they set to work in drawing up this compromise program!

Instead of the indefinite concluding phrase of the paragraph—"the removal of all social and political inequality"—it ought to have been said that with the abolition of class differences all the social and political inequality arising from them would disappear of itself.

III.

"The German Workers' Party, in order *to pave the way to the solution of the social question,* demands the establishment of producers' co-operative societies with state aid under the democratic control of the *toiling people.* The producers' co-operative societies *are to be called into being* for industry and agriculture in such dimensions *that the socialist organization of the total labor will arise from them.*"

After the Lassallean "iron law of wages," the remedy of the prophet. The way to it is "paved" in worthy fashion. In place of the existing class struggle appears a newspaper scribbler's phrase: "the social *question,*" to the *"solution"* of which one *"paves the way."* Instead of the revolutionary process of transformation of society, the "socialist organization of the total labor" "arises" from the "state aid" that the state gives to the producers' co-operative societies and which the state, not the worker, *"calls into being."* This is worthy of Lassalle's imagination that one can build a new society by state loans just as well as a new railway!

From the remnants of a sense of shame, "state aid" has been put—under the democratic control of the "toiling people."

In the first place the majority of the "toiling people" in Germany consists of peasants and not of proletarians.

Secondly, "democratic" is in German *"volksherrschaftlich"* ("by the rule of the people"). But what does "control by the rule of the people of the toiling people" mean? And particularly in the case of a toiling people which, through these demands that it puts to the state, expresses its full consciousness that it neither rules nor is ripe for ruling!

It would be superfluous to deal here with the criticism of the recipe prescribed by Buchez in the reign of Louis Philippe in *opposition* to the French Socialists and accepted by the reactionary workers of the *Atelier.* The chief offense does not lie in having inscribed these specific nostrums in the program, but in that in general a retrograde step from the standpoint of a class movement to that of a sectarian movement is being taken.

That the workers desire to establish the conditions of co-operative production on a social, and first of all on a national, scale in their own country, only means that they are working to revolutionize the present conditions of production, and has nothing in common with the foundation of co-operative societies with state aid. But as far as the present co-operative societies are concerned, they are of value *only* in so far as they are the independent creations of the workers and not protégés either of the government or of the bourgeoisie.

IV.

I come now to the democratic section.

A. *"The free basis of the state."*

First of all, according to II, the German Workers' Party strives for the "free state."

Free state—what is this?

It is by no means the aim of the workers, who have got rid of the narrow mentality of humble subjects, to set the state free. In the German empire the "state" is almost as "free" as in Russia. Freedom consists in converting the state from an organ standing above society into one completely subordinated to it, and today also the forms of the state are more free or less free to the extent that they restrict the "freedom of the state."

The German Workers' Party—at least if it adopts the program—shows that its socialist ideas are not even skin-deep, in that, instead of treating existing society (and this holds good of any future one) as the *basis* of the existing state (or of the future state in the case of future society), it treats the state rather as an independent entity that possesses its own *intellectual, moral, and free basis.*

And what of the riotous misuse which the program makes of the words *"present-day state," "present-day society,"* and of the still more riotous misconception that it achieves in regard to the state to which it addresses its demands?

"Present-day society" is capitalist society, which exists in all civilized countries, more or less free from medieval admixture, more or less modified by the special historical development of each country and more or less developed. On the other hand, the "present-day state" changes with a country's frontier. It is different in the Prusso-German empire from what it is in Switzerland, it is different in England from what it is in the United States. The "present-day state" is therefore a fiction.

Nevertheless, the different states of the different civilized countries, in spite of their manifold diversity of form, all have this in common, that they are based on modern bourgeois society, only one more or less capitalistically developed. They have, therefore, also certain essential features in common. In this sense it is possible to speak of the "present-day state," in contrast to the future in which its present root, bourgeois society, will have died away.

The question then arises: what transformation will the state undergo in Communist society? In other words, what social functions will remain in existence there that are analogous to the present functions of the state? This question can only be answered scientifically and one does not get a flea-hop nearer to the problem by a thousandfold combination of the word *people* with the word *state*.

Between capitalist and Communist society lies the period of the revolutionary transformation of the one into the other. There corresponds to this also a political transition period in which the state can be nothing but *the revolutionary dictatorship of the proletariat*.

Now the program does not deal with this nor with the future state in Communist society.

Its political demands contain nothing beyond the old familiar democratic litany: universal suffrage, direct legislation, people's justice, a people's militia, etc. They are a mere echo of the bourgeois People's Party, of the League of Peace and Freedom. They are all demands which, in so far as they are not exaggerated in fanciful presentation, have already been *realized*. Only the state to which they belong does not lie within the frontiers of the German empire, but in Switzerland, the United States, etc. This sort of "state of the future" is a present-day state, although existing outside the "framework" of the German empire.

But one thing has been forgotten. Since the German

Workers' Party expressly declares that it acts within "the present-day national state," hence *its own state*, the Prusso-German empire—its demands would indeed otherwise be largely meaningless, since one only demands what one has not got—it should not have forgotten the chief thing, namely, that all those pretty little toys rest on the recognition of the so-called sovereignty of the people and hence there is only room for them in a *democratic republic*.

Since one has not the courage—and wisely, for the circumstances demand caution—to demand the democratic republic, as the French workers' program under Louis Philippe and under Louis Napoleon did, one should not have taken refuge either in the subterfuge, neither "honorable" nor "worthy," of demanding things which have meaning only in a democratic republic from a state which is nothing but a police-guarded military despotism, embellished with parliamentary forms, alloyed with a feudal admixture, bureaucratically constructed and already influenced by the bourgeoisie, and then to assure this state into the bargain that one thinks one will be able to extort these things from it "by legal means."

Even vulgar democracy, which sees the millennium in the democratic republic and has no suspicion that it is precisely in this last state form of bourgeois society that the class struggle has to be fought out to a conclusion—even it towers mountains above this kind of democratism within the limits of what is permitted by the police and what is logically impermissible.

That, in fact, by the word "state" the government machinery is understood, or the state in so far as it forms a special organism separated from society through division of labor, is already shown by the words "the German Workers' Party demands *as the economic basis of the state:* a single progressive income tax, etc." Taxes are the economic basis of the government machinery and of nothing else. In the state of the future as it exists in Switzerland, this demand has been pretty well fulfilled. Income tax presupposes the various sources of income of the various social classes, and hence capitalist society. It is, therefore, not extraordinary that the Liverpool financial reformers, bourgeois headed by Gladstone's brother, are putting forward the same demand as the program.

B. "The German Workers' Party demands as the intellectual and moral basis of the state:

1. Universal and *equal elementary education* through the state. Universal compulsory school attendance. Free instruction."

Equal elementary education? What idea lies behind these words? Is it believed that in present-day society (and it is only with this one has to deal) education can be *equal* for all classes? Or is it demanded that the upper classes also shall be compulsorily reduced to the modicum of education—the elementary school—that alone is compatible with the economic conditions not only of the wage workers but of the peasants as well.

"Universal compulsory school attendance. Free instruction." The former exists even in Germany, the second in Switzerland and in the United States in the case of elementary schools. If in some states of the latter country the higher educational institutions are also "free," that only means in fact defraying the cost of the education of the upper classes from the general tax receipts. Incidentally, the same holds good for "free administration of justice" demanded under A:5.* Criminal justice is to be had free everywhere; civil justice is concerned almost exclusively with conflicts over property and hence affects almost exclusively the possessing classes. Should they carry on their litigation at the expense of the national treasury?

The paragraph on the schools should at least have demanded technical schools (theoretical and practical) in combination with the elementary school.

"Elementary education through the state" is altogether objectionable. Defining by a general law the financial means of the elementary schools, the qualifications of the teachers, the branches of instruction, etc., and, as happens in the United States, supervising the fulfillment of these legal prescriptions by means of state inspectors, is a very different thing from appointing the state as the educator of the people! Government and

* Point 5 under A of Section IV of the Program.

church should rather be equally excluded from any influence on the school. Particularly, indeed, in the Prusso-German empire (and one cannot take refuge in the rotten subterfuge that one is speaking of a "state of the future," we have seen what that is) the state has need, on the contrary, of a very stern education by the people.

But the whole program, for all its democratic clang, is tainted through and through by the servile belief in the state of Lassalle's sect, or, what is no better, by democratic miracle-faith, or rather it is a compromise between these two kinds of miracle-faith, both equally remote from socialism.

"Freedom of science" says a paragraph of the Prussian constitution. Why then here?

"Freedom of conscience"! If one desires at this time of the *Kulturkampf* to remind liberalism of its old catchwords, then it surely could have been done in the following form: Everyone should be able to attend to his religious as well as his bodily needs without the police sticking their noses in. But the Workers' Party ought at any rate in this connection to have expressed its consciousness of the fact that bourgeois "freedom of conscience" is nothing but the toleration of all possible kinds of *religious freedom of conscience,* and that for its part it endeavors rather to liberate the conscience from the specter of religion. But there is a desire not to transgress the "bourgeois" level.

I have now come to the end, for the appendix that now follows in the program does not constitute a characteristic component part of it. Hence I can be very brief here.

2. *"Normal working day."*

In no other country has the Workers' Party restricted itself to such an indefinite demand, but has always fixed the length of the working day that it considers normal under the given circumstances.

3. "Restriction of women's labor and prohibition of child labor."

The standardization of the working day must already include the restriction of women's labor, in so far as it relates to the duration, intervals, etc., of the working day; otherwise it could only mean the exclusion of women's labor from branches of industry that are specifically unhealthy for the female body or are objectionable morally for the female sex. If that is what was meant, then it ought to have been stated.

"Prohibition of child labor"! Here it was absolutely essential to state the age limits.

A *general prohibition* of child labor is incompatible with the existence of large-scale industry and hence an empty, pious aspiration.

Its realization—if it were possible—would be reactionary, since, with a strict regulation of the working time according to the different age groups and other safety measures for the protection of children, an early combination of productive labor with education is one of the most potent means for the transformation of present-day society.

4. "State supervision of factory, workshop, and domestic industry."

In regard to the Prusso-German state it should definitely have been demanded that the inspectors are only to be removable by a court of law; that any worker can denounce them to the courts for neglect of duty; that they must belong to the medical profession.

5. "Regulation of prison labor."

A petty demand in a general workers' program. In any case, it should have been clearly stated that there is no intention from fear of competition to allow ordinary criminals to be treated like beasts, and especially that there is no desire to deprive them of their sole means of betterment, productive labor. This was surely the least one might have expected from Socialists.

6. "An effective liability law."

It should have been stated what is understood by an "effective" liability law.

Incidentally, in connection with the normal working day, the part of factory legislation that deals with health regulations and safety measures has been overlooked.

The liability law only comes into operation when these regulations are infringed.

In short, this appendix also is distinguished by slovenly editing.

Dixi et salvavi animam meam.

THE PROGRAM OF THE RUSSIAN SOCIAL-DEMOCRATIC LABOR PARTY

ADOPTED AT THE SECOND CONGRESS OF THE PARTY, AUGUST, 1903

The development of exchange has established such close ties among all the peoples of the civilized world that the great proletarian movement toward emancipation was bound to become—and has long since become—international.

Considering itself one of the detachments of the universal army of the proletariat, the Russian Social-Democracy is pursuing the same ultimate goal as that for which the Social-Democrats in other countries are striving. This ultimate goal is determined by the character of modern bourgeois society and by the course of its development. The chief feature of such a society is production for the market on the basis of capitalist production relations whereby the largest and most important part of the means of production and exchange of commodities belongs to a numerically small class of people, while the overwhelming majority of the population consists of proletarians and semi-proletarians who, by their economic situation, are forced either continually or at intervals to sell their labor power, *i.e.*, to hire themselves out to the capitalists, and by their labor to create the incomes of the upper classes of society.

The expansion of the capitalist system of production runs parallel to technical progress, which, by increasing the economic importance of large enterprises, tends to eliminate the small independent producers, to convert some of them into proletarians, to reduce the socio-economic role of others and, in some localities, to place them in more or less complete, more or less open, more or less onerous dependence on capital.

Moreover, the same technical progress enables the enterprisers to utilize to an ever-greater extent woman and child labor in the process of production and exchange of commodities. And since, on the other hand, technical improvements lead to a decrease in the enterpriser's demand for human labor power, the demand for labor power necessarily lags behind the supply, and there is in consequence greater dependence of hired labor upon capital, and increased exploitation of the former by the latter.

Such a state of affairs in the bourgeois countries, as well as the ever-growing competition among those countries on the world market, render the sale of goods which are produced in greater and greater quantities ever more difficult. Overproduction with the resulting more or less acute industrial crises, which in turn are followed by more or less protracted periods of industrial stagnation, are the inevitable consequences of the development of the productive forces in bourgeois society. Crises and periods of industrial stagnation in their turn tend still further to impoverish the small producers, still further to enhance the dependence of hired labor upon capital, still further to accelerate the relative, and sometimes the absolute, deterioration of the condition of the working class.

Thus, technical progress, signifying increased productivity of labor and greater social wealth, becomes in bourgeois society the cause of more striking social inequalities, of more unbridgeable gulfs between the wealthy and the poor, of greater insecurity of existence, of unemployment, and of numerous privations for ever larger and larger masses of toilers.

But together with the growth and development of all these contradictions inherent in bourgeois society, there is the concomitant growth of dissatisfaction with the present order among the toiling and exploited masses, the concomitant growth in the number and solidarity of the proletarians, as well as the sharpening of their struggle against the exploiters. At the same time, technical progress, by concentrating the means of production and exchange, by socializing the process of labor in capitalist enterprises, creates more and more rapidly the material possibility for replacing capitalist production relations by Socialist ones, *i.e.*, the possibility for a Socialist revolution, which is the ultimate aim of all the activities of international Social-Democracy as the class-conscious expression of the proletarian movement.

By introducing social, instead of private, ownership of the means of production and exchange, by introducing well-regulated organization in the social process of production so that the well-being and the many-sided development of all members of society may be insured, the social revolution of the proletariat will abolish the division of society into classes and thus emancipate all oppressed humanity, and will put an end to all forms of exploitation of one part of society by another.

A necessary condition for this social revolution is the dictatorship of the proletariat, *i.e.*, the conquering by the proletariat of such political power as would enable it to crush any resistance offered by the exploiters. In its effort to make the proletariat capable of fulfilling its great historical mission, international Social-Democracy organizes it into an independent political party in opposition to all bourgeois parties, directs all the manifestations of its class struggle, discloses before it the irreconcilable conflict between the interests of the exploiters and those of the exploited, and clarifies for it the historical significance of the imminent social revolution, and the conditions necessary for its coming. At the same time, it reveals to the other sections of the toiling and the exploited masses the hopelessness of their condition in capitalist society and the need of a social revolution if they wish to be free of the capitalist yoke. The party of the working class, the Social-Democracy, calls upon all strata of the toiling and exploited population to join its ranks in so far as they adopt the point of view of the proletariat.

On the road toward their common final goal which is conditioned by the prevalence of the capitalist system of production throughout the civilized world, the Social-Democrats of different countries must needs devote themselves to different immediate tasks—first, because the capitalist system is not everywhere developed to the same degree; secondly, because in different countries its development takes place in a different socio-political setting.

In Russia, where capitalism has already become the dominant mode of production, there are still preserved numerous vestiges of the old pre-capitalist order, when the toiling masses were the serfs of the rich landowners, the state, or the head of the state.

Greatly hampering economic progress, these vestiges interfere with the many-sided development of the class struggle of the proletariat, help to preserve and strengthen the most barbarous forms of exploitation which the state and the propertied classes foist upon millions and millions of peasants, and keep the whole people in darkness and subjection.

The most outstanding among these relics of the past, the mightiest bulwark of all this barbarism, is the tsarist monarchy. In its very nature it is bound to be inimical to any social movement, cannot but be bitterly opposed to all the aspirations of the proletariat toward freedom.

By reason of the above, the first and immediate task put before itself by the Russian Social-Democratic Labor Party is to overthrow the tsarist monarchy and to create a democratic republic whose constitution would guarantee the following:

1. The sovereignty of the people, *i.e.*, the concentration of all supreme state power in the hands of a legislative assembly, consisting of the people's representatives, and forming one chamber.

2. Universal, equal, and direct suffrage for all male and female citizens, twenty years old or over, at all elections to the legislative assembly and to the various local organs of self-government; the secret ballot at elections; the right of every voter to be elected into any representative institution; biennial parliaments; salaries to be paid to the people's representatives.

3. Local self-government on a wide scale; home rule for all localities where the population is of a special composition and characterized by special conditions of life.

4. Inviolability of person and dwelling.

5. Unlimited freedom of religion, speech, press, assembly, strikes, and unions.

6. Freedom of movement and occupation.

7. Abolition of feudal estate; equal rights for all citizens, irrespective of sex, creed, race, or nationality.

8. The right of any people to receive instruction in its own tongue, this to be secured by creating schools at the expense of the state and the local organs of self-government; the right of every citizen to use his native language at meetings; introduction of the use of the native language on a par with the state language in all local, public, and state institutions.

9. The right of self-determination for all nations included in the composition of the state.

10. The right of any person to sue any official in the regular way before a jury.

11. Election of judges by the people.

12. Replacement of the standing army by a general arming of the people.

13. Separation of church and state, and of school and church.

14. Free and compulsory general and professional education for all children of both sexes up to the age of sixteen; the state to provide poor children with food, clothing, and school supplies.

As a basic condition for the democratization of our state economy, the Russian Social-Democratic Labor Party demands the abolition of all indirect taxes and the establishment of a progressive tax on incomes and inheritances.

In order to safeguard the working class against physical and moral degeneration, as well as to insure the development of its powers to carry on the struggle for freedom, the party demands the following:

1. Eight-hour work day for all hired labor.

2. A law providing a weekly uninterrupted forty-two-hour respite for all hired labor, both male and female, in all the branches of national industry.

3. Complete prohibition of overtime work.

4. Prohibition of night work (from 9 P.M. to 6 A.M.) in all the branches of national economy, with the exception of those in which this is absolutely necessary because of technical considerations approved by labor organizations.

5. Prohibition of the employment of children of

school age (up to sixteen) and restriction of the working day of minors (from 16 to 18) to six hours.

6. Prohibition of woman labor in all branches of industry injurious to women's health; relief from work four weeks before and six weeks after childbirth, with regular wages paid during all this period.

7. Nurseries for babies to be established in all shops, factories, and other enterprises that employ women; recesses to be granted of at least half-hour duration, at three-hour intervals, to all nursing mothers.

8. Old-age state insurance, also insurance against total or partial disability; such insurance to be based on a special fund formed from a tax levied on the capitalists for this purpose.

9. Payment of wages in kind to be prohibited; establishment of regular weekly pay days when all wages should be paid in money in absolute conformity with all the agreements relating to the hire of workers; wages to be paid during working hours.

10. Deductions by employers from workers' wages, on any ground or for any purpose (fines, spoilage, etc.), are to be prohibited.

11. An adequate number of factory inspectors to be appointed in all branches of national industry, and their supervision to be extended to all enterprises employing hired labor, including government enterprises (domestic service also to be within the sphere of their supervision); special women inspectors to be appointed in those industries where woman labor is employed; participation of representatives, elected by the workers and paid by the state, in supervising the enforcement of the factory laws, the fixing of wage scales, in accepting or rejecting the finished products and other results of labor.

12. Organs of local self-government, together with representatives elected by the workers, to have control over sanitation in the dwellings assigned to the workers by the employers, as well as over the inside arrangements in those dwellings and the renting conditions—this for the purpose of shielding the workers against the employers' interference with their life and activity as private citizens.

13. Establishment of regularly organized sanitary control over all undertakings employing hired labor, the

medico-sanitary organization to be entirely independent of the employers; in time of sickness, free medical aid to be supplied to the workers at the expense of the employers, with the workers retaining their wages.

14. Employers' infringement upon the laws intended to protect the workers to be punished as a crime.

15. Establishment of industrial courts in all branches of national industry, the courts to be composed of equal numbers of representatives from workers' and employers' organizations.

16. Imposition upon the organs of local self-governments of the duty of establishing employment bureaus (labor exchanges) to deal with the hire of local and out-of-town labor in all branches of industry; workers' and employers' representatives to participate in their administration.

Having as its aim the removal of the vestiges of serfdom that fall directly and heavily upon the peasants, wishing to encourage the free development of the class struggle in the villages, the Russian Social-Democratic Labor Party demands:

1. Removal from the peasants of all feudal estate restrictions relative to persons and property.

2. Removal of all payments and duties connected with the feudal estate disqualification of the peasantry, and abolition of all debts imposing usurers' burdens.

3. Confiscation of all church lands, monastery lands, appanages, and crown lands, as well as of all state lands, and their transfer to the higher organs of local self-government combining the urban and the rural districts; lands needed for the migration fund, and also forests and waters of importance to the state, to be transferred to the democratic state.

4. Confiscation of privately owned lands, excepting small land-holds, and transfer of their management to democratically elected higher organs of local self-government. The minimum size of an estate subject to confiscation to be determined by the higher organs of local self-government. While supporting all revolutionary actions of the peasantry, including confiscation of large estates, the Russian Social-Democratic Labor Party will always and unconditionally oppose any intent at hindering the natural development of economic progress.

While striving, in case of a victorious development of the revolution, to transfer all confiscated lands to the democratic institutions of local self-government, the Russian Social-Democratic Labor Party is ready, if circumstances prove unfavorable for such a transfer, to advocate that all privately owned estates which are actually managed on a petty-economy basis or which are indispensable for rounding out the peasants' holdings, be divided among the peasants.

Under all circumstances, and under whatever conditions the democratic agrarian reform may occur, the party will unswervingly strive for an independent class organization of the rural proletariat, it will endeavor to disclose to it the irreconcilable conflict between its interests and those of the peasant bourgeoisie, to warn it against the seduction of the petty-economy system which, as long as commodity production exists, can never eliminate the poverty of the masses, and, finally, to reveal to it the need for a complete Socialist overturn, as the only way of abolishing all poverty and all exploitation.

Striving to achieve its immediate ends, the Russian Social-Democratic Labor Party supports all oppositional or revolutionary movements directed against the present social and political order in Russia, but at the same time it definitely rejects all reformist projects which look toward the widening or strengthening of the guardianship of the police and bureaucracy over the laboring classes.

On its own part, the Russian Social-Democratic Labor Party is firmly convinced that a full, consistent, and thorough realization of the indicated political and social changes can only be attained by the overthrow of autocracy and by the convocation of a Constituent Assembly freely elected by the entire people.

THE PROGRAM OF THE ALL-RUSSIAN COMMUNIST PARTY (BOLSHEVIKS)

Adopted at the Eighth Congress of the Party, March, 1919

The October Revolution of October 25 (November 7), 1917, realized the dictatorship of the proletariat, which assisted by poorest peasantry or semi-proletariat, began to lay the foundation of a Communist society. The course of development of revolutions in Germany and Austria-Hungary, the growth of the revolutionary movement of the proletariat in all advanced countries, the spreading of the Soviet form of this movement, that is, a form that is directed to the immediate realization of the dictatorship of the proletariat—all this proved that there had begun the era of a world-wide proletarian Communist revolution.

This revolution was the inevitable outcome of the development of capitalism which still prevails in the majority of the civilized countries. Our old program, except for the incorrect designation of the party as the Social-Democratic Party, quite correctly characterizes the nature of capitalism and of bourgeois society in the following theses:

The chief feature of such a [capitalist] society is production for the market on the basis of capitalist production relations whereby the largest and most important part of the means of production and exchange of commodities belongs to a numerically small class of people, while the overwhelming majority of the population consists of proletarians and semi-proletarians who, by their economic situation, are forced either continually or at intervals to sell their labor power, *i.e.*, to hire themselves out to the capitalists, and by their labor to create the incomes of the upper classes of society.

The expansion of the capitalist system of production runs parallel to technical progress, which, by increasing the economic importance of large enterprises, tends to eliminate the small independent producers, to convert some of them into proletarians, to reduce the socio-economic role of others and in some localities, to place them in more or less complete, more or less open, more or less onerous dependence on capital.

Moreover, the same technical progress enables the enterprisers to utilize to an ever greater extent woman and child labor in the process of production and exchange of commodities. And since, on the other hand, technical improvements lead to a decrease in the enterpriser's demand for human labor power, the demand for labor power necessarily lags behind the supply, and there is in consequence greater dependence of hired labor upon capital, and increased exploitation of the former by the latter.

Such a state of affairs in the bourgeois countries, as well as the ever-growing competition among those countries on the world market, render the sale of goods which are produced in greater and greater quantities ever more difficult. Overproduction with the resulting more or less acute industrial crises, which in turn are followed by more or les protracted periods of industrial stagnation, are the inevitable consequences of the development of the productive forces in bourgeois society. Crises and periods of industrial stagnation in their turn tend still further to impoverish the small producers, still further to enhance the dependence of hired labor upon capital, still further to accelerate the relative, and sometimes the absolute, deterioration of the condition of the working class.

Thus, technical progress, signifying increased productivity of labor and greater social wealth, becomes in bourgeois society the cause of more striking social inequalities, of more unbridgeable gulfs between the wealthy and the poor, of greater insecurity of existence, of unemployment, and of numerous privations for ever larger and larger masses of toilers.

But together with the growth and development of all these contradictions inherent in bourgeois society, there is the concomitant growth of dissatisfaction with the present order among the toiling and exploited masses, the concomitant growth in the number and solidarity of the proletarians, as well as the sharpening of their struggle against the exploiters. At the same time, technical progress, by concentrating the means of production and exchange, by socializing the process of labor in capitalist enterprises, creates more and more rapidly the material possibility for replacing capitalist production relations by Socialist ones, *i.e.*, the possibility for a Socialist revolution, which is the ultimate aim of all the activities of international Social-Democracy as the class-conscious expression of the proletarian movement.

By introducing social, instead of private, ownership of the means of production and exchange, by introducing well-regulated organization in the social process of production so that the well-being and the many-sided development of all members of society may be insured, the social revolution of the proletariat will abolish the division of society into classes and thus emancipate all of oppressed humanity, and will put an end to all forms of exploitation of one part of society by another.

A necessary condition for this social revolution is the dictatorship of the proletariat, *i.e.,* the conquering by the proletariat of such political power as would enable it to crush any resistance offered by the exploiters. In its effort to make the proletariat capable of fulfilling its great historical mission, international Social-Democracy organizes it into an independent political party in opposition to all bourgeois parties, directs all the manifestations of its class struggle, discloses before it the irreconcilable conflict between the interests of the exploiters and those of the exploited, and clarifies for it the historical significance of the imminent social revolution, and the conditions necessary for its coming. At the same time, it reveals to the other sections of the toiling and the exploited masses the hopelessness of their condition in capitalist society and the need of a social revolution if they wish to be free of the capitalist yoke. The party of the working class, the Social-Democracy, calls upon all strata of the toiling and exploited population to join its ranks in so far as they adopt the point of view of the proletariat.

At the beginning of the twentieth century, the process of concentration and centralization of capital, destroying free competition, led to the creation of great capitalist monopolies, syndicates, cartels, trusts, which dominated economic life. The same process brought about the amalgamation of bank capital with highly concentrated industrial capital, and to the increased exportation of capital abroad. The trusts, uniting whole groups of capitalist states, began the economic partition of the world, the territories of which had already been divided between the richest countries. This period of financial capital, in which the struggle between the capitalist countries inevitably grows sharper, is the period of imperialism.

Imperialist wars therefore become inevitable, wars for

markets for the sale of goods, [wars] for spheres for investing capital, for raw material and for labor power, *i.e.*, [wars] for world domination and for power over small and weak nations. Such was the nature of the first great imperialist war of 1914-1918.

The exceedingly high stage of development of world capitalism, the replacement of free competition by capitalist, state monopolies, the setting up by banks and also by groups of capitalists of an apparatus for the regulation of production and distribution, the resulting rise in cost of living, the pressure of the combinations on the working class and the oppression of the working class by the imperialist state, the tremendous difficulties for the proletariat to carry on an economic and political struggle, and all the horrors, misery, and destruction which an imperialist war brings—all this makes the failure of capitalism and the transition to the higher type of public economy inevitable.

The bourgeois governments could finish the imperialist war neither by the conclusion of a just peace nor of any kind of stable peace. Capitalism has reached the point where an imperialist war must inevitably become transformed, and is becoming transformed, into a civil war between the exploited toiling masses, headed by the proletariat, against the bourgeoisie.

The increasing pressure of the proletariat, particularly its victories in individual countries, strengthens the resistance of the exploiters and compels them to create new forms of international capitalist solidarity (League of Nations, etc.), which, by organizing the systematic exploitation of all peoples on a world scale, direct all their efforts to the immediate suppression of the revolutionary movement of the proletariat of all countries.

All this inevitably leads to the blending of civil war within individual countries with the defensive wars of revolutionary countries, and the struggles of oppressed nations against the yoke of imperialist powers.

Under such conditions, the watchwords of pacifism, international disarmament, courts of arbitration, etc., are not merely reactionary Utopias, but deception of the toiling classes, directed to the disarming of the proletariat and to diverting it from its own task of disarming the exploiters.

Only the proletarian Communist revolution is able to lead humanity out of the blind alley which was created by the imperialists and imperialist wars. In spite of all the difficulties the revolution will have to face—temporary failures, waves of counterrevolution—the final victory of the proletariat is inevitable.

To attain the victory of the world proletarian revolution, the fullest confidence, the closest unity and co-ordination of all revolutionary activity of the working class in all advanced countries are necessary.

These conditions cannot be realized without a complete break with and bitter opposition to the bourgeois perversion of socialism which has obtained the upper hand in the higher circles of the official Social-Democratic and Socialist parties.

One form of this perversion is the current of opportunism and social-chauvinism—socialism in name, but chauvinism in fact—disguising the defense of the interests of the bourgeoisie under the false watchwords of defense of the fatherland, particularly during the imperialist war of 1914–1918. This current of opportunism is due to the opportunities created by the robbery of colonial and weak nations by advanced capitalist states; the surplus profits acquired therefrom by the bourgeoisie enables it to bribe the upper strata of the working class by placing them in a privileged position and guaranteeing them in time of peace a tolerable existence and taking their leaders into its service. The opportunists and the social-chauvinists are the servants of the bourgeoisie and the direct enemies of the proletariat, especially now, when together with the capitalists they are suppressing by armed force the revolutionary movement of the proletariat in their own and in foreign countries.

The other form of perversion is the so-called "Center," which is also a bourgeois perversion of socialism. This current is observed in equal degrees in all capitalist countries, and fluctuates between social-chauvinists and Communists, the latter striving to preserve unity with the former and trying to revive the bankrupt Second International. The new Third Communist International alone conducts the struggle of the proletariat for its emancipation, and the All-Russian Communist Party is

one of its sections. This International was in fact created
when the real proletarian elements of former Socialist
parties in different countries, particularly in Germany,
formed Communist parties, and was formally established
in March, 1919, at the First Congress in Moscow. The
Communist International, which is more and more gaining the sympathies of the masses of the proletariat of all
countries, not only in words but by deeds, by its political content and ideology returns to Marxism and
realizes the revolutionary teaching of Marx, now
cleansed of all bourgeois-opportunistic perversions.

The All-Russian Communist Party, developing the
concrete aims of the dictatorship of the proletariat with
reference to Russia, the chief characteristic of which is
that the majority of the population consists of petty-
bourgeois strata, defines these aims as follows:

General Politics

1. A bourgeois republic, even the most democratic,
sanctified by such watchwords as "will of the people,"
"will of the nation," "no class privilege," remains in
fact, owing to the existence of private property in land
and other means of production, the dictatorship of the
bourgeoisie, an instrument for exploitation and oppression of the broad masses of workers by a small group of
capitalists. In opposition to this, proletarian or Soviet
democracy transformed mass organizations precisely of
the classes oppressed by capitalism, of proletarian and
poorest peasantry or semi-proletarian, *i.e.,* the vast
majority of the population, into a single and permanent
basis of the state apparatus, local and central. By this
act, the Soviet state realized among other things local
and regional autonomy without the appointment of authorities from above, on a much wider scale than is
practiced anywhere. The aim of the Party is to exert
the greatest efforts in order to realize fully this highest
type of democracy, which to function accurately requires a continually rising standard of culture, organization, and activity on the part of the masses.

2. In contrast to bourgeois democracy, which concealed the class character of the state, the Soviet authority openly acknowledges that every state must

inevitably bear a class character until the division of society into classes has been abolished and all government authority disappears. By its very nature, the Soviet state directs itself to the suppression of the resistance of the exploiters, and the Soviet constitution does not stop at depriving the exploiters of their political rights, bearing in mind that any kind of freedom is a deception if it is opposed to the emancipation of labor from the yoke of the capitalist. The aim of the Party of the proletariat consists in carrying on a determined suppression of the resistance of the exploiters, in struggling against the deeply rooted prejudices concerning the absolute character of bourgeois rights and freedom, and at the same time explaining that deprivation of political rights and any kind of limitation of freedom are necessary as temporary measures in order to defeat the attempts of the exploiters to retain or to re-establish their privileges. With the disappearance of the possibility of the exploitation of one human being by another, the necessity for these measures will also gradually disappear, and the Party will aim to reduce and completely abolish them.

3. Bourgeois democracy has limited itself to formally extending political rights and freedom, such as the right of combination, freedom of speech, freedom of press, equality of citizenship. In practice, however, particularly in view of the economic slavery of the working masses, it was impossible for the workers to enjoy these rights and privileges to any great extent under bourgeois democracy.

Proletarian democracy on the contrary, instead of formally proclaiming those rights and freedoms, actually grants them first of all to those classes which have been oppressed by capitalism, *i.e.*, to the proletariat and to the peasantry. For that purpose the Soviet state expropriates premises, printing offices, supplies of paper, etc., from the bourgeoisie, placing these at the disposal of the working masses and their organizations. The aim of the All-Russian Communist Party is to encourage the working masses to enjoy democratic rights and liberties, and to offer them every opportunity for doing so.

4. Bourgeois democracy through the ages proclaimed equality of persons, irrespective of religion, race, or

nationality, and the equality of the sexes, but capitalism prevented the realization of this equality and in its imperialist stage developed race and national suppression. The Soviet Government, by being the authority of the toilers, for the first time in history could in all spheres of life realize this equality, destroying the last traces of woman's inequality in the sphere of marriage and the family. At the present moment the work of the Party is principally intellectual and educational with the aim of abolishing the last traces of former inequality and prejudices, especially among the backward sections of the proletariat and peasantry.

The Party's aim is not to limit itself to the formal proclamation of woman's equality, but to liberate woman from all the burdens of antiquated methods of housekeeping, by replacing them by house-communes, public kitchens, central laundries, nurseries, etc.

5. The Soviet Government, guaranteeing to the working masses incomparably more opportunities to vote and to recall their delegates in the most easy and accessible manner than they possessed under bourgeois democracy and parliamentarism, at the same time abolishes all the negative features of parliamentarism, especially the separation of legislative and executive powers, the isolation of the representative institutions from the masses, etc.

In the Soviet state not a territorial district, but a productive unit (factory, mill) forms the electoral unit and the unit of the state. The state apparatus is thus brought near to the masses.

The aim of the Party consists in endeavoring to bring the Government apparatus into still closer contact with the masses, for the purpose of realizing democracy more fully and strictly in practice, by making Government officials responsible to, and placing them under the control of, the masses.

6. The Soviet state includes in its organs—the Soviets—workmen and soldiers on a basis of complete equality and unity of interests whereas bourgeois democracy, in spite of all its declarations, transformed the army into an instrument of the wealthy classes, separated it from the masses, and set it against them, depriving the soldiers of any opportunity of exercising their political

rights. The aim of the Party is to defend and develop this unity of the workmen and soldiers in the Soviets and to strengthen the indissoluble ties between the armed forces and the organizations of the proletariat and semi-proletariat.

7. The urban industrial proletariat, being the more concentrated, united, and educated section of the toiling masses, hardened in battle, played the part of leader in the whole Revolution. This was evidenced while the Soviets were being created, as well as in the course of development of the Soviets into organs of authority. Our Soviet constitution reflects this in certain privileges it confers upon the industrial proletariat, in comparison with the more scattered petty-bourgeois masses in the village.

The All-Russian Communist Party, explaining the temporary character of these privileges, which are historically connected with difficulties of socialist organization of the village, must try undeviatingly and systematically to use this position of the industrial proletariat in order closer to unite the backward and the scattered masses of the village proletarians and semi-proletarians, as well as the middle-class peasantry, as a counterbalance to narrow craft professional interests, which were fostered by capitalism among the workmen.

8. The proletarian revolution, owing to the Soviet organization of the state, was able at one stroke finally to destroy the old bourgeois, official and judicial state apparatus. The comparatively low standard of culture of the masses, the absence of necessary experience in state administration on the part of responsible workers who are elected by the masses, the pressing necessity, owing to the critical situation of engaging specialists of the old school, and the calling up to military service of the more advanced section of city workmen, all this led to the partial revival of bureaucratic practices within the Soviet system.

The All-Russian Communist Party, carrying on a resolute struggle with bureaucratism, suggests the following measures for overcoming this evil:

(1) Every member of the Soviet is obliged to perform a certain duty in state administration.

(2) These duties must change in rotation, so as grad-

ually to embrace all the branches of administrative work.

(3) All the working masses without exception must be gradually induced to take part in the work of state administration.

The complete realization of these measures will carry us in advance of the Paris Commune, and the simplification of the work of administration, together with the raising of the level of culture of the masses, will eventually lead to the abolition of state authority.

Relations of Nationalities

9. With reference to the nationality question the All-Russian Communist Party is guided by the following theses:

(1) The principal aim is to bring into closer relations the proletarians and semi-proletarians of different nationalities, for the purpose of carrying on a general revolutionary struggle for the overthrow of the land-lords and the bourgeoisie.

(2) In order to remove mistrust on the part of the working masses of the oppressed countries toward the proletariat of those states which formerly oppressed them, it is necessary to abolish all privileges of any national group, to proclaim the fullest equality of all nationalities, and to recognize the rights of colonies and oppressed nations to political separation.

(3) For the same purpose, as a temporary measure toward achieving the unity of nations, the Party suggests a federative combination of all states organized on the Soviet basis.

(4) The All-Russian Communist Party regards the question as to which class expresses the desire of a nation for separation from a historical point of view, taking into consideration the level of historical development of the nation, *i.e.*, whether the nation is passing from medievalism toward bourgeois democracy or from bourgeois democracy toward Soviet or proletarian democracy, etc.

In any case, particular care and attention must be exercised by the proletariat of those nations which were oppressing nations toward the prevailing national feelings of the working masses of the oppressed nations, or nations which are limited in their rights. Only by such a policy is it possible to create favorable conditions for a voluntary and real unity of different national elements of the international proletariat, as has been proved by the combination of different national Soviet republics around Soviet Russia.

Military Affairs

10. The aims of the Party with reference to military matters are defined by the following fundamental theses:

(1) In the period when imperialism is decaying and civil war is spreading, it is possible neither to retain the old army nor to construct a new one on a so-called national and non-class basis. The Red Army, as the instrument of the proletarian dictatorship, is compelled to have an undisguised class character, *i.e.*, its ranks must be filled exclusively with proletarians and semi-proletarian sections of the peasantry. Only with the abolition of classes will this kind of army be transformed into national Socialist militia.

(2) All proletarians and semi-proletarians must undergo thorough courses of military training. Military training must be introduced into the schools.

(3) The work of military training and of education of the Red Army is conducted on the basis of class solidarity and Socialist education. Therefore, political commissaries chosen from devoted and trustworthy Communists are as necessary as military chiefs, and Communist groups must be organized in all sections of the army, in order to establish class-conscious discipline and an intellectual link with the Party.

(4) As a counterbalance to the old order of things in the army, the following changes are necessary: shorter periods of barrack training, barracks to be nearer to the type of military and military-political schools, closer connection between military formations and mills, factories, trade unions, and organizations of the poorest peasantry.

(5) Only commanding corps, of which at first at least the lower ranks are drawn from among class-conscious workmen and peasants, can give the necessary organiza-

tion and stability to the young revolutionary army. Therefore, one of the principal aims in the construction of the army is the training of the most energetic and capable soldiers devoted to the cause of socialism, for the duties of commanders.

(6) It is necessary to make use of, and adopt on a wide scale, the practical and technical experience of the last world war. In connection with this it is necessary to attract military specialists who have gone through the training of the old army, for the organization of the army and for conducting military operations. At the same time this use of military specialists may be made on condition that political guidance and full control over military officials is concentrated in the hands of the working class.

(7) The demand that the commanding corps should be elective had great significance with reference to the bourgeois army where the military commanders were selected and trained to become an instrument of class oppression of soldiers, and through them of the working masses. This demand has no significance with reference to the Red Army, composed of class-conscious workmen and peasants. The possibility of combining the election and appointment of the commanders of the revolutionary class army is determined exclusively by practical considerations, and depends upon the standard of organization attained, the degree of solidarity of the parts of the army, the effective supply of commanders, etc.

Jurisprudence

11. Proletarian democracy, taking power into its own hands and finally abolishing the organs of domination of the bourgeoisie—the former courts of justice—has replaced the formula of bourgeois democracy: "judges elected by the people," by the class watchword: "judges elected from the working masses and only by the working masses," and has applied the latter in the organization of law courts, having extended equal rights to both sexes, both in the election of judges and in the exercise of the functions of judges.

In order to induce the broad masses of the proletariat and the poorest peasantry to take part in the administration of justice, a bench of jury-judges sitting in rotation under guidance of a permanent judge is introduced and various labor organizations and trade unions must impanel their delegates.

The Soviet Government has replaced the former endless series of courts of justice with their various divisions, by a very simplified, uniform system of Peoples' Courts, accessible to the population, and freed of all useless formalities of procedure.

The Soviet Government, abolishing all the laws of the overthrown Governments, commissioned the judges elected by the Soviets to carry out the will of the proletariat in compliance with its decrees, and in cases of absence or incompleteness of decrees, to be guided by Socialist conscience.

Constructed on such a basis, the courts of justice have already led to a fundamental alteration of the character of punishment, introducing conditional sentences on a wide scale, applying public censure as a form of punishment by obligatory labor with the retention of freedom, and prisons by institutions for training, and applying the principle of comradely tribunals.

The All-Russian Communist Party, in order to assist the further development of the courts of justice on these lines, will strive to induce all workmen without exception to perform judicial duties and finally replace the system of punishment by measures of an educational character.

Public Education

12. The All-Russian Communist Party in the field of education sets itself the task of bringing to fulfillment the work begun by the October Revolution of 1917, of transforming the school from an instrument of class domination of the bourgeoisie into an instrument for the abolition of the class divisions of society, into an instrument for a Communist regeneration of society.

In the period of the dictatorship of the proletariat, *i.e.,* in the period of preparation of conditions suitable for the realization of communism, the school must be not only the conductor of Communist principles, but it must become the conductor of the intellectual, organizational, and educational influences of the proletariat to the semi-proletariat and non-proletarian sections of the toiling masses, in order to educate a generation capable of establishing communism. The immediate aim in this direction is at the present time the further development of the following principles of school and educational work, already established by the Soviet Government:

(1) The introduction of free and compulsory general and technical education (instruction in the theory and practice of the principal branches of production) for all children of both sexes up to the age of 17.

(2) The establishment of a system of preschool institutions: nurseries, kindergartens, homes, etc., to improve the social development of women and assist in their emancipation.

(3) Full realization of the principle of a uniform industrial school with instruction in the native language, with coeducation for children of both sexes, free from religious influence; a school where tuition is closely connected with socially useful labor and which prepares members of a Communist society.

(4) The supply of all pupils with food, clothes, boots, and school appliances at the cost of the state.

(5) The preparation of a new staff of teachers who are imbued with the ideas of communism.

(6) Bringing the toiling masses to take an active part in educational work (the development of councils of public education, mobilization of educated people, etc.).

(7) General state assistance to self-education and the intellectual development of workers and peasants (creation of a system of institutions for education outside of the schools, such as libraries, schools for adults, people's palaces and universities, courses of lectures, cinemas, studios, etc.).

(8) Spreading on a large scale of professional education for persons from the age of 17, in connection with technical knowledge.

(9) Making all universities accessible to all desiring to study, particularly to workmen; attracting all people able to lecture to become instructors in these universities; abolishing all artificial barriers standing in the way of young scientists reaching professional chairs; financial support of students in order to offer the prole-

tarians and the peasants the fullest opportunity to take advantage of the universities.

(10) Opening and making accessible to the toiling classes all the art treasures which were created by the exploitation of their labor, and which were formerly at the exclusive disposal of the exploiters.

(11) The development of the propaganda of Communist ideas on a wide scale and for that purpose the utilization of state resources and apparatus.

Religion

13. With reference to religion, the All-Russian Communist Party does not content itself with the already decreed separation of church from state, *i.e.*, measures which are one of the items of the programs of bourgeois democracy, which was, however, never fulfilled owing to many and various ties binding capital with religious propaganda.

The All-Russian Communist Party is guided by the conviction that only the realization of conscious and systematic social and economic activity of the masses will lead to the disappearance of religious prejudices. The aim of the Party is finally to destroy the ties between the exploiting classes and the organization of religious propaganda, at the same time helping the toiling masses actually to liberate their minds from religious superstitions, and organizing on a wide scale scientific-educational and anti-religious propaganda. It is, however, necessary carefully to avoid offending the religious susceptibilities of believers, which leads only to the strengthening of religious fanaticism.

Economics

1. Undeviatingly to continue and finally to realize the expropriation of the bourgeoisie which was begun and which has already been largely completed, the transforming of all means of production and exchange into the property of the Soviet republic, *i.e.*, the common property of all toilers.

2. All possible increase of the productive forces of the country must be considered the fundamental and

principal point upon which the economic policy of the Soviet Government is based. In view of the disorganization of the country, everything in other spheres of life must be subordinated to the practical aim immediately and at all costs to increase the quantity of products required by the population. The successful functioning of every Soviet institution connected with public economy must be gauged by the practical results in this direction.

At the same time it is necessary in the first place to pay attention to the following:

3. The decaying imperialist system of economy left to the Soviet state a heritage of chaos in the organization and management of production, which hampered it in the first period of construction. The more imperative therefore becomes the fundamental task of concentrating all the economic activity of the country according to a general state plan; the greatest concentration of production for the purpose of amalgamating it into various branches and groups of branches, and centralizing it in the most productive units, and for the purpose of rapidity in carrying out economic achievements; the most efficient arrangement of the productive apparatus and a rational and economical utilization of all material resources of the country.

It is necessary to extend economic co-operation and political ties with other nations, and try at the same time to establish a general economic plan with those which have already adopted the Soviet system.

4. It is necessary to utilize small-scale and handicraft industry to the widest extent by placing Government orders with handicraftsmen; to include handicraft and small-scale industry in the general scheme of supplying raw materials and fuel, as well as financial assistance, on condition that individual handicraftsmen, handicraft associations, productive co-operative societies, and small enterprises amalgamate into large productive and industrial units; to encourage such amalgamations by offering them economic privileges, which together with other measures are aimed at defeating the aspirations of the handicraftsmen to become small manufacturers, and thus painlessly replace the backward forms of production by a higher form of large-scale mechanized industry.

5. The organizing apparatus of socialized industry

must first of all rest upon the trade unions. The latter must free themselves from their narrow guild outlook and transform themselves into large productive combinations which will unite the majority, and finally all the workmen of a given branch of production.

Trade unions, being already according to the laws of the Soviet Republic and established practice participants in all local and central organs for managing industry, must actually concentrate in their hands the management of the whole system of public economy as an economic unit. The trade unions, thus securing an indissoluble union between the central state administration, the public system of economy, and the masses of toilers, must induce the latter to take part in the immediate management of production. The participation of trade unions in the management of production and the attraction by them of the broad masses are, moreover, the principal means to carry on a struggle against bureaucracy in the economic apparatus of the Soviet state, and afford the opportunity of establishing a really democratic control over the results of production.

6. A maximum utilization of all labor power existing in the state, its regular distribution and redistribution among various territorial regions as well as among various branches of production is necessary for the systematic development of public economy, and must be the immediate aim in the economic policy of the Soviet Government. This aim can be attained in closest co-operation with the trade unions. For the purpose of performing certain social duties, a general mobilization of all capable of work must be carried out by the Soviet Government, aided by the trade unions, on a much wider scale and more systematically than has been done hitherto.

7. In the state of the complete disorganization of the capitalist system of labor, the productive forces of the country can be restored and developed, and a Socialist system of production strengthened, only on the basis of the comradely discipline of toilers, maximum activity on their part, responsibility, and the strictest mutual control over the productivity of labor.

Persistent systematic effort directed to the re-education of the masses is necessary to attain this aim. This work is now made easier as the masses in reality see the abolition of capitalists, landowners, and merchants, and from their own experience draw the conclusion that the level of their prosperity depends entirely upon the productivity of their own labor.

The trade unions play the principal part in the work of establishing a new Socialist discipline. Breaking with old conventions, they must put into practice and try various measures, such as the establishment of control, standards of production, the introduction of responsibility of the workmen before special labor tribunals, etc., for the realization of this aim.

8. Moreover, for the development of the productive forces the immediate wide and full utilization of all specialists in science and technology left to us by capitalism is necessary, in spite of the fact that the majority of the latter are inevitably imbued with bourgeois ideas and habits. The Party considers that the period of sharp struggle with this group, owing to organized sabotage on their part, is ended as the sabotage is in the main subdued. The Party, in closest contact with the trade unions, will follow its former line of action, *i.e.*, on the one hand it will make no political concessions to this bourgeois section and mercilessly suppress any counter-revolutionary moves on its part, and on the other hand it will carry on a merciless struggle against the pseudo-radical but, in reality, ignorant and conceited opinion that the working class can overcome capitalism and the bourgeois order without the aid of bourgeois specialists or taking advantage of their knowledge, without passing, together with them, through a thorough schooling of hard work.

While striving toward equal remuneration of labor and to realize communism, the Soviet Government does not regard the immediate realization of such equality possible at the moment, when only the first steps are being taken toward replacing capitalism by communism. It is therefore necessary to maintain a higher remuneration for specialists in order that they should work not worse but better than before, and for that purpose it is not possible to abandon the system of bonuses for the most successful, particularly for work of organization.

To the same degree, it is necessary to place the bourgeois experts in a setting of comradely common effort, working hand in hand with the mass of average workers, led by class-conscious Communists, and thus to assist the mutual understanding and unity between manual and intellectual workers formerly separated by capitalism.

9. The Soviet authority has already adopted a number of measures directed to the development of science and for bringing it into closer contact with production, *viz.*, the creation of a number of new scientific institutions, laboratories, stations for research and experimental production, in order to verify new technical methods, improvements, and inventions, taking stock of and organizing all scientific forces. The All-Russian Communist Party, supporting all these measures, strives to attain their further development and to create more favorable conditions for scientific work in connection with the increase of the productive forces of the country.

Agriculture, Rural Economy

10. The Soviet Government, having carried out the complete abolition of private property in land, has already begun to carry out a series of measures directed to the organization of Socialist agriculture on a wide scale. The principal measures are the following: (1) The establishment of Soviet farms, *i.e.*, large Socialist economic enterprises; (2) Assistance to societies as well as associations for common land cultivation; (3) Organization by the state of the cultivation of all uncultivated acreage; (4) State mobilization of all agricultural forces for the purpose of taking the most energetic measures to increase agricultural productivity; (5) The support of agricultural communes as absolutely voluntary associations of agricultural laborers for the purpose of conducting a communal system of economy on a large scale.

The All-Russian Communist Party, considering all these measures as the only way toward the absolutely indispensable increase of productivity of agricultural labor, strives to extend them to the more backward regions of the country, and as further steps in this direction the All-Russian Communist Party particularly supports:

(1) All possible encouragement by the state of agricultural co-operative societies engaged in the processing of agricultural products.

(2) The introduction of a system of melioration on a wide scale.

(3) The systematic supply on a wide scale of agricultural implements through special establishments, to the poorest and the middle-class peasantry.

The All-Russian Communist Party, taking into consideration that the small-scale system of agriculture will continue for a considerable time, strives to carry out a series of measures directed to the increase of productivity of the peasant enterprise. The measures are: (1) The regulation of the exploitation of land by the peasants (abolition of scattered fields, etc.); (2) The supply to the peasantry of improved seeds and artificial manure; (3) The improvement of the breed of cattle; (4) The dissemination of agricultural information; (5) Agricultural aid to the peasantry; (6) The repair of peasants' agricultural implements in Soviet workshops; (7) The establishment of loan centers, experimental stations, exhibition fields, etc.; (8) The improvement of peasant lands.

11. The opposition between the town and the village is one of the chief causes of the economic and cultural backwardness of the village. In periods of serious crisis, such as the present, this opposition places the town as well as the village before the immediate danger of degeneration and destruction. The All-Russian Communist Party sees in the abolition of this opposition one of the principal tasks of Communist construction, and among other measures considers essential the systematic attraction of industrial workmen to Communist construction in agriculture, and greater activity on the part of the already established "Workmen's Committees of Assistance," etc.

12. The All-Russian Communist Party in its work in the village, as formerly, looks for support to the proletarian and semi-proletarian groups in it, and in the first place organizes these into an independent force, creating Party circles in the village, organizations of the rural

poor, special types of trade unions of village proletarians and semi-proletarians, and so on, bringing them into closer contact with the urban proletarians, freeing them from the influence of the rural bourgeoisie and the interests of small property-holders.

The relation of the All-Russian Communist Party to the rural bourgeois elements is one of carrying on a resolute struggle against their attempts at exploitation, and suppressing their resistance to the Soviet policy.

The policy of the All-Russian Communist Party with reference to the middle-class peasantry consists in gradually and systematically attracting it to the work of Socialist construction. The Party's aim is to separate this section from the kulaks (rich peasants) by giving consideration to its needs, to bring it over to the side of the proletariat, to struggle against its backwardness by means of education and not by means of suppression, in all cases where the vital interests of this section are involved to come to an agreement with it, making concessions to it on questions related to methods of realizing Socialist reorganization.

Distribution

13. In the field of distribution, the task of the Soviet Government at the present time is undeviatingly to replace private trade by a systematic distribution of products on a national scale. The aim is to organize the population into a single network of consumers' communes, which will be able with the greatest rapidity, systematically, economically, and with the least expenditure of labor, to distribute all necessary products, strictly centralizing the whole apparatus for distribution.

The already existing general and workmen's co-operative societies, which are the largest organizations of consumers and which the development of capitalism has made a most efficient apparatus for distribution on a large scale, will become the basis of the communes of consumers and their groupings.

The All-Russian Communist Party, considering more correct on principle the further Communist development of the co-operative apparatus and not its abolition, must systematically continue its policy: to make the work in co-operative societies obligatory for all members of the Party, to conduct them with the aid of trade unions on a Communist basis, to develop among the workers in co-operative societies initiative and discipline, to strive toward the aim that the whole population belong to co-operative societies, combined into one co-operative embracing all Soviet Russia, and finally—and most essential—to see that the influence of the proletariat on other groups or toilers should always prevail, and introduce measures facilitating and realizing the transformation of petty-bourgeois co-operatives of the old capitalist type into communes of consumers conducted by the proletariat and semi-proletariat.

Money and Banking

14. The Soviet Government in Russia, avoiding the mistakes of the Paris Commune, immediately expropriated the State Bank, then proceeded to the nationalization of private commercial banks and combined the nationalized banks and savings banks with the State Bank, thus laying the foundation of a single national bank of the Soviet Republic and transforming the banks from an instrument of economic domination of financial capital and of the political domination of exploiters, into an organ of power of the workers, and a lever of economic revolution. The All-Russian Communist Party considers its aim to be the final accomplishment of the work begun by the Soviet Government and regards the following principles as paramount:

(1) The monopolization of all banking by the Soviet state.

(2) A complete alteration and simplification of bank transactions by transforming the banks into an apparatus for uniform accounting and general bookkeeping of the Soviet Republic. The organization of a systematic public economy will lead to the abolition of the bank and to the transformation of it into a central bookkeeping department of the Communist society.

15. In the first period of transition from capitalism to communism, while Communist production and distribution of products is not yet organized, it is impossible to abolish money. Under such conditions the bour-

geois sections of society are able to utilize money, which still remains private property, for the purpose of speculation, profiteering, and robbery of the toilers. The All-Russian Communist Party strives toward the adoption of a series of measures which will render it possible to extend the field of operations without the aid of money and which will lead to the abolition of money, such as the compulsory depositing of money in the public bank, the introduction of budget books, the replacing of money by checks, short-term tickets for procuring products, and so on.

Finance

16. In the period of the beginning of the socialization of the means of production expropriated from the capitalists, the state ceases to be a parasitic apparatus ruling the process of production; it begins to become transformed into an organization performing the function of managing the economic system of the country, and to that extent the state budget becomes the budget of public economy as a whole.

Under such circumstances the balancing of state revenues and expenditures can be realized on the condition that state production and distribution of products are arranged in the most efficient manner. The All-Russian Communist Party, with reference to the covering of immediate state expenditure in the period of transition, defends the transition from the system of levies imposed on the capitalists which was historically necessary and legal in the period of social revolution, to the progressive income and property tax. As this tax becomes obsolete, owing to the general expropriation of the propertied class, state expenditure must be met by the direct conversion of a part of the income derived from the various state monopolies into state revenue.

Housing

17. The Soviet Government, in trying to solve the housing problem which was particularly sharpened during the war, has expropriated completely all the houses of capitalist owners, and handed them over to the municipal Soviets; has removed in mass the workmen from

the suburbs into bourgeois houses; handed over the best houses to the workmen's organization, undertaking the maintenance of these at the expense of the state; and has arranged for the supply of furniture to workmen's families.

The aim of the All-Russian Communist Party is to exert the greatest effort for the improvement of the housing conditions of the toiling masses without infringing on the interests of non-capitalist home-ownership; the abolition of overcrowding in unsanitary quarters; the abolition of inadequate housing, the rebuilding of old, and the building of new houses which will be in conformity with the new conditions of life of the working masses, and the rational resettlement of the working masses.

Protection of Labor and Social Security

The establishment of the dictatorship of the proletariat for the first time made it possible to realize fully the minimum program of all Socialist parties in the sphere of the protection of labor.

The Soviet Government has introduced by legislative enactment and ratified in the "Code of Labor Laws" a minimum eight-hour day for all workmen, and a six-hour day for persons under 18 years of age and those working in unhealthy branches of production, and for miners; a 42-hour uninterrupted rest every week for all toilers; the prohibition of continuous overtime; the prohibition of employment of young persons under 16; the prohibition of night work, particularly in harmful branches of production, for all women and males under 18; the exemption from work of pregnant women eight weeks before and eight weeks after confinement, with the maintenance of full wages together with free medical assistance and medicine; permission to working women of not less than half an hour every three hours for nursing their babies, and supplementary subsidies to all nursing mothers; factory and sanitary inspection elected by the trade union councils.

The Soviet Government by legislative enactment has introduced complete social maintenance of all workmen not exploiting the labor of others, and in all cases of loss of capacity for work, and for the first time in the world, has introduced unemployment insurance of workmen at the cost of employers and of the state, granting complete self-administration to those who are maintained and with the participation of trade unions.

Moreover, the Soviet Government in some respects has gone further than the minimum program and provided in the same "Code of Labor Laws" for the participation of the workmen's organizations in the discussion of questions referring to the hiring and discharging of workmen; a month's holiday for all workmen who have worked continually for not less than a year, with the maintenance of wages; the state regulation of ' wages according to rates worked out by trade unions; the duty of certain organs such as the Soviet and trade-union departments for the distribution and regulation of labor power, to provide work for unemployed workmen.

The extreme destruction caused by the war and the pressure of world imperialism have compelled the Soviet Government to depart from the code in the following instances: to allow overtime in exceptional cases, but not exceeding 50 days in the course of one year; to permit youths between 14 and 16 to work, but the length of their working day not to exceed four hours; temporarily to reduce holidays from a month to a fortnight; to increase the hours of night work to seven.

The All-Russian Communist Party must carry on an extensive propaganda for the participation of all workmen in the realization of all these measures for the protection of labor, for which purpose it is necessary:

(1) To make the work of organization and extension of labor inspection more intensive by choosing and preparing for that purpose active workers from among the workmen and to extend inspection to small-scale and home industry.

(2) To abolish completely child labor and further to decrease the working hours for young persons.

In addition the All-Russian Communist Party's task is to establish:

(1) With the general increase of productivity of labor the six-hour working day as a maximum without reduction of wages, but on condition that all workers must devote two hours' overtime without pay to the study of

the theory of trade and industry, to practical training for state administration, and to military drill.

(2) The introduction of the premium bonus system for the increase of labor productivity.

The All-Russian Communist Party in the sphere of social security strives to organize on a large scale the state support not only of war victims and victims of various catastrophes, but the victims of abnormal social relations. The Party also conducts a struggle against parasitism and idleness and sets itself the task of bringing back to a life of work any who have been dislodged from work.

Protection of Public Health

The All-Russian Communist Party proposes, as the starting point in its work for the protection of public health, the realization of sanitary measures on a large scale for the purpose of preventing the spreading of disease. The dictatorship of the proletariat has already made it possible to carry out a series of measures, the realization of which was impossible in bourgeois society: the nationalization of drugstores, of large private medical institutions, of health resorts, compulsory work for all medical men and women, and so on.

In conformity with the above the All-Russian Communist Party sets as its immediate task:

(1) To carry out, in the interests of the toilers, sanitary measures on a large scale, such as:

(a) Sanitation of centers of population (guarding of soil, water, and air).

(b) Setting up communal feeding on a scientific and hygienic basis.

(c) The organization of measures preventing the development and spreading of infectious diseases.

(d) The introduction of sanitary legislation.

(2) The struggle with social diseases (consumption, venereal diseases, alcoholism, etc.)

(3) Free trained medical assistance and medical supplies accessible to all.

THE PROGRAM OF THE COMMUNIST PARTY OF THE SOVIET UNION (DRAFT), 1961

CONTENTS

101

THE PROGRAM OF THE COMMUNIST PARTY OF THE SOVIET UNION (DRAFT), 1961

INTRODUCTION

The great October Socialist Revolution ushered in a new era in the history of mankind, the era of the downfall of capitalism and the establishment of communism. Socialism has triumphed in the Soviet Union and has achieved decisive victories in the people's democracies; socialism has become a cause of practical significance to hundreds of millions of people, and the banner of the revolutionary movement of the working class throughout the world.

More than 100 years ago Karl Marx and Friedrich Engels, the great teachers of the proletariat, wrote in the Communist Manifesto: "A specter is haunting Europe, the specter of communism." The courageous and selfless struggle of the proletariat of all countries brought mankind nearer to communism. First, dozens and hundreds of people, then thousands and millions, inspired by the ideals of communism, stormed the old world. The Paris Commune, the October Revolution, the Socialist revolutions in China and in a number of European and Asian countries are the major historical stages in the heroic battle fought by the international working class for the victory of communism. A tremendously long road, a road drenched in the blood of fighters for the happiness of the people, a road of glorious victories and temporary reverses, had to be traversed before communism, which had once seemed a mere specter, became the greatest force of modern times, a society that is being built up over vast areas of the globe.

In the early twentieth century the center of the international revolutionary movement shifted to Russia. Russia's heroic working class, led by the Bolshevik Party headed by Vladimir Ilyich Lenin, became its vanguard. The Communist Party inspired and led the Socialist revolution; it was the organizer and leader of the first workers' and peasants' state in history. The brilliant genius of Lenin, whose name will live forever, illumines mankind's road to communism.

On entering the arena of political struggle, the Leninist-Communist Party raised high the banner of revolutionary Marxism over the whole world. Marxism-Leninism became a powerful ideological weapon for the revolutionary transformation of society. At every stage of historical progress, the Party, taking guidance from the theory of Marx-Engels-Lenin, accomplished the tasks scientifically formulated in its programs.

In adopting its first program at its Second Congress in 1903 the Bolshevik Party called on the working class and all working people of Russia to fight for the overthrow of the Czarist autocracy and then of the bourgeois-landlord system and for the establishment of the dictatorship of the proletariat. In February, 1917, the Czarist regime was swept away. In October, 1917, the proletarian revolution abolished the capitalist system so hated by the people. A Socialist country came into being for the first time in history. The creation of a new world began.

The first program of the Party had been carried out.

Adopting its second program at the Eighth Congress in 1919, the Party promulgated the task of building a Socialist society. Treading on unexplored ground and overcoming difficulties and hardships, the Soviet people under the leadership of the Communist Party put into practice the plan for Socialist construction drawn up by Lenin. Socialism triumphed in the Soviet Union completely and finally.

The second program of the Party has likewise been carried out.

The gigantic revolutionary exploit accomplished by the Soviet people roused and inspired the masses in all countries and continents. A mighty purifying thunderstorm marking the springtime of mankind is raging over the earth. The Socialist revolution in European and Asian countries has resulted in the establishment of the world Socialist system. A powerful wave of national liberation revolutions is sweeping away the colonial system of imperialism.

One-third of mankind is building a new life under the banner of scientific communism. The first contingents of the working class to shake off capitalist oppression are facilitating victory for fresh contingents of their class brothers. The Socialist world is expanding; the capitalist world is shrinking. Socialism will inevitably succeed capitalism everywhere. Such is the objective law of social development. Imperialism is powerless to check the irresistible process of emancipation.

Our epoch, whose main content is the transition from capitalism to socialism, is an epoch of struggle between the two opposing social systems, an epoch of Socialist and national liberation revolutions, of the breakdown of imperialism and the abolition of the colonial system, an epoch of the transition of more and more people to the Socialist path, of the triumph of socialism and communism on a world-wide scale. The central factor of the present epoch is the international working class and its main creation, the world Socialist system.

Today the Communist Party of the Soviet Union (C.P.S.U.) is adopting its third program, a program for the building of Communist society. The new program is a constructive generalization of the experience of Socialist development; it takes account of the experience of the revolutionary movement throughout the world and, giving expression to the collective opinion of the Party, defines the main tasks and principal stages of Communist construction.

The supreme goal of the Party is to build a Communist society on whose banner will be inscribed: "From each according to his ability, to each according to his needs." The Party's motto, "Everything in the name of man, for the benefit of man," will be put into effect in full.

The Communist Party of the Soviet Union, true to proletarian internationalism, always follows the militant slogan: "Workers of all countries, unite!" The Party regards Communist construction in the U.S.S.R. as the Soviet people's great internationalist task, in keeping with the interests of the world Socialist system as a whole, and with the interests of the international proletariat and all mankind.

Communism accomplishes the historic mission of delivering all men from social inequality, from every form of oppression and exploitation, from the horrors of war, and proclaims peace, labor, freedom, equality, and happiness for all peoples of the earth.

Part One

THE TRANSITION FROM CAPITALISM TO COMMUNISM IS THE ROAD OF HUMAN PROGRESS

1. The Historical Necessity of the Transition from Capitalism to Socialism

The epoch-making turn of mankind from capitalism to socialism, initiated by the October Revolution, is a natural result of the development of society. Marxism-Leninism discovered the objective laws of social development and revealed the contradictions inherent in capitalism, the inevitability of their bringing about a revolutionary explosion and of the transition of society to communism.

Capitalism is the last exploiting system. Having developed its productive forces to an enormous extent, it became a tremendous obstacle to social progress. Capitalism alone is responsible for the fact that the twentieth century, a century of colossal growth of the productive forces and of great scientific progress, has not yet put an end to the poverty of hundreds of millions of people, has not provided an abundance of material and spiritual values for all men on earth. The growing conflict between productive forces and production relations imperatively demands that mankind should break the decayed capitalist shell, release the powerful productive forces created by man, and use them for the good of society as a whole.

Whatever the specific character of the rise and development of capitalism in any country, that system has everywhere common features and objective laws.

The development of world capitalism and of the

revolutionary struggle of the working class has fully confirmed the correctness of the Marxist-Leninist analysis of capitalism and its highest stage, imperialism, given in the first and second programs of the party. The basic propositions of this analysis are also given in the present program.

Under capitalism, the basic and decisive means of production belong to the numerically small capitalist class, while the vast majority of the population consists of proletarians and semi-proletarians, who own no means of production and are therefore compelled to sell their labor-power and by their labor create profits and riches for the ruling classes of society. The bourgeois state, whatever its form, is an instrument of the domination of labor by capital.

The development of large-scale capitalist production—production for profit, for the appropriation of surplus value—leads to the elimination of small independent producers, makes them wholly dependent on capital. Capitalism extensively exploits female and child labor. The economic laws of its development necessarily give rise to a huge reserve army of unemployed, which is constantly replenished by ruined peasants and urban petty bourgeoisie. The exploitation of the working class and all working people is continuously increasing, social inequality is becoming more and more marked, the gulf between the haves and have-nots is widening, and the sufferings and privation of the millions are growing worse.

Capitalism, by concentrating millions of workers in its factories, socializing the process of labor, imparts a social character to production; nevertheless it is the capitalists who appropriate the fruits of labor. This fundamental contradiction of capitalism—the contradiction between the social character of production and the private-capitalist form of appropriation—manifests itself in production anarchy and in the fact that the purchasing power of society falls short of the expansion of production and leads periodically to destructive economic crises. Crises and periods of industrial stagnation, in turn, are still more ruinous to small producers, increase the dependence of wage-labor on capital, and lead more rapidly to a relative, and sometimes an absolute, deterioration of the condition of the working class.

The growth and development of the contradictions of bourgeois society are accompanied by the growing discontent of the working people and the exploited masses with the capitalist system, by an increase in the number of proletarians and their greater unity, and by a sharpening of their class struggle against the exploiters. At the same time there is an accelerated creation of the material conditions that make possible the replacement of capitalist by Communist production relations, that is, the accomplishment of the social revolution which is the aim of the Communist Party, the politically conscious exponent of the class movement of the proletariat.

The working class, which is the most consistent revolutionary class, is the chief motive force of the revolutionary transformation of the world. In the course of class struggles it becomes organized, sets up its trade unions and political parties, and wages an economic, political, and theoretical struggle against capitalism. In fulfilling its historic mission as the revolutionary remaker of the old society and creator of a new system, the working class has become the exponent, not only of its own class interests, but of the interests of all working people. It is the natural leader of all forces fighting against capitalism.

The dictatorship of the proletariat and the leadership of the Marxist-Leninist party are indispensable conditions for the triumph of the Socialist revolution and the building of socialism.

The process of concentration and centralization of capital, while destroying free competition, led in the early twentieth century to the establishment of powerful capitalist monopoly associations—syndicates, cartels, and trusts—which acquired decisive importance in the economy, led to the merging of bank capital and immensely concentrated industrial capital, and to intensive export of capital. The trusts, which encompassed entire groups of capitalist powers, began the economic division of a world already divided territorially among the wealthiest countries. Capitalism had entered its final stage, the stage of monopoly capitalism, of imperialism.

The period of a more or less smooth spread of capitalism all over the globe gave way to spasmodic, cataclysmic development causing an unprecedented growth and aggravation of all the contradictions of capitalism—economic, political, class, and national. The imperialist powers' struggle for markets, for spheres of capital investment, for raw materials and labor, and for world domination became more intense than ever. In an epoch of the undivided rule of imperialism, that struggle necessarily led to devastating wars.

Imperialism is decaying and moribund capitalism; it is the eve of the Socialist revolution. The world capitalist system as a whole is ripe for the social revolution of the proletariat.

The exceedingly high degree of development of world capitalism in general; the replacement of free competition by state-monopoly capitalism; the establishment, by banks as well as associations of capitalists, of machinery for the social regulation of the production and the distribution of products; the growing cost of living and the oppression of the working class by the syndicates, connected with the growth of capitalist monopolies; the enslavement of the working class by the imperialist state, the growing difficulty of the economic and political struggle of the proletariat; and the horrors, hardships, and ruination brought about by imperialist war have all made inevitable the downfall of capitalism and the transition to a higher type of social economy.

The revolutionary defeat of imperialism does not take place all over the world simultaneously. The uneven character of the economic and political development of the capitalist countries under imperialism leads to revolutions occurring at different periods in different countries.

V. I. Lenin developed the theory of the Socialist revolution in new historical conditions; he elaborated the theory of the possibility of socialism triumphing first in one capitalist country taken singly.

Russia was the weakest link in the imperialist system and the focal point of all its contradictions. On the other hand, she had all the conditions necessary for the victory of socialism. Her working class was the most revolutionary and best organized in the world and had considerable experience of class struggle. It was led by a Marxist-Leninist party armed with an advanced revolutionary theory and steeled in class battles.

The Bolshevik Party brought together in one revolutionary torrent the struggle of the working class for socialism, the country-wide peace movement, the peasants' struggle for land, and the national-liberation movement of the oppressed peoples of Russia, and directed these forces to the overthrow of capitalism.

II. The Historic Significance of the October Revolution and of the Victory of Socialism in the U.S.S.R.

The great October Revolution breached the imperialist front in Russia, one of the world's largest countries, firmly established the dictatorship of the proletariat, and created a new type of state—the Soviet state—and a new type of democracy—democracy for the working people.

Workers' and peasants' power, born of the revolution, took Russia out of the bloodbath of the imperialist war, saved her from the national catastrophe to which the exploiting classes had doomed her, and delivered her peoples from the danger of enslavement by foreign capital.

The October Revolution undermined the economic basis of a system of exploitation and social injustice. Soviet power nationalized industry, the railways, banks, and the land. It abolished landed proprietorship and fulfilled the peasants' age-long dream of land.

The October Revolution smashed the chains of national oppression; it proclaimed and put into effect the right of nations to self-determination, up to and including the right to secede. The revolution completely abolished the social-estate and class privileges of the exploiters. For the first time in history, it emancipated women and granted them the same rights as men.

The Socialist revolution in Russia shook the entire structure of world capitalism to its very foundations; the world split into two opposing systems.

For the first time there emerged in the international arena a state which put forward the great slogan of peace and began carrying through new principles in relations between peoples and countries. Mankind acquired a reliable bulwark in its struggle against wars of conquest, for peace and the security of the peoples.

The October Revolution led the country on to the road of socialism. The path which the Soviet people were to traverse was an unexplored and arduous one. The reactionary forces of the old world did all they could to strangle the Soviet state at its birth. The young Soviet Republic had to cope with intervention and civil war, economic blockade and disruption, conspiracies, sabotage, subversion, terrorism, and numerous other trials. Socialist construction was rendered incredibly difficult by the socio-economic, technical, and cultural backwardness of the country.

The victorious workers and peasants lacked knowledge of state administration and the experience necessary for the construction of a new society. The difficulties of Socialist construction were greatly increased by the fact that for almost thirty years the U.S.S.R. was the world's only Socialist state, and was subjected to incisive attacks by the hostile capitalist environment. The class struggle in the period of transition from capitalism to socialism was therefore acute.

The enemies of Leninism maintained that Russia was not mature enough for a Socialist revolution, that it was impossible to build socialism in one country. But the enemies of Leninism were put to shame.

A wise, discerning policy, the greatest stanchness, organization, and deep faith in their own strength and in the strength of the people were required of the Party and the working class. It was necessary to steer the right course in Socialist construction and insure the victory of socialism, despite the highly complicated international situation and a relatively weak industrial basis, in a country whose economy had been badly ravaged by war and where small-commodity production was overwhelmingly predominant.

The Party proved equal to that historic task. Under the leadership of Lenin it worked out a plan for the radical transformation of the country, for the construction of socialism. On the basis of a thorough scientific analysis, Lenin elaborated the policy of the proletarian state for the entire period of transition from capitalism to socialism. He evolved the New Economic Policy (N.E.P.), designed to bring about the victory of socialism. The main elements of the Lenin plan for the building of a Socialist society were industrialization of the country, agricultural co-operation, and the cultural revolution.

The Party upheld that plan in an acute struggle against skeptics and capitulators, against the Trotskyists, Right opportunists, nationalist-deviators, and other hostile groups. It rallied the whole of the Soviet people to put Lenin's program into practice.

The point at issue at the time was: either perish or forge full steam ahead and overtake the capitalist countries economically.

The Soviet state had first of all to solve the problem of industrialization. In a historically brief period, without outside help, the Soviet Union built up a large-scale modern industry. By the time it had fulfilled three five-year plans (1928-1941) the Soviet Union had become a mighty industrial power that had achieved complete economic independence from the capitalist countries. Its defense capacity had increased immeasurably. The industrialization of the U.S.S.R. was a great exploit performed by the working class and the people as a whole, for they spared no effort or means, and consciously made sacrifices to lift the country out of its backward state.

The destiny of socialism in a country like the U.S.S.R. largely depended on the solution of a most difficult problem, namely, the transition from a small-scale, dispersed peasant economy to Socialist co-operation. Led by the Party, aided and fully supported by the working class, the peasantry took the road of socialism. Millions of small individual farms went into voluntary association to form collective farms. A large number of Soviet state farms and machine and tractor stations were established. The introduction in the Soviet countryside of large-scale Socialist farming meant a far-reaching revolution in economic relations, in the entire way of life of the peasantry. Collectivization forever delivered the countryside from kulak bondage, from class differentiation, ruin, and poverty. The real solution of the eternal peasant question was provided by the Lenin co-operative plan.

To build socialism it was necessary to raise the cultural level of the people; that task too was accomplished. A cultural revolution was carried out in the country. It freed the working people from spiritual slavery and ignorance and gave them access to the cultural values accumulated by mankind. The country, the bulk of whose population had been illiterate, made breathtaking progress in science and culture.

Socialism, which Marx and Engels scientifically predicted as inevitable and the plan for the construction of which was mapped out by Lenin, has become a reality in the Soviet Union.

Socialism has done away forever with the supremacy of private ownership of the means of production, that source of the division of society into antagonistic classes. Socialist ownership of the means of production has become the solid economic foundation of society. Unlimited opportunities have been afforded for the development of the productive forces.

Socialism has solved a great social problem—it has abolished the exploiting classes and the causes engendering the exploitation of man by man. There are now two friendly classes in the U.S.S.R.—the working class and the peasantry. And these classes, furthermore, have changed. The common character of the two forms of Socialist property has brought the working class and the collective-farm peasantry close together; it has strengthened their alliance and made their friendship indestructible.

A new intelligentsia, coming from the people and devoted to socialism, has emerged. The one-time antithesis between town and countryside, between labor by hand and by brain, has been abolished. The indestructible socio-political and ideological unity of the Soviet people has been built on the basis of the common vital interests of the workers, peasants, and intellectuals.

The Socialist principle "From each according to his abilities, to each according to his work" has been put into effect in the Soviet Union. This principle insures that the members of society have a material interest in the fruits of their labor; it makes it possible to harmonize personal and social interests in the most effective way and serves as a powerful stimulus for increasing productivity of labor, developing the economy, and raising the people's standard of living.

The awareness that they work for themselves and their society and not for exploiters inspires the working people with labor enthusiasm; it encourages their effort for innovation, their creative initiative and mass Socialist emulation. Socialism is living creativity by the working masses. The growing activity of the people in the building of a new life is a law of the Socialist epoch.

The aim of socialism is to meet the growing material and cultural requirements of the people ever more fully by continuously developing and improving social production.

The entire life of Socialist society is based on the principle of broad democracy. Working people take an active part, through the Soviets, trade unions, and other mass organizations, in managing the affairs of the state and in solving problems of economic and cultural advancement. Socialist democracy includes both political freedoms—freedom of speech, of the press, and of assembly, the right to elect and to be elected, and also social rights—the right to work, to rest and leisure, to education, to material security in old age and in case of illness or disability; equality of citizens of all races and nationalities; equal rights for women and men in all spheres of political, economic, and cultural activity. Socialist democracy, unlike bourgeois democracy, does not merely proclaim the rights of the people, but makes it really possible for the people to exercise them. Soviet society insures the real liberty of the individual. The highest manifestation of this liberty is man's emancipation from exploitation, which is what primarily constitutes genuine social justice.

Socialism has created conditions for the rapid progress of science. The achievements of Soviet science clearly show the superiority of the Socialist system and testify to the unlimited possibilities of scientific progress and to the growing role of science under socialism. It is only logical that the country of victorious socialism should have ushered in the era of the utilization of atomic energy for peaceful purposes, and that it should have blazed a trail into outer space. The man-made satellites of the earth and the sun, powerful space rockets and interplanetary space ships, atomic power stations and the first triumphal orbiting of the globe, accomplished by a Soviet citizen, which are a source of pride to all mankind, have become symbols of the creative energy of ascendant communism.

The solution of the national question is one of the greatest achievements of socialism. This question is of especial importance to a country like the Soviet Union, inhabited by more than a hundred nations and nationalities. Socialist society has not only guaranteed the political equality of nations, but has also abolished the economic and cultural backwardness inherited from the old system. With reciprocal fraternal assistance, primarily from the great Russian people, all the Soviet non-Russian republics have set up their own modern industries, trained their own national working class and intelligentsia, and developed a culture that is national in form and Socialist in content.

Many nations which in the past were backward have achieved socialism, by-passing the capitalist stage of development. The union and consolidation of equal peoples on a voluntary basis in a single multi-national state—the Union of Soviet Socialist Republics—their close co-operation in state, economic, and cultural development, their fraternal friendship and a flourishing economy and culture constitute the most important result of the Leninist national policy.

The Soviet people were destined by history to start on a new road, to blaze a new path of social development. This required special efforts of them, a continuous quest for forms and methods of building the new society which had to be tested in the crucible of practice. For nearly two out of little more than four decades, the Soviet people were compelled to devote their energies to the repulsion of invasions by the imperialist powers and to post-war economic rehabilitation. The Soviet system was put to a particularly severe test during the Great Patriotic War, the most trying war in history. By winning that war, the Soviet people proved that there are no forces in the world capable of stopping the progress of Socialist society.

What are the principal lessons to be learned from the experience of the Soviet people?

Soviet experience has shown that the peoples are able to achieve socialism only as a result of the Socialist revolution and the establishment of the dictatorship of the proletariat. Despite certain specific features due precisely to the historical conditions of Socialist construction in the Soviet Union, then in a hostile capitalistic encirclement, this experience has fully confirmed the fundamental principles of Socialist revolution and Socialist construction, principles which are of universal significance.

Soviet experience has shown that socialism alone can put an end to the exploitation of man by man, production anarchy, economic crises, unemployment, and the poverty of the people, and insure planned, continuous, and rapid development of the economy and steady improvement of the people's standard of living.

Soviet experience has shown that the working class can fulfill its historic mission as the builder of a new society only in a sound alliance with the non-proletarian working masses, primarily the peasantry.

Soviet experience has shown that the victory of the Socialist revolution alone provides all possibilities and conditions for the abolition of all national oppression, for the voluntary union of free and equal nations and nationalities in a single state.

Soviet experience has shown that the Socialist state is the main instrument for the Socialist transformation of society. The state organizes and unites the masses, exercises planned leadership of economic and cultural construction, and safeguards the revolutionary gains of the people.

Soviet experience has shown that socialism and peace are inseparable. The might of socialism serves peace. The Soviet Union saved mankind from Fascist enslavement. The Soviet state, which champions peace and implements the Leninist principle of peaceful existence, is a mighty barrier to imperialist aggression.

Soviet experience has fully borne out the Marxist-Leninist theory that the Communist Party plays a decisive role in the formation and development of Socialist society. Only a Party that steadfastly pursues a class proletarian policy, and is equipped with progressive, revolutionary theory, only a Party solidly united and closely linked with the masses, can organize the people and lead them to the victory of Socialism.

Soviet experience has shown that fidelity to the principles of Marxism-Leninism, of proletarian internationalism, their firm and unswerving implementation, and defense of those principles against opportunists and all other enemies are imperative conditions for the victory of socialism.

The world's greatest revolution and the Socialist reorganization of society, which has attained unprecedented heights in its development and prosperity, have confirmed in practice the historic truth of Leninism and have delivered a crushing blow to social-reformist ideology.

As a result of the devoted labor of the Soviet people and the theoretical and practical activities of the Communist Party of the Soviet Union, there exists in the world a Socialist society that is a reality and a science of Socialist construction that has been tested in practice. The highroad to Socialism has been paved. Many peoples are already marching along it, and it will be taken sooner or later by all peoples.

III. The World Socialist System

The Soviet Union is not pursuing the tasks of Communist construction alone but in fraternal community with the other Socialist countries.

The defeat of German fascism and Japanese militarism in World War II, in which the Soviet Union played a decisive part, created favorable conditions for the overthrow of capitalist and landlord rule by the peoples in a number of European and Asian countries. The peoples of Albania, Bulgaria, China, Czechoslovakia, the Democratic Republic of Vietnam, the German Democratic Republic, Hungary, the Korean People's Democratic Republic, Poland and Rumania, and still earlier the people of the Mongolian People's Republic, adopted the path of Socialist construction and, together with the Soviet Union, formed the Socialist camp. Yugoslavia likewise took the Socialist path. But the Yugoslav leaders by their revisionist policy contraposed Yugoslavia to the Socialist camp and the international Communist movement, thus threatening the loss of the revolutionary gains of the Yugoslav people.

The Socialist revolutions in Europe and Asia dealt imperialism a further powerful blow. The victory of the revolution in China was of special importance. The revolutions in European and Asian countries are the biggest event in world history since October, 1917.

A new form of political organization of society, people's democracy, a variety of the dictatorship of the proletariat, emerged. It reflected the distinctive development of Socialist revolution at a time when imperialism had been weakened and the balance of forces had tilted in favor of socialism. It also reflected the distinctive historical and national features of the countries concerned.

There emerged a world Socialist system, a social, economic, and political community of free sovereign peoples pursuing the Socialist and Communist path, united by common interests and goals and the close bonds of international Socialist solidarity.

In the people's democracies Socialist production relations are dominant and the socio-economic possibility of capitalist restoration has been eliminated. The successes of these countries have conclusively proved that true progress in all lands, irrespective of the level of their economic development, their area and population, is feasible only under socialism.

The combined forces of the Socialist camp guarantee each Socialist country against encroachments of imperialist reaction. The consolidation of the Socialist countries in a single camp, its increasing unity and steadily growing strength, insure the complete victory of socialism within the framework of the system as a whole.

The countries of the Socialist system have accumulated considerable collective experience in the remolding of the lives of hundreds of millions of people and have contributed many new and specific features to the forms of political and economic organization of society. This experience is a most valuable asset to the international revolutionary movement.

It has been borne out in practice and recognized by all Marxist-Leninist parties that the processes of Socialist revolution and construction are founded on a number of basic objective laws applicable to all countries entering upon the Socialist path.

The world Socialist system is a new type of economic and political relationship between countries. The Socialist countries have the same type of economic basis —social ownership of the means of production; the same type of political system—rule of the people with the working class at their head; a common ideology—Marxism-Leninism; common interests in the defense of their revolutionary gains and national independence from encroachments by the imperialist camp; and a great common goal—communism. This socio-economic and political community of purpose is the objective groundwork for lasting and friendly inter-governmental relations within the Socialist camp. The distinctive features of the relations existing between the countries of the Socialist community are complete equality, respect for independence and sovereignty, and fraternal mutual assistance. In the Socialist camp or, which is the same thing, in the world community of Socialist countries, none have, nor can have, any special rights or privileges.

The experience of the world Socialist system has confirmed the need for the closest unity of countries that fall away from capitalism, for their united effort in the building of socialism and communism. The line of Socialist construction in isolation, detached from the world community of Socialist countries, is theoretically untenable because it conflicts with the objective laws governing the development of Socialist society. It is harmful economically because it causes waste of social labor, retards the rates of growth of production, and makes the country dependent upon the capitalist world. It is reactionary and politically dangerous because it does not unite, but divides the peoples in face of the united front of imperialist forces, because it nourishes bourgeois-nationalist tendencies and may ultimately lead to the loss of the Socialist gains.

As they combine their effort in the building of a new society, the Socialist states give active support to and extend their political, economic, and cultural co-operation with countries that have cast off colonial rule. They maintain—and are prepared to maintain—broad mutually advantageous trade relations and cultural contacts with the capitalist countries.

The development of the world Socialist system and of the world capitalist system is governed by diametrically opposed laws. The world capitalist system emerged and developed in fierce struggle between the countries composing it, through the subjection and exploitation of the weaker countries by the strong, through the enslavement of hundreds of millions of people and the reduction of entire continents to the status of colonial appendages of the imperialist metropolitan countries. The formation and development of the world Socialist system, on the other hand, proceeds on the basis of sovereignty and free will and in conformity with the fundamental interests of the working people of all the countries of that system.

Whereas the world capitalist system is governed by the law of uneven economic and political development that leads to conflicts between countries, the world Socialist system is governed by opposite laws, which ensure the rapid, steady, and balanced growth of the economies of all the countries belonging to that system. Growth of production in a country belonging to the capitalist world deepens the contradiction between countries and intensifies competitive rivalries. The development of each Socialist country, on the other hand, promotes the general progress and consolidation of the world Socialist system as a whole. The economy of world capitalism develops at a slow rate, and goes through crises and upheavals. Typical of the economy of world socialism, on the other hand, are high and stable rates of growth and the common unintermittent economic progress of all Socialist countries.

All the Socialist countries make their contribution to the building and development of the world Socialist system and the consolidation of its might. The existence of the Soviet Union greatly facilitates and accelerates the building of socialism in the people's democracies. The Marxist-Leninist parties and the peoples of the Socialist countries proceed from the fact that the successes of the world Socialist system as a whole depend on the contribution and effort made by each country, and therefore consider the greatest possible development of the productive forces of their country an internationalist duty.

The co-operation of the Socialist countries enables each country to use its resources and develop its productive forces to the full and in the most rational manner. A new type of international division of labor is taking shape in the process of the economic, scientific, and technical co-operation of the Socialist countries, the co-ordination of their economic plans, the specialization and combination of production.

The establishment of the Union of Soviet Socialist Republics and, later, of the world Socialist system is the commencement of the historical process of an all-round association of peoples. With the disappearance of class antagonisms in the fraternal family of Socialist countries, national antagonisms also disappear. The rapid cultural progress of the peoples of the Socialist community is attended by a progressive mutual enrichment of the national cultures, and an active molding of the internationalist features typical of man in Socialist society.

The experience of the peoples of the world Socialist community has confirmed that their fraternal unity and co-operation conform to the supreme national interests of each country. The strengthening of the unity of the world Socialist system on the basis of proletarian internationalism is an imperative condition for the further progress of all its member countries.

The Socialist system has to cope with certain difficulties, deriving chiefly from the fact that most of the countries in that system had a medium or even low level of economic development in the past, and also from the fact that world reaction is doing its utmost to impede the building of socialism.

The experience of the Soviet Union and the people's democracies has confirmed the accuracy of Lenin's thesis that the class struggle does not disappear in the period of the building of socialism. The general development of the class struggle within the Socialist countries in conditions of successful Socialist construction leads to consolidation of the position of the Socialist forces and weakens the resistance of the remnants of the hostile classes. But this development does not follow a straight line. Changes in the domestic or external situation may cause the class struggle to intensify in specific periods. This calls for constant vigilance in order to frustrate in good time the designs of hostile forces within and without, who persist in their attempts to undermine people's power and sow strife in the fraternal community of Socialist countries.

Nationalism is the chief political and ideological weapon used by international reaction and the remnants of the domestic reactionary forces against the unity of the Socialist countries. Nationalist sentiments and national narrow-mindedness do not disappear automatically with the establishment of the Socialist system. Nationalist prejudice and survivals of former national strife are a province in which resistance to social progress may be most protracted and stubborn, bitter and insidious.

The Communists consider it their prime duty to educate working people in a spirit of internationalism, Socialist patriotism, and intolerance of all possible manifestations of nationalism and chauvinism. Nationalism is harmful to the common interests of the Socialist community and, above all, the people of the country where it obtains, since isolation from the Socialist camp holds up that country's development, deprives it of the advantages deriving from the world Socialist system, and encourages the imperialist powers to make the most of the nationalist tendencies for their own ends. Nationalism can gain the upper hand only where it is not consistently combated.

The Marxist-Leninist internationalist policy and determined efforts to wipe out the survivals of bourgeois nationalism and chauvinism are an important condition for the further consolidation of the Socialist community. Yet while they oppose nationalism and national egoism, Communists always show utmost consideration for the national feelings of the masses.

The world Socialist system is advancing steadfastly toward decisive victory in its economic competition with capitalism. It will shortly surpass the world capitalist system in aggregate industrial and agricultural production. Its influence on the course of social development in the interests of peace, democracy, and socialism is growing more and more.

The magnificent edifice of the new world being built by the heroic labors of the free peoples on vast areas of Europe and Asia is a prototype of a new society, of the future of all mankind.

IV. CRISIS OF WORLD CAPITALISM

Imperialism has entered the period of decline and collapse. The inexorable process of decay has seized capitalism from top to bottom—its economic and political system, its politics and ideology. Imperialism has forever lost its power over the bulk of mankind. The main content, main trend, and main features of the historical development of mankind are being determined by the world Socialist system, by the forces fighting against imperialism, for the Socialist reorganization of society.

World War I and the October Revolution ushered in the general crisis of capitalism. The second stage of this crisis developed at the time of World War II and the Socialist revolutions in a number of European and Asian countries. World capitalism has now entered a new, third stage of that crisis, the principal feature of which is that its development is not tied to a world war.

The breakaway from capitalism of more and more countries; the weakening of imperialist positions in the economic competition with socialism; the breakup of the imperialist colonial system; the intensification of imperialist contradictions with the development of state-monopoly capitalism and the growth of militarism; the mounting internal instability and decay of capitalist economy evidenced by the increasing inability of capitalism to make full use of the productive forces (low rates of production growth, periodic crises, continuous under-capacity operation of production plant, and chronic unemployment); the mounting struggle between labor and capital; an acute intensification of contradictions within the world capitalist economy; an unprecedented growth of political reaction in all spheres, rejection of bourgeois freedoms, and establishment of Fascist and despotic regimes in a number of countries, and the profound crisis of bourgeois policy and ideology—all these are manifestations of the general crisis of capitalism.

In the imperialist stage state-monopoly capitalism develops on an extensive scale. The emergence and growth of monopolies leads to the direct intervention of the state, in the interests of the financial oligarchy, in the process of capitalist reproduction. It is in the interests of the financial oligarchy that the bourgeois state institutes various types of regulation and resorts to the nationalization of some branches of the economy. World wars, economic crises, militarism, and political upheavals have accelerated the development of monopoly capitalism into state-monopoly capitalism.

The oppression of finance capital keeps growing. Giant monopolies controlling the bulk of social production dominate the life of the nation. A handful of millionaires and multi-millionaires wield arbitrary power over the entire wealth of the capitalist world and make the life of entire nations mere small change in their selfish deals. The financial oligarchy is getting fabulously rich.

The state is becoming a committee for the management of the affairs of the monopoly bourgeoisie. The bureaucratization of the economy is rising steeply. State-monopoly capitalism combines the strength of the monopolies and that of the state into a single mechanism whose purpose is to enrich the monopolies, suppress the working-class movement and the national-liberation struggle, save the capitalist system, and launch aggressive wars.

The right-wing Socialists and revisionists are making out state-monopoly capitalism to be almost socialism. The facts give the lie to this contention. State-monopoly capitalism does not change the nature of imperialism. Far from altering the position of the principal classes in the system of social production, it widens the rift between labor and capital, between the majority of the nation and the monopolies.

Attempts at state regulation of the capitalist economy cannot eliminate competition and anarchy of production, cannot ensure the planned development of the economy on a nationwide scale because capitalist ownership and exploitation of wage-labor remain the basis of production. The bourgeois theories of "crisis-free" and "planned" capitalism have been laid in the dust by the development of contemporary capitalist economy. The dialectics of state-monopoly capitalism is such that instead of shoring up the capitalist system, as the bourgeoisie expects, it aggravates the contradictions of capitalism and undermines its foundations. State-monopoly capitalism is the fullest material preparation for socialism.

The new phenomena in imperialist development corroborate the accuracy of Lenin's conclusions on the principal objective laws of capitalism in its final stage and on its increasing decay. Yet this decay does not signify complete stagnation, a palsy of its productive forces, and does not rule out growth of capitalist economy at particular times and in particular countries.

All in all, capitalism is increasingly impeding the development of the contemporary productive forces. Mankind is entering the period of a great scientific and technical revolution bound up with the conquest of nuclear energy, space exploration, the development of chemistry, automation, and other major achievements of science and engineering. But the relations of production under capitalism are much too narrow for a scientific and technical revolution. Socialism alone is capable of effecting it and of applying its fruits in the interests of society.

Technical progress under the rule of monopoly capital is turning against the working class. By using new forms, the monopolies intensify the exploitation of the working class. Capitalist automation is robbing the worker of his daily bread. Unemployment is rising, the living standard is dropping. Technical progress is continuously throwing more sections of small producers overboard. Imperialism is using technical progress chiefly for military purposes. It is turning the achievements of human genius against humanity. As long as imperialism exists, mankind cannot feel secure about its future.

Modern capitalism has made the market problem extremely acute. Imperialism is incapable of solving it, because lag of effective demand behind growth of production is one of its objective laws. Moreover, it retards the industrial development of the underdeveloped countries. The world capitalist market is shrinking relative to the more rapidly expanding production capacity. It is partitioned by countless customs barriers and restrictive fences and split into exclusive currency and finance zones. An acute competitive struggle for markets, spheres of investment, and sources of raw materials is under way in the imperialist camp. It is becoming doubly acute since the territorial sphere of capitalist domination has been greatly narrowed.

Monopoly capital has, in the final analysis, doomed bourgeois society to low rates of production growth that in some countries barely keep ahead of the growth of population. A considerable part of the production plant stands idle, while millions of unemployed wait at the factory gates. Farm production is artificially restricted, although millions are underfed in the world. People suffer want in material goods, but imperialism is squandering them on war preparations.

Abolition of the capitalist system in a large group of countries, the developing and strengthening of the world Socialist system, the disintegration of the colonial system and the collapse of old empires, the commencing reorganization of the colonial economic structure in the newly free countries and the expanding economic connections between the latter and the Socialist world—all these factors intensify the crisis of the world capitalist economy.

State-monopoly capitalism stimulates militarism to an unheard-of degree. The imperialist countries maintain immense armed forces even in peacetime. Military expenditures devour an ever-growing portion of the state budgets. The imperialist countries are turning into militarist states run by the army and the police. Militarization pervades the life of bourgeois society.

While enriching some groups of the monopoly bourgeoisie, militarism leads to the exhaustion of nations, to the ruin of the peoples languishing under an excessive tax burden, mounting inflation, and a high cost of living. Within the lifetime of one generation imperialism plunged mankind into the abyss of two destructive world wars. In the First World War the imperialists annihilated ten million and crippled twenty million people. The Second World War claimed nearly fifty million human lives. In the course of these wars entire countries were ravaged, thousands of towns and villages were demolished, and the fruits of the labor of many generations were destroyed. The new war being hatched by the imperialists threatens mankind with unprecedented human losses and destruction. Even the preparations for it bring suffering and privation to millions of people.

The progress achieved in the development of the productive forces and the socialization of labor is being usurped by the contemporary capitalist state in the interest of the monopolies.

The monopoly bourgeoisie has become a useless growth on the social organism, one unneeded in production. The industries are run by hired managers, engineers, and technicians. The monopolists lead a parasitical life and with their menials consume a substantial portion of the national income created by the toil of proletarians and peasants.

Fear of revolution, the successes of the Socialist countries, and the pressure of the working-class movement compel the bourgeoisie to make partial concessions with respect to wages, labor conditions, and social security. But more often than not mounting prices and inflation reduce these concessions to nought. Wages lag behind the daily material and cultural requirements of the worker and his family which grow as society develops.

Even the relatively high standard of living in the small group of capitalistically developed countries rests upon the poverty of the Asian, African, and Latin-American peoples, upon non-equivalent exchange, discrimination against female labor, brutal oppression of Negroes and immigrant workers, and also upon the intensified exploitation of the working people in those countries.

The bourgeois myth of "full employment" has proved to be sheer mockery, for the working class is suffering continuously from mass unemployment and insecurity. In spite of some successes in the economic struggle, the condition of the working class in the capitalist world is, on the whole, deteriorating.

The development of capitalism has dissipated the

legend of the stability of small peasant farming once and for all. The monopolies have seized dominant positions in agriculture as well. Millions of farmers and peasants are being driven off the land, and their farms are being brought under the hammer. Small farms survive at the price of appalling hardships, excessive labor, and the peasants' underconsumption. The peasantry is groaning under the burden of mounting taxes and debts. Agrarian crises are bringing even greater ruin to the countryside. Unspeakable want and poverty fall to the lot of the peasantry in the colonial and dependent countries; it suffers the dual oppression of the landlords, and the monopoly bourgeoisie.

The monopolies are also ruining small urban proprietors. Handicrafts are going under. Small-scale industrial and commercial enterprises are fully dependent upon the monopolies.

Life has fully confirmed the Marxist thesis of increasing proletarization in capitalist society. The expropriated masses have no other prospect of acquiring property than the revolutionary establishment of the social ownership of the means of production, that is, making them the property of the whole people.

The uneven development of capitalism alters the balance of forces between countries and makes the contradictions between them more acute. The economic and with it the political and military center of imperialism has shifted from Europe to the United States. United States monopoly capital, gorged on war profits and the arms race, has seized the main sources of raw materials, the markets and the spheres of investment, has built up a covert colonial empire and become the biggest international exploiter. Taking cover behind spurious professions of freedom and democracy, United States imperialism is in effect performing the function of world gendarme, supporting reactionary dictatorial regimes and decayed monarchies, opposing democratic, revolutionary changes, and launching aggressions against peoples fighting for independence.

The United States monopoly bourgeoisie is the mainstay of international reaction. It has assumed the role of "savior" of capitalism. The United States financial tycoons are engineering a "holy alliance" of imperialists and founding aggressive military blocs. American troops and war bases are stationed at the most important points of the capitalist world.

But the facts reveal the utter incongruity of the United States imperialist claims to world domination. Imperialism has proved incapable of stemming the Socialist and national-liberation revolutions. The hopes which American imperialism pinned on its atomic-weapons monopoly fell through. The United States monopolies have not been able to retain their share in the economy of the capitalist world, although they are still its chief economic, financial, and military force. The United States, the strongest capitalist power, is past its zenith and has entered the stage of decline. Imperialist countries such as Great Britain, France, Germany, and Japan have also lost their former power.

The basic contradiction of the contemporary world, that between socialism and imperialism, does not eliminate the deep contradictions rending the capitalist world. The aggressive military blocs founded under the aegis of the United States of America are time and again faced with crises. The international state-monopoly organizations springing up under the motto of "integration," of mitigation of the market problem, are in reality new forms of the redivision of the world capitalist market and are becoming seats of acute strain and conflict.

The contradictions between the principal imperialist powers are growing deeper. The economic rehabilitation of the imperialist countries defeated in the Second World War leads to the revival of the old and the emergence of new knots of imperialist rivalry and conflict. The Anglo-American, Franco-American, Franco-German, American-German, Anglo-German, Japanese-American, and other contradictions will inevitably arise and grow in the imperialist camp.

The American monopolies and their British and French allies are openly assisting the resurgence of West German imperialism which is cynically advocating aggressive aims of revenge and preparing a war against the Socialist countries and other European states. A dangerous center of aggression, imperiling the peace and security of all peoples, is being revived in the heart of

Europe. In the Far East the American monopolies are reviving Japanese militarism, another dangerous hotbed of war threatening the countries of Asia and, above all, the Socialist countries.

The interests of the small group of imperialist powers are incompatible with the interests of the other countries, the interests of all peoples. Deep-rooted antagonism divides the imperialist countries from the countries that have won national independence and those that are fighting for liberation.

Contemporary capitalism is inimical to the vital interests and progressive aspirations of all mankind. Capitalism with its exploitation of man by man, with its chauvinist and racist ideology, with its moral degradation, its rampage of profiteering, corruption, and crime is defiling society, the family, and man.

The bourgeois system came into being with the alluring slogans of liberty, equality, fraternity. But the bourgeoisie made use of these slogans merely to elbow out the feudal gentry and to assume power. Instead of equality a new gaping abyss of social and economic inequality appeared. Not fraternity but ferocious class struggle reigns in bourgeois society.

Monopoly capital is revealing its reactionary, antidemocratic substance more and more strikingly. It does not tolerate even the former bourgeois-democratic freedoms, although it proclaims them for its demagogic ends. In the current stage of historical development it is getting harder for the bourgeoisie to propagate, as heretofore, slogans of equality and liberty. The upswing of the international labor movement restricts the maneuvers of finance capital. Finance capital can no longer squash revolutionary sentiments and cope with the inexorably growing anti-imperialist movement by means of the old slogans and by bribing the labor bureaucracy.

Having taken full possession of the principal material values, monopoly capital refuses to share political power with anyone. It has established a dictatorship, the dictatorship of the minority over the majority, the dictatorship of the capitalist monopolies over society.

The ideologists of imperialism hide the dictatorship of monopoly capital behind specious slogans of freedom and democracy. They declare the imperialist powers to be countries of the "free world" and represent the ruling bourgeois circles as opponents of all dictatorship. In reality, however, freedom in the imperialist world signifies nothing but freedom to exploit the working class, the working people, not only at home, but in all the other countries that fall under the iron heel of the monopolies.

The bourgeoisie gives extensive publicity to the allegedly democratic nature of its election laws, singing special praise to its multi-party system and the possibility of nominating many candidates. In reality, however, the monopolists deprive the masses of the opportunity to express their will and elect genuine champions of their interests. Being in control of such potent means as capital, the press, radio, cinema, television, and also of their henchmen in the trade unions and other mass organizations, they mislead the masses, imposing their own candidates upon the electorate. The different bourgeois parties are usually no more than different factions of the ruling bourgeoisie.

The dictatorship of the bourgeoisie also grossly violates the will of the electorate. Whenever the bourgeoisie sees that the working people are likely to use their constitutional rights to elect a considerable number of the champions of their interests to the legislative organs, it brazenly alters the election system and arbitrarily limits the number of working people's representatives in Parliament.

The financial oligarchy resorts to the establishment of Fascist regimes, banking on the army, police, and gendarmerie as a last refuge from the people's wrath, when the masses try to make use even of their democratic rights, albeit curtailed, to uphold their interests and end the all-pervading power of the monopolies. Although the vicious German and Italian fascism has crashed, Fascist regimes still survive in some countries and fascism is being revived in new forms in others.

Thus, the world imperialist system is rent by deep-rooted and acute contradictions. The antagonism of labor and capital, the contradictions between the people and the monopolies, growing militarism, the breakup of the colonial system, contradictions between the imperialist countries, conflicts and contradictions between the young national states and the old colonial powers, and —most important of all—the rapid growth of world socialism, are sapping and destroying imperialism, leading to its weakening and collapse.

Not even nuclear weapons can protect the monopoly bourgeoisie from the unalterable course of historical development. Mankind has learned the true face of capitalism. Hundreds of millions of people see that capitalism is a system of economic chaos and periodical crises, chronic unemployment, mass poverty and indiscriminate waste of productive forces, a system constantly fraught with the danger of war. Mankind does not want to, and will not, tolerate the historically outdated capitalist system.

v. The International Revolutionary Movement of the Working Class

The international revolutionary movement of the working class has achieved epoch-making victories. Its chief gain is the world Socialist system. The example of victorious socialism has a revolutionizing effect on the minds of the working people of the capitalist world; it inspires them to fight against imperialism and greatly facilitates their struggle.

Social forces that are to ensure the victory of socialism are taking shape, multiplying and becoming steeled in the womb of capitalist society. A new contingent of the world proletariat—the young working-class movement of the newly free dependent and colonial countries of Asia, Africa, and Latin America—has entered the world arena. Marxist-Leninist parties have arisen and grown. They are becoming a universally recognized national force enjoying ever greater prestige and followed by large sections of the working people.

The international revolutionary movement has accumulated vast experience in the struggle against imperialism and its placement in the ranks of the working class. It has become more mature ideologically and possesses great organized might and a militantly dynamic spirit. The trade union movement, which unites vast masses of working people, is playing an increasing role.

The capitalist countries are continuously shaken by class battles. Militant actions of the working class in defense of its economic and political interests are growing in number. The working class and all working people have frequently imperiled the class rule of the bourgeoisie. In an effort to maintain its power, the finance oligarchy, in addition to methods of suppression, uses diverse ways of deceiving and corrupting the working class and its organizations, and of splitting the trade union movement on a national and international scale.

It bribes the top stratum of trade unions, co-operative, and other organizations and swells the labor bureaucracy, to which it allots lucrative positions in industry, the municipal bodies, and the government apparatus. Anti-Communist and anti-labor legislation, the banning of Communist Parties, wholesale dismissal of Communists and other progressive workers, blacklisting in industry, government employee loyalty screening, police reprisals against the democratic press, and the suppression of strikes by military force have all become routine methods of action for the governments of the imperialist bourgeoisie in its efforts to preserve its dictatorship.

The reactionary forces in individual capitalist countries can no longer cope with the growing forces of democracy and socialism. Struggle and competition between the capitalist states do not preclude, however, a certain unity among them in the face of the increasing strength of socialism and the working-class movement. The imperialists form reactionary alliances; they enter into mutual agreements and set up military blocs and bases spearheaded not only against the Socialist countries, but also against the revolutionary working-class and national-liberation movement. The reactionary bourgeoisie in a number of European states have in peacetime opened the doors of their countries to foreign troops.

The bourgeoisie seeks to draw definite lessons from the October Revolution and the victories of socialism. It is using new methods to cover up the ulcers and vices of the capitalist system. Although all these methods render the activities of the revolutionary forces in the capitalist countries more difficult, they cannot reduce the contradictions between labor and capital.

The world situation today is more favorable to the working-class movement. The achievements of the U.S.S.R. and the world Socialist system as a whole, the deepening crisis of world capitalism, the growing influence of the Communist Parties among the masses, and the ideological breakdown of reformism have brought about a substantial change in the conditions of class struggle that is to the advantage of the working people. Even in those countries where reformism still holds strong positions, appreciable shifts to the Left are taking place in the working-class movement.

In the new historical situation, the working class of many countries can, even before capitalism is overthrown, compel the bourgeoisie to carry out measures that transcend ordinary reforms and are of vital importance to the working class and the progress of its struggle for socialism, as well as to the majority of the nation. By uniting large sections of the working people, the working class can make ruling circles cease preparations for a new world war, renounce the idea of starting local wars, and use the economy for peaceful purposes; it can beat back the offensive of Fascist reaction and bring about the implementation of a national program for peace, national independence, democratic rights, and a certain improvement of the living standard of the people.

The capitalist monopolies are the chief enemy of the working class. They are also the chief enemy of the peasants, handicraftsmen, and other small urban proprietors, of most office workers, intellectuals, and small capitalists, and even of a section of the middle capitalists.

The working class directs its main blow against the capitalist monopolies. All the main sections of a nation have a vital interest in abolishing the unlimited power of the monopolies. This makes it possible to unite all the democratic movements opposing the oppression of the finance oligarchy in a mighty anti-monopoly torrent.

The proletariat advances a program for combating the power of the monopolies with due regard to the present as well as the future interests of its allies. It advocates broad nationalization on terms most favorable to the people, control by parliament, the trade unions, and other democratic representative bodies over the nationalized industries and over the entire economic activity of the state. It backs the peasants' demands for radical land reforms and works for the realization of the slogan: "The land to those who till it."

The proletariat, together with other sections of the people, wages a resolute struggle for broad democracy. It mobilizes the masses for effective action against the policy of the finance oligarchy, which strives to abolish democratic freedoms, restrict the power of parliament, revise the constitution with the aim of establishing the personal power of monopoly puppets, and to go over from the parliamentary system to some variety of fascism.

It is in this struggle that the alliance of the working class and all working people is shaped. The working class unites the peasantry, its chief ally, to combat the survivals of feudalism and monopoly domination. Large sections of the office workers and a considerable section of the intelligentsia, whom capitalism reduces to the status of proletarians and who realize the need of changes in the social sphere, become allies of the working class.

General democratic struggles against the monopolies do not delay the Socialist revolution but bring it nearer. The struggle for democracy is a component of the struggle for socialism. The more profound the democratic movement, the higher becomes the level of the political consciousness of the masses and the more clearly they see that only socialism clears for them the way to genuine freedom and well-being. In the course of this struggle, Right-Socialist, reformist illusions are dispelled and a political army of the Socialist revolution is brought into being.

Socialist revolutions, anti-imperialist national-liberation revolutions, people's democratic revolutions, broad peasant movements, popular struggles to overthrow Fascist and other despotic regimes, and general democratic movements against national oppression—all these merge in a single world-wide revolutionary process undermining and destroying capitalism.

The proletarian revolution in any country, being part of the world Socialist revolution, is accomplished by the working class of that country and the masses of its people. The revolution is not made to order. It cannot be imposed on the people from without. It results from the profound internal and international contradictions of capitalism. The victorious proletariat cannot impose any "felicity" on another people without thereby undermining its own victory.

Together with the other Marxist-Leninist parties, the Communist Party of the Soviet Union regards it as its internationalist duty to call on the peoples of all countries to rally, muster all their internal forces, take vigorous action, and drawing on the might of the world Socialist system, forestall or firmly repel imperialist interference in the affairs of the people of any country risen in revolt and thereby prevent imperialist export of counterrevolution.

It will be easier to prevent export of counterrevolution if the working people, defending the national sovereignty of their country, work to bring about the abolition of foreign military bases on their territory and to make their country dissociate itself from aggressive military blocs.

Communists have never held that the road to revolution lies necessarily through wars between countries. Socialist revolution is not necessarily connected with war. Although both world wars, which were started by the imperialists, culminated in Socialist revolutions, revolutions are quite feasible without war. The great objectives of the working class can be realized without world war. Today the conditions for this are more favorable than ever.

The working class and its vanguard—the Marxist-Leninist parties—prefer to achieve the transfer of power from the bourgeoisie to the proletariat by peaceful means, without civil war. Realization of this possibility would meet the interests of the working class and the people as a whole; it would accord with the national interests of the country.

The working class, supported by the majority of the people and firmly repelling opportunist elements incapable of renouncing the policy of compromise with the capitalists and landlords, can defeat the reactionary, anti-popular forces, win a solid majority in parliament, transform it from a tool serving the class interests of the bourgeoisie into an instrument serving the working people, launch a broad mass struggle outside parliament, smash the resistance of the reactionary forces, and provide the necessary conditions for a peaceful Socialist revolution. This can be done only by extending and continuously developing the class struggle of the workers and peasants and the middle strata of the urban population against big monopoly capital and reaction, for far-reaching social reforms, for peace and socialism.

Where the exploiting classes resort to violence against the people, the possibility of a non-peaceful transition to socialism should be borne in mind. Leninism maintains, and historical experience confirms, that the ruling classes do not yield power of their own free will. Hence, the degree of bitterness of the class struggle and the forms it takes will depend not so much on the proletariat as on the strength of the reactionary groups' resistance to the will of the overwhelming majority of the people, and on the use of force by these groups at a particular stage of the struggle for socialism. In each particular country the actual applicability of one method of transition to socialism or the other depends on concrete historical conditions.

It may well be that as the forces of socialism grow, the working-class movement gains strength, and the positions of capitalism are weakened, there will arise in certain countries a situation in which it will be preferable for the bourgeoisie, as Marx and Lenin foresaw it, to agree to the means of production being purchased from it and for the proletariat to "pay off" the bourgeoisie.

The success of the struggle which the working class wages for the victory of the revolution will depend on how well the working class and its party master the use of all forms of struggle—peaceful and non-peaceful, parliamentary and extra-parliamentary—and how well they are prepared to replace one form of struggle by another as quickly and unexpectedly as possible.

While the principal law-governed processes of the Socialist revolution are common to all countries, the diversity of the national peculiarities and traditions that have arisen in the course of history creates specific conditions for the revolutionary process and for the variety of forms and rates of the proletariat's advent to power. This predetermines the possibility and necessity, in a number of countries, of transition stages in the struggle for the dictatorship of the proletariat, and a variety of forms of political organization of the society building socialism. But whatever the form in which the transition from capitalism to socialism is effected, that transition can come about only through revolution. However varied the forms of a new, people's state power, in the period of Socialist construction, their essence will be the same—dictatorship of the proletariat, which represents genuine democracy, democracy for the working people.

A bourgeois republic, however democratic, however hallowed by slogans purporting to express the will of the people or nation as a whole, or an extra-class will, inevitably remains in practice—owing to the existence of private capitalist ownership of the means of production—a dictatorship of the bourgeoisie, a machine for the exploitation and suppression of the vast majority of the working people by a handful of capitalists. In contrast to the bourgeoisie, which conceals the class character of the state, the working class does not deny the class character of the state.

The dictatorship of the proletariat is a dictatorship of the overwhelming majority over the minority; it is directed against the exploiters, against the oppression of peoples and nations, and is aimed at abolishing all exploitation of man by man. The dictatorship of the proletariat expresses not only the interests of the working class, but also those of all working people; its chief content is not violence but creation, the building of a new, classless society, and the defense of its gains against the enemies of socialism.

Overcoming the split in its ranks is an important condition for the working class to fulfill its historic mission. No bastion of imperialism can withstand a closely knit working class that exercises unity of action. The Communist Parties favor co-operation with the Social-Democratic parties not only in the struggle for peace, for better living conditions for the working people, and for the preservation and extension of their democratic rights and freedoms, but also in the struggle to win power and build a Socialist society.

At the same time Communists criticize the ideological positions and Right-opportunist practice of social-democracy and expose the Right Social-Democratic leaders, who have sided openly with the bourgeoisie and renounced the traditional Socialist demands of the working class.

The Communist Parties are the vanguard of the world revolutionary movement. They have demonstrated the vitality of Marxism-Leninism and their ability not only to propagate the great ideals of scientific communism, but also to put them into practice. Today the international Communist movement is so powerful that the combined forces of reaction cannot crush it.

The Communist movement grows and becomes steeled as it fights against various opportunist trends. Revisionism, Right opportunism, which is a reflection of bourgeois influence, is the chief danger within the Communist movement today. The revisionists, who mask their renunciation of Marxism with talk about the necessity of taking account of the latest developments in society and the class struggle, in effect play the role of peddlers of bourgeois-reformist ideology within the Communist movement. They seek to rob Marxism-Leninism of its revolutionary spirit, to undermine the faith which the working class and all working people have in the Socialist cause, to disarm and disorganize them in their struggle against imperialism. The revisionists deny the historical necessity of the Socialist revolution and of the dictatorship of the proletariat, deny the leading role of the Marxist-Leninist party, undermine the foundations of proletarian internationalism, and drift to nationalism. The ideology of revisionism is most fully embodied in the program of the League of Communists of Yugoslavia.

Another danger is dogmatism and sectarianism, which cannot be reconciled with a creative development of revolutionary theory, and which lead to the dissociation and isolation of Communists from the masses of the working people, doom them to passive expectation or incite them to Leftist adventurist actions in the revo lutionary struggle, and hinder a correct appraisal of the changing situation and the use of new opportunities for the benefit of the working class and all democratic forces. Dogmatism and sectarianism, unless steadfastly combated, can also become the chief danger at a particular stage in the development of individual parties.

The Communist Party of the Soviet Union holds that an uncompromising struggle against revisionism, dogmatism, and sectarianism, against all departures from Leninism, is a necessary condition for the further strengthening of the unity of the world Communist movement and for the consolidation of the Socialist camp.

The Communist Parties are independent and they shape their policies with due regard to the specific conditions prevailing in their own countries. They base relations between themselves on equality and the principles of proletarian internationalism. They co-ordinate their actions, consciously and of their own free will, as components of a single international army of labor. The Communist Party of the Soviet Union, like the other Communist Parties, regards it as its internationalist duty to abide by the appraisals and conclusions which the fraternal parties have reached jointly concerning their common tasks in the struggle against imperialism, for peace, democracy, and socialism, and by the declarations and the statements adopted by the Communist Parties at their international meetings.

Vigorous defense of the unity of the world Communist movement in line with the principles of Marxism-Leninism and proletarian internationalism, and the prevention of any action likely to disrupt that unity are an essential condition for victory in the struggle for national independence, democracy, and peace, for the successful accomplishment of the tasks of the Socialist revolution, for the construction of socialism and communism.

The C.P.S.U. will continue to strengthen the unity and cohesion of the ranks of the great army of Communists of all countries.

VI. THE NATIONAL-LIBERATION MOVEMENT

The world is experiencing a period of stormy national-liberation revolutions. Imperialism suppressed the national independence and freedom of the majority of the peoples and put the fetters of brutal slavery on them, but the rise of socialism marks the advent of the era of emancipation of the oppressed peoples. A powerful wave of national-liberation revolutions is sweeping away the colonial system and undermining the foundations of imperialism. Young sovereign states have arisen, or are arising, in one-time colonies or semi-colonies. Their peoples have entered a new period of development. They have emerged as makers of a new life and as active participants in world politics, as a revolutionary force destroying imperialism.

But the struggle is not yet over. The peoples who are throwing off the shackles of colonialism have attained different degrees of freedom. Many of them, having established national states, are striving for economic sovereignty and durable political independence. The peoples of those formally independent countries that in reality depend on foreign monopolies politically and economically are rising to fight against imperialism and reactionary pro-imperialist regimes. The peoples who have not yet cast off the chains of colonial slavery are conducting a heroic struggle against their foreign enslavers.

The young sovereign states do not belong either to the system of imperialist states or to the system of Socialist states. But the overwhelming majority of them have not yet broken free from the world capitalist economy even though they occupy a special place in it. They constitute that part of the world which is still being exploited by the capitalist monopolies. As long as they have not put an end to their economic dependence on imperialism, they will be playing the role of a "world countryside," and will remain objects of semi-colonial exploitation.

The existence of the world Socialist system and the weakening of imperialism offer the peoples of the newly free countries the prospect of a national renascence, of ending age-long backwardness and poverty, and achieving economic independence.

The interests of a nation call for the elimination of the remnants of colonialism, the eradication of imperialist rule, the ousting of foreign monopolies, the founding of a national industry, the abolition of the feudal system and its survivals, the implementation of radical land reforms with the participation of the entire peasantry and in its interests, the pursuit of an independent foreign policy of peace, the democratization of the life of society, and the strengthening of political independence. All patriotic and progressive forces of the nation are interested in the solution of national problems. That is the basis on which the latter can be unified.

Foreign capital will retreat only before a broad union of patriotic democratic forces pursuing an anti-imperialist policy. The pillars of feudalism will crumble only under the impact of a general democratic movement. None but far-reaching agrarian reforms and a broad peasant movement can sweep away those remnants of medievalism that fetter the development of the productive forces, and solve the food problem that stares the peoples of Asia, Africa, and Latin America so starkly in the face. Political independence can be made secure only by a nation that has won democratic rights and freedoms and is taking an active part in governing the state.

A consistent struggle against imperialism is a paramount condition for the solution of national tasks. Imperialism seeks to retain one-time colonies and semicolonies within the system of capitalist economy and perpetuate their underprivileged position in it. United States imperialism is the chief bulwark of modern colonialism.

The imperialists are using new methods and new forms to maintain colonial exploitation of the people. They have recourse to whatever means they can (colonial wars, military blocs, conspiracies, terrorism, subversion, economic pressure, bribery) to control the newly free countries and to reduce the independence they have won to mere form or to deprive them of that independence. Under the guise of "aid," they are trying to retain their old positions in those countries and capture new ones, to extend their social basis, lure the national bourgeoisie to their side, implant military despotic regimes, and put obedient puppets in power. Using the poisoned weapon of national and tribal strife, the imperialists seek to split the ranks of the national-liberation movement; reactionary groups of the local exploiting classes play the role of allies of imperialism.

Imperialism thus remains the chief enemy, and the chief obstacle to the solution of the national problems facing the young sovereign states and all dependent countries.

A national-liberation revolution does not end with the winning of political independence. Independence will be unstable and will become fictitious unless the revolution brings about radical changes in the social and economic spheres and solves the pressing problems of national rebirth.

The working class is the most consistent fighter for the consummation of the revolution, for national interests and social progress. As industry develops, its ranks will swell and its role on the socio-political scene will increase. The alliance of the working class and the peasantry is the fundamental condition for the success of the struggle to carry out far-reaching democratic changes and achieve economic and social progress. This alliance must form the core of a broad national front.

The extent to which the national bourgeoisie will take part in the anti-imperialist and anti-feudal struggle will depend in considerable measure on the solidity of the alliance of the working class and the peasantry. The national front also embraces the urban petty bourgeoisie and the democratic intelligentsia.

In many countries, the liberation movement of the peoples that have awakened proceeds under the flag of nationalism. Marxists-Leninists draw a distinction between the nationalism of the oppressed nations and that of the oppressor nations. The nationalism of an oppressed nation contains a general democratic element directed against oppression, and Communists support it because they consider it historically justified at a given stage. That element finds expression in the striving of the oppressed peoples to free themselves from imperialist oppression, to gain national independence and bring about a national renascence. But the nationalism of an oppressed nation has yet another aspect, one expressing the ideology and interests of the reactionary exploiting top stratum.

The national bourgeoisie is dual in character. In modern conditions the national bourgeoisie in those colonial, one-time colonial, and dependent countries where it is not connected with the imperialist circles is objectively interested in accomplishing the basic tasks of an anti-imperialist and anti-feudal revolution. Its progressive role and its ability to participate in the solution of pressing national problems are, therefore, not yet spent.

But as the contradictions between the working people and the propertied classes grow and the class struggle inside the country becomes more aggravated, the national bourgeoisie shows an increasing inclination to compromise with imperialism and domestic reaction.

The development of the countries which have won their freedom may be a complex multi-stage process. By virtue of varying historical and socio-economic conditions in the newly free countries, the revolutionary effort of the masses will impart distinctive features to the forms and rates of their social progress.

One of the basic issues confronting these peoples is, which road of development the countries that have freed themselves from colonial tyranny are to take, whether the capitalist road or the noncapitalist.

What can capitalism bring them?

Capitalism is the road of suffering for the people.

It will not insure rapid economic progress nor eliminate poverty; social inequality will increase. The capitalist development of the countryside will ruin the peasantry still more. The workers will be fated either to engage in back-breaking labor to enrich the capitalists, or to swell the ranks of the disinherited army of the unemployed. The petty bourgeoisie will be crushed in competition with big capital. The benefits of culture and education will remain out of reach of the people. The intelligentsia will be compelled to trade its talent.

What can socialism bring the peoples?

Socialism is the road to freedom and happiness for the peoples. It insures rapid economic and cultural progress. It transforms a backward country into an industrial country within the lifetime of one generation and not in the course of centuries. Planned Socialist economy is an economy of progress and prosperity by its very nature. Abolition of the exploitation of man by man does away with social inequality. Unemployment disappears completely. Socialism provides all peasants with land, helps them to develop farming, combines their labor efforts in voluntary co-operatives, and puts modern agricultural machinery and agronomy at their disposal. Peasant labor becomes more productive and the land is made more fertile. Socialism provides a high material and cultural standard of living for the working class and all working people. Socialism lifts the people out of darkness and ignorance and gives them access to modern culture. The intelligentsia is offered ample opportunities for creative effort for the benefit of the people.

It is for the peoples themselves to decide which road they are to choose. In view of the present balance of the world forces and the actual feasibility of powerful support on the part of the world Socialist system, the peoples of the former colonies can decide this question in their own interest. Their choice will depend on the balance of the class forces. The noncapitalist road of development is insured by the struggle of the working class and the masses of the people, by the general democratic movement, and meets the interests of the absolute majority of the nation. This road will require concessions from the bourgeoisie, but those will be concessions on behalf of the nation. All sections of the population can find application for their energies, if they follow the noncapitalist road of development.

Establishing and developing national democracies opens vast prospects for the peoples of the underdeveloped countries. The political basis of a national democracy is a bloc of all the progressive, patriotic forces fighting to win complete national independence and broad democracy, and to consummate the anti-imperialist, anti-feudal, democratic revolution.

A steady growth of the class and national consciousness of the masses is a characteristic of the present stage of social development. The imperialists persist in distorting the idea of national sovereignty, trying to rob it of its main content and to use it as a means of fomenting national egoism, implanting a spirit of national exclusiveness and increasing national antagonisms.

The democratic forces establish the idea of national sovereignty in the name of equality for the peoples, of their mutual trust, friendship, and assistance, and of closer relations between them, in the name of social progress. The idea of national sovereignty in its democratic sense becomes more and more firmly established; it acquires increasing significance and becomes an important factor in the progressive development of society.

The Communist Parties are steadfastly carrying on an active struggle to consummate the anti-imperialist, antifeudal, democratic revolution, to establish a state of national democracy and achieve social progress. The Communists' aims are in keeping with the supreme interests of the nation. The attempts of reactionary circles to disrupt the national front under the guise of anti-communism, and their persecution of Communists lead to the weakening of the national liberation movement and run counter to the national interests of the peoples; they threaten the loss of the gains achieved.

The national states become ever more active as an independent force on the world scene; objectively, this force is in the main a progressive, revolutionary, and anti-imperialist force. The countries and peoples that are now free from colonial oppression are to play a prominent part in the prevention of a new world war—the focal problem of today. The time is past when imperialism could freely use the manpower and material resources of those countries in its predatory wars. The time has come when the peoples of those countries, breaking the resistance of the reactionary circles and those connected with the colonialists and overcoming the vacillation of the national bourgeoisie, can put their resources at the service of universal security and become a new bulwark of peace. This is what their own fundamental interests and the interests of all peoples demand.

The joining of the efforts of the newly free peoples and of the peoples of the Socialist countries in the struggle against the war danger is a major factor for world peace.

This mighty front, which expresses the will and strength of two-thirds of mankind, can force the imperialist aggressors into retreat.

The Socialist countries are sincere and true friends of peoples fighting for their liberation and of those that have freed themselves from imperialist tyranny and render them all-around support. They stand for the abolition of all forms of colonial oppression and vigorously promote the strengthening of the sovereignty of the states rising on the ruins of colonial empires.

The C.P.S.U. considers fraternal alliance with the peoples who have thrown off colonial or semi-colonial tyranny to be a cornerstone of its international policy. This alliance is based on the common vital interests of world socialism and the world national-liberation movement. The C.P.S.U. regards it as its internationalist duty to assist the peoples who have set out to win and strengthen their national independence, all peoples who are fighting for the complete abolition of the colonial system.

VII. The Struggle Against Bourgeois and Reformist Ideology

A grim struggle is going on between two ideologies—Communist and bourgeois—in the world today. This struggle is a reflection, in the spiritual life of mankind, of the historic process of transition from capitalism to socialism.

The new historic epoch has brought the revolutionary world outlook of the proletariat a genuine triumph. Marxism-Leninism has gripped the minds of progressive mankind.

Bourgeois doctrines and schools have failed in the test of history. They have been and still are unable to furnish scientific answers to the questions posed by life. The bourgeoisie is no longer in a position to put forward ideas that will induce the masses to follow it. Bourgeois ideology is experiencing a grave crisis.

A revolutionary change in the minds of vast human masses is a long and complex process. The more victories the world Socialist system achieves, the deeper the crisis of world capitalism, and the sharper the class struggle, the more important becomes the role of the Marxist-Leninist ideas in unifying and mobilizing the masses to fight for communism. The ideological struggle is a most important element of the class struggle of the proletariat.

Imperialist reaction mobilizes every possible means to exert ideological influence on the masses as it attempts to denigrate communism and its noble ideas and to defend capitalism. The chief ideological and political weapon of imperialism is anti-communism, which consists mainly in slandering the Socialist system and distorting the policy and objectives of the Communist Parties and Marxist-Leninist theory.

Under cover of anti-communism, imperialist reaction persecutes and hounds all that is progressive and revolutionary; it seeks to split the ranks of the working people and to paralyze the proletarians' will to fight. Rallied to this black banner today are all the enemies of social progress: the finance oligarchy and the military, the Fascists and reactionary clericals, the colonialists and landlords, and all the ideological and political vehicles of imperialist reaction. Anti-communism is a reflection of the extreme decadence of bourgeois ideology.

The defenders of the bourgeois system, seeking to keep the masses in spiritual bondage, invent new "theories" designed to mask the exploiting character of the bourgeois system and to embellish capitalism. They assert that modern capitalism has changed its nature, and that it has become "people's capitalism" in which property is "diffused" and capital becomes "democratic," that classes and class contradictions are disappearing, that "incomes are being equalized" and economic crises are being eliminated.

In reality, however, the development of modern capitalism confirms the accuracy of the Marxist-Leninist theory of the growing contradictions and antagonisms in capitalist society and of the aggravation of the class struggle within it.

The advocates of the bourgeois state call it a "welfare state." They propagate the illusion that the capitalist state opposes monopolies and can achieve social harmony and universal well-being. But the masses see from their own experience that the bourgeois state is an obedient tool of the monopolies and that the vaunted "welfare" is welfare for the magnates of finance capital, but suffering and torture for hundreds of millions of working men.

The "theoreticians" of anti-communism describe modern imperialism as the "free world." In reality the "free world" is a world of exploitation and lack of rights, a world where human dignity and national honor are trampled underfoot, a world of obscurantism and political reaction, of rabid militarism and bloody reprisals against the working people.

Monopoly capital is reviving Fascist ideology—the ideology of extreme chauvinism and racism. Fascism in power is an open terroristic dictatorship of the most reactionary, most chauvinistic, and most imperialistic elements of finance capital. Fascism begins everywhere and always with vicious anti-communism to isolate and rout the parties of the working class, to split the forces of the proletariat and defeat them piecemeal, and then to do away with all the other democratic parties and organizations and turn the people into the blind tool of the policy of the capitalist monopolies.

Fascism strikes first of all at the Communist Parties since they are the most consistent, stanch, and incorruptible defenders of the interests of the working class and all working people.

Imperialist reaction makes extensive use of chauvinism to incite nationalist conflicts, persecute entire nationalities and national groups (anti-Semitism, racial discrimination against Negroes and the peoples of the underdeveloped countries), blunt the class consciousness of the working people, and divert the proletariat and its allies from the class struggle.

Clericalism is acquiring ever greater importance in the political and ideological arsenal of imperialism. The clericals do not confine themselves to using the Church and its ramified machinery. They now have their own big political parties which in many capitalist countries are in power. They set up their own trade-union, youth, women's, and other organizations and split the ranks of the working class and all working people. The monopolies lavishly subsidize clerical parties and organizations, which exploit the religious sentiments of the working people and their superstitions and prejudices.

Bourgeois ideology assumes a variety of forms and uses the most diverse methods and means of deceiving the working people. But they all amount to the same—defense of the declining capitalist system. The ideas running through the political and economic theories of the modern bourgeoisie, through its philosophy and sociology, through its ethics and aesthetics, substantiate monopoly domination, justify exploitation, defame social property and collectivism, glorify militarism and war, whitewash colonialism and racism, and foment enmity and hatred among the peoples.

Anti-communism is becoming the main instrument of reaction in its struggle against the democratic forces of Asia, Africa, and Latin America. It is the meeting ground of imperialist ideology and the ideology of the feudal, pro-imperialist elements and the reactionary groups of the bourgeoisie of the countries which have gained their freedom from colonial tyranny.

The anti-popular circles of those countries seek to tone down the general democratic content of nationalism, to play up its reactionary aspect, to push aside the democratic forces of the nation, to prevent social progress, and to hinder the spread of scientific socialism.

At the same time they advance theories of "socialism of the national type," propagate socio-philosophical doctrines that are, as a rule, so many variations of the petty-bourgeois illusion of socialism, an illusion which rules out the class struggle. These theories mislead the people, hamper the development of the national-liberation movement, and imperil its gains.

National-democratic, anti-imperialist ideas are becoming widespread in the countries which have liberated themselves from colonial oppression. The Communists and other proponents of these ideas patiently explain to the masses the untenability of the illusion that it is possible to insure national independence and social progress without an active struggle against imperialism and internal reaction. They come out actively against chauvinism and other manifestations of reactionary ideology, which justify despotic regimes and the suppression of democracy. At the same time the Communists act as exponents of the Socialist ideology, rallying the masses under the banner of scientific socialism.

The ideological struggle of the imperialist bourgeoisie is spearheaded primarily against the working class and its Marxist-Leninist parties. Social-democratism in the working-class movement and revisionism in the Communist movement reflect the bourgeois influence on the working class.

The contemporary Right-wing Social-Democrats are the most important ideological and political prop of the bourgeoisie within the working-class movement. They eclectically combine old opportunist ideas with the "latest" bourgeois theories. The Right wing of Social-Democracy has completely broken with Marxism and contraposed so-called democratic socialism to scientific socialism. Its adherents deny the existence of antagonistic classes and the class struggle in bourgeois society; they forcefully deny the necessity of the proletarian revolution and oppose the abolition of the private ownership of the means of production. They assert that capitalism is being "transformed" into socialism.

The Right-wing Socialists began by advocating social reforms in place of the Socialist revolution and went as far as to defend state-monopoly capitalism. In the past they impressed on the minds of the proletariat that their differences with revolutionary Marxism bore not so much on the ultimate goal of the working-class movement as on the ways of achieving it.

Now they openly renounce socialism. Formerly the Right-wing Socialists refused to recognize the class struggle to the point of not recognizing the dictatorship of the proletariat. Today they deny, not only the existence of the class struggle in bourgeois society, but also the very existence of antagonistic classes.

Historical experience has shown the bankruptcy of both the ideology and the policy of Social-Democracy. Even when reformist parties come to power they limit themselves to partial reforms that do not affect the rule of the monopoly bourgeoisie. Anti-communism has brought social reformism to an ideological and political impasse. This is one of the main reasons for the crisis of Social-Democracy.

Marxism-Leninism is winning more and more victories. It is winning them because it expresses the vital interests of the working class, of the vast majority of mankind, which seeks peace, freedom, and progress, and because it expresses the ideology of the new society succeeding capitalism.

VIII. PEACEFUL COEXISTENCE AND THE STRUGGLE FOR WORLD PEACE

The C.P.S.U. considers that the chief aim of its foreign-policy activity is to provide peaceful conditions for the building of a Communist society in the U.S.S.R. and developing the world Socialist system and together with the other peace-loving peoples to deliver mankind from a world war of extermination.

The C.P.S.U. maintains that forces capable of preserving and promoting world peace have arisen and are growing in the world. Possibilities are arising to establish essentially new relations between states.

Imperialism knows no relations between states other than those of domination and subordination, of oppression of the weak by the strong. It bases international relations on diktat and intimidation, on violence and arbitrary rule. It regards wars of aggression as a natural means of settling international issues. For the imperialist countries, diplomacy has been, and remains, a tool for imposing their will upon other nations and preparing wars. At the time of the undivided rule of imperialism the issue of war and peace was settled by the finance and industrial oligarchy in the utmost secrecy from the peoples.

Socialism, in contrast to imperialism, advances a new type of international relations. The foreign policy of the Socialist countries, which is based on the principle of peace, the equality and self-determination of nations, and respect for the independence and sovereignty of all countries, as well as the fair, humane methods of Socialist diplomacy, are exerting a growing influence on the world situation. At a time when imperialism no longer plays a dominant role in international relations while the Socialist system is playing an increasing role, and when the influence of the countries that have won national independence and of the masses of the people in the capitalist countries has grown very considerably, it is becoming possible for the new principles advanced by socialism to gain the upper hand over the principles of aggressive imperialistic policy.

For the first time in history, a situation has arisen in which not only the big states, but also the small ones, the countries which have chosen independent development, and all the states which want peace, are in a position, irrespective of their strength, to pursue an independent foreign policy.

The issue of war and peace is the principal issue of today. Imperialism is the only source of the war danger. The imperialist camp is making preparations for the worst crime against mankind—a world thermonuclear war that can bring unprecedented destruction to entire countries and wipe out entire nations. The problem of war and peace has become a life-and-death problem for hundreds of millions of people.

The peoples must concentrate their efforts on curbing the imperialists in good time and preventing them from making use of lethal weapons. The main thing is to ward off a thermonuclear war, to prevent it from breaking out. This can be done by the present generation.

The consolidation of the Soviet state and the formation of the world Socialist system were historic steps toward the realization of mankind's age-old dream of banishing wars from the life of society. In the Socialist part of the world there are no classes or social groups interested in starting a war. Socialism, outstripping capitalism in a number of important branches of science and technology, has supplied the peace-loving peoples with powerful material means of curbing imperialist aggression.

Capitalism established its rule with fire and sword, but socialism does not require war to spread its ideals. Its weapon is its superiority over the old system in social organization, political system, economy, the improvement of the standard of living, and spiritual culture.

The Socialist system is a natural center of attraction for the peace-loving forces of the globe. The principles of its foreign policy are gaining ever greater international recognition and support. A vast peace zone has taken shape on earth. In addition to the Socialist countries, it includes a large group of non-Socialist countries that for various reasons are not interested in starting a war. The emergence of those countries in the arena of world politics has substantially altered the balance of forces in favor of peace.

There is a growing number of countries that adhere to a policy of neutrality and strive to safeguard themselves against the hazards of participation in military blocs.

In the new historical epoch the masses have a far greater opportunity of actively intervening in the settlement of international issues. The peoples are taking the solution of the problem of war and peace into their own hands more and more vigorously. The anti-war movement of the masses, which takes various forms, is a major factor in the struggle for peace. The international working class, the most uncompromising and most consistent fighter against imperialist war, is the great organizing force in this struggle of the people as a whole.

It is possible to avert a world war by the combined efforts of the mighty Socialist camp, the peace-loving non-Socialist countries, the international working class, and all the forces championing peace. The growing superiority of the Socialist forces over the forces of imperialism, of the forces of peace over those of war, will make it actually possible to banish world war from the life of society even before the complete victory of socialism on earth, with capitalism surviving in a part of the world. The victory of socialism throughout the world will do away completely with the social and national causes of all wars. To abolish war and establish everlasting peace on earth is a historical mission of communism.

General and complete disarmament under strict international control is a radical way of guaranteeing a durable peace. Imperialism has imposed an unprecedented burden of armaments on the people. Socialism sees its duty toward mankind in delivering it from this absurd waste of national wealth. The solution of this problem would have historical significance for mankind. By an active and determined effort the peoples can and must force the imperialists into disarmament.

Socialism has offered mankind the only reasonable principle of maintaining relations between states at a time when the world is divided into two systems—the principle of the peaceful coexistence of states with different social systems, put forward by Lenin.

Peaceful coexistence of the Socialist and capitalist

countries is an objective necessity for the development of human society. War cannot and must not serve as a means of settling international disputes. Peaceful coexistence or disastrous war—such is the alternative offered by history. Should the imperialist aggressors nevertheless venture to start a new world war, the peoples will no longer tolerate a system which drags them into devastating wars. They will sweep imperialism away and bury it.

Peaceful coexistence implies renunciation of war as a means of settling international disputes, and their solution by negotiation; equality, mutual understanding and trust between countries; consideration of mutual interests; non-interference in internal affairs; recognition of the right of every people to solve all the problems of their country by themselves; strict respect for the sovereignty and territorial integrity of all countries; promotion of economic and cultural co-operation on the basis of complete equality and mutual benefit.

Peaceful coexistence serves as a basis for the peaceful competition between socialism and capitalism on an international scale and constitutes a specific form of class struggle between them. As they consistently pursue the policy of peaceful coexistence, the Socialist countries are steadily strengthening the positions of the world Socialist system in its competition with capitalism. Peaceful coexistence affords more favorable opportunities for the struggle of the working class in the capitalist countries and facilitates the struggle of the people of the colonial and dependent countries for their liberation.

Support for the principle of peaceful coexistence is also in keeping with the interests of that section of the bourgeoisie which realizes that a thermonuclear war would not spare the ruling classes of capitalist society either. The policy of peaceful coexistence is in accord with the vital interests of all mankind, except the big monopoly magnates and the militarists.

The Soviet Union has consistently pursued and will continue to pursue the policy of peaceful coexistence of states with different social systems.

The Communist Party of the Soviet Union advances the following tasks in the field of international relations:

To use, together with the other Socialist countries, peaceful states and peoples, every means of preventing war and providing conditions for the complete elimination of war from the life of society;

To pursue a policy of establishing sound international relations, and work for the disbandment of all military blocs opposing each other, the discontinuance of the "cold war" and the propaganda of enmity and hatred among the nations, and the abolition of all air, naval, rocket, and other military bases on foreign territory;

To work for general and complete disarmament under strict international control;

To strengthen relations of fraternal friendship and close co-operation with the countries of Asia, Africa, and Latin America which are fighting to attain or consolidate national independence, with all peoples and states that advocate the preservation of peace;

To pursue an active and consistent policy of improving and developing relations with all capitalistic countries, including the United States of America, Great Britain, France, the Federal Republic of Germany, Japan, Italy, and other countries, with a view to safeguarding peace;

To contribute in every way to the militant solidarity of all contingents and organizations of the international working class, which oppose the imperialist policy of war;

Steadfastly to pursue a policy of consolidating all the forces fighting against war. All the organizations and parties that strive to avert war, the neutralist and pacifist movements and the bourgeois circles that advocate peace and normal relations between countries will meet understanding and support on the part of the Soviet Union;

To pursue a policy of developing international co-operation in the fields of trade, cultural relations, science, and technology;

To be highly vigilant with regard to the aggressive circles, which are intent on violating peace; to expose, in good time, the initiators of military adventures; to take all necessary steps to safeguard the security and inviolability of our Socialist country and the Socialist camp as a whole.

The C.P.S.U. and the Soviet people as a whole will continue to oppose all wars of conquest, including wars between capitalist countries, and local wars aimed at strangling people's emancipation movements, and consider it their duty to support the sacred struggle of the oppressed peoples and their just anti-imperialist wars of liberation.

The Communist Party of the Soviet Union will hold high the banner of peace and friendship among the nations.

Part Two

THE TASKS OF THE COMMUNIST PARTY OF THE SOVIET UNION IN BUILDING A COMMUNIST SOCIETY

COMMUNISM—THE BRIGHT FUTURE OF ALL MANKIND

The building of a Communist society has become an immediate practical task for the Soviet people. The gradual development of socialism into communism is an objective law; it has been prepared by the development of Soviet Socialist society throughout the preceding period.

What is communism?

Communism is a classless social system with one form of public ownership of the means of production and full social equality of all members of society; under it, the all-round development of people will be accompanied by the growth of the productive forces through continuous progress in science and technology, all sources of public wealth will gush forth abundantly, and the great principle, "From each according to his ability, to each according to his needs," will be implemented. Communism is a highly organized society of free, socially conscious working people in which public self-government will be established, in which labor for the good of society will become the prime and vital requirement of everyone, a necessity recognized by one and all, and the ability of each person will be employed to the greatest benefit of the people.

A high degree of Communist consciousness, industry, discipline, and devotion to the public interest are qualities typifying the man of Communist society.

Communism insures the continuous development of

social production and high labor productivity through rapid scientific and technological progress; it equips man with the best and most powerful machines, greatly increases his power over nature, and enables him to control its elemental forces to an ever greater extent. The social economy reaches the highest stage of planned organization, and the most effective and rational use is made of the material wealth and labor reserves to meet the growing requirements of the members of society.

Under communism, the classes, and the socio-economic and cultural distinctions, and differences in living conditions, between town and countryside disappear completely; the countryside rises to the level of the town in the development of the productive force and the nature of work, the forms of production relations, living conditions, and the well-being of the population. With the victory of communism mental and physical labor will merge organically in the production activity of people. The intelligentsia will no longer be a distinct social stratum, since workers by hand will have risen in cultural and technological standards to the level of workers by brain.

Thus, communism puts an end to the division of society into classes and social strata, whereas the whole history of mankind, with the exception of its primitive period, was one of class society in which division into opposing classes led to the exploitation of man by man, class struggle, and antagonisms between nations and states.

Under communism all people will have equal status in society, will stand in the same relation to the means of production, will enjoy equal conditions of work and distribution, and will actively participate in the management of public affairs. Harmonious relations will be established between the individual and society on the basis of the unity of public and personal interests. For all their diversity, the requirements of people will express the sound, reasonable requirements of perfectly developed persons.

The purpose of Communist production is to insure uninterrupted progress of society and to provide all its members with material and cultural benefits according to their growing needs, their individual requirements and tastes.

People's requirements will be satisfied from public sources. Articles of personal use will come into the full ownership of each member of society and will be at his disposal.

Communist society, which is based on highly organized production and advanced technology, alters the character of work, but it does not release the members of society from work. It will by no means be a society of anarchy, idleness, and inactivity. Everyone will participate in social labor and thereby insure the steady growth of the material and spiritual wealth of society. Thanks to the changed character of labor, its greater mechanization and the high degree of consciousness of all members of society, the latter will work willingly for the public benefit according to their own inclinations.

Communist production demands high standards of organization, precision, and discipline, which are insured, not by compulsion, but thanks to an understanding of public duty, and are determined by the whole tenor of life in Communist society. Labor and discipline will not be a burden to people, labor will no longer be a mere source of livelihood—it will be a genuinely creative process and a source of happiness.

Communism represents the highest form of organization of public life. All production units and self-governing associations will be harmoniously interlinked by a common planned economy and a uniform rhythm of social labor.

Under communism the nations will draw closer and closer together in all spheres on the basis of a complete identity of economic, political, and spiritual interests, of fraternal friendship and co-operation.

Communism is the system under which the abilities and talents of free man, his best moral qualities, blossom forth and reveal themselves in full. Family relations will be freed from material considerations and will be based solely on mutual love and friendship.

In defining the basic tasks to be accomplished in building a Communist society, the party is guided by Lenin's great formula: "Communism is Soviet power plus the electrification of the whole country."

The C.P.S.U., being a party of scientific communism, proposes and fulfills the task of Communist construction in step with the preparation and maturing of the material and spiritual prerequisites, considering that it would be wrong to jump over necessary stages of development, and that it would be equally wrong to halt at an achieved level and thus check progress. The building of communism must be carried out by successive stages.

In the current decade (1961–1970), the Soviet Union, in creating the material and technical basis of communism, will surpass the strongest and richest capitalist country, the U.S.A., in production per head of population. The people's standard of living and their cultural and technical standards will improve substantially, everyone will live in easy circumstances, all collective and state farms will become highly productive and profitable enterprises, the demand of the Soviet people for well-appointed housing will, in the main, be satisfied, hard physical work will disappear, the U.S.S.R. will become the country with the shortest working day.

In the next decade (1971-1980), the material and technical basis of communism will be created and there will be an abundance of material and cultural benefits for the whole population. Soviet society will come close to a stage where it can introduce the principle of distribution according to needs, and there will be a gradual transition to one form of ownership—public ownership. Thus, a Communist society will, on the whole, be built in the U.S.S.R. The construction of Communist society will be fully completed in the subsequent period.

The majestic edifice of communism is being erected by the persevering effort of the Soviet people—the working class, the peasantry, and the intelligentsia. The more successful their work, the closer the great goal—Communist society.

I. The Tasks of the Party in the Field of Economic Development and in the Creation and Promotion of the Material and Technical Basis of Communism

The main economic task of the Party and the Soviet people is to create the material and technical basis of communism within two decades. This means the complete electrification of the country and the perfection on this basis of the techniques, technologies, and organization of social production in industry and agriculture, the comprehensive mechanization of production operations and a growing degree of their automation, the widespread use of chemistry in the national economy, the vigorous development of new, economically effective branches of production, new types of power and new materials, the all-round and rational utilization of natural resources, the organic fusion of science and production, and rapid scientific and technical progress, a high cultural and technical level for the working people, substantial superiority over the more developed capitalist countries in productivity of labor, which constitutes a most important prerequisite for the victory of the Communist system.

As a result, the U.S.S.R. will possess productive forces of unparalleled might, it will surpass the technical level of the most developed countries and occupy first place in the world in per capita production. This will serve as a basis for the gradual transformation of Socialist social relations into Communist social relations and for a development of industry and agriculture that will make it possible to meet in abundance the requirements of society and all its members.

In contrast to capitalism, the planned Socialist system of economy combines accelerated technical progress with the full employment of all able-bodied citizens. Automation and comprehensive mechanization serve as a material basis for the gradual development of Socialist labor into Communist labor. Technical progress will require higher standards of production and a higher level of the vocational and general education of all workers. The new machinery developed will be used to improve radically the Soviet people's working conditions, and make them easier, to reduce the length of the working day, to improve living conditions, eliminate hard physical work and, subsequently, all unskilled labor.

The material and technical basis will develop and improve continuously together with the evolution of society toward the complete triumph of communism. The level of development of science and technology, and the degree of mechanization and automation of production operations, will steadily rise.

The creation of the material and technical basis of

communism will call for huge investments. The task is to utilize these investments most rationally and economically, with the maximum effect and gain of time.

(1) The Development of Industry; Its Role in Creating the Productive Forces of Communism.

The creation of the material and technical basis of communism, the task of making Soviet industry technologically the best and strongest in the world, calls for the further development of heavy industry. On this basis, all the other branches of the national economy—agriculture, the consumer goods industries, the building industry, transport and communications, as well as the branches directly concerned with services for the population—trade, public catering, health, housing, and communal services—will be technically re-equipped.

A first-class heavy industry, the basis for the country's technical progress and economic might, has been built up in the Soviet Union. The C.P.S.U. will continue to devote unflagging attention to the growth of heavy industry, which insures the development of the country's productive forces and defense potential. In the new period of the Soviet Union's development, the growth and technological progress of heavy industry must insure the expansion of those branches of economy producing consumer goods to meet ever more fully the requirements of the people.

Thus, the main task of heavy industry is to meet the needs of the country's defense in full and to satisfy the daily requirements of the man of Soviet society better and more fully.

With these aims in view, the C.P.S.U. plans the following increases in total industrial output:

Within the current ten years, by approximately 150 per cent, exceeding the contemporary level of U.S. industrial output.

Within twenty years, by not less than 500 per cent, leaving the present over-all volume of U.S. industrial output far behind.

To achieve this, it is necessary to raise productivity of labor in industry by more than 100 per cent within ten years, and by 300 to 350 per cent within twenty years. In twenty years' time labor productivity in Soviet industry will exceed the present level of labor productivity in the

U.S.A. by roughly 100 per cent, and considerably more in terms of per-hour output, due to the reduction of the working day in the U.S.S.R.

Such an intensive development of industry will call for major progressive changes in its structure. The role of new branches insuring the greatest technical progress will grow very considerably. The less effective fuels, types of power, raw and semi-manufactured materials will be increasingly superseded by highly effective ones, and their comprehensive use will increase greatly. The share of synthetic materials, metals, and alloys with new properties will increase considerably. New types of automatic and electronic machinery, instruments, and apparatus will be rapidly introduced on a large scale.

Electrification, which is the backbone of the economy of Communist society, plays a key role in the development of all economic branches and in all modern technological progress.

It is therefore important to insure the priority development of electric power output. The plan for the electrification of the country provides for an almost threefold increase in the use of electricity to equip industrial labor within the present decade, a considerable expansion of industries with a high rate of power consumption through the supply of cheap power, and extensive electrification of transport, agriculture, and the household in town and countryside. The electrification of the whole country will on the whole be completed in the course of the second decade.

The annual output of electricity must be brought up to 900,000-1,000,000 million kilowatt-hours by the end of the first decade, and to 2,700,000-3,000,000 million kwh by the end of the second decade. For this it will be necessary in the course of twenty years to increase accordingly the installed capacities of electric power plants and to build hundreds of thousands of kilometers of high-tension transmission and distribution lines throughout the country. A single power grid for the whole U.S.S.R. will be built and will have sufficient capacity reserves to transmit electric power from the eastern regions to the European part of the country. It will link up with the power grids of other Socialist countries.

As atomic energy becomes cheaper, the construction of

atomic power stations will be expanded, especially in areas poor in other power sources, and the use of atomic energy for peaceful purposes in the national economy, in medicine and science will increase.

The further rapid expansion of the output of metals and fuels, the basis of modern industry, remains one of the major economic tasks. Within twenty years metallurgy will develop sufficiently to produce about 250,000,000 metric tons of steel a year. Steel output must cover the growing requirements of the national economy in accordance with the technological progress achieved in that period. The output of light, nonferrous, and rare metals will grow very appreciably; the output of aluminum and its use in electrification, engineering, building, and the household will considerably increase. A steady effort will be made to insure priority output of oil and gas which will be used increasingly as raw materials for the chemical industry. Oil output must meet the requirements of the national economy in full.

One of the most important tasks is the all-round development of the chemical industry, and the full use in all economic fields of the achievements of modern chemistry. This provides greater opportunities to increase the national wealth and the output of new, better, and cheaper capital and consumer goods. Metal, wood, and other building materials will be increasingly replaced by economical, durable, light synthetic materials. The output of mineral fertilizers and chemical weed and pest killers will rise sharply.

Of primary importance for the technical re-equipment of the entire national economy is the development of mechanical engineering, with special stress laid on the accelerated production of automated production lines and machines, automatic, telemechanic, and electronic devices and precision instruments. The designing of highly efficient machines consuming less raw materials and power and leading to higher productivity will make rapid progress. The requirements of the national economy in all types of modern machinery, machine tools, and instruments must be met in full.

The development of mechanical engineering in the first decade will serve as the basis for comprehensive mechanization in industry, agriculture, building, transport, loading and unloading operations and in the municipal economy. Comprehensive mechanization will exclude manual labor from both basic and auxiliary operations.

Within the twenty-year period the comprehensive automation of production will be effected on a large scale, with more and more shops and plants being fully automated. The introduction of highly efficient automatic control systems will be accelerated. Cybernetics, computers, and control systems must be introduced on a large scale in industry, research, designing, planning, accounting, statistics, and management.

The vast scope of capital construction calls for the rapid development and technological modernization of the building industry, a substantial increase in the output of better and cheaper building materials, the maximum acceleration of the rate and reduction of building costs through steady industrialization and the use of prefabricated elements.

The C.P.S.U. will concentrate its efforts on insuring a rapid increase in the output of consumer goods. The growing resources of industry must be used more and more to meet fully all the requirements of the Soviet people and to build and equip enterprises and establishments catering to the household and cultural needs of the population. Along with the accelerated development of all branches of the light and food industries, the share of consumer goods in the output of heavy industry will also increase. More electricity and gas will be supplied to the population.

The growth of the national economy will call for the accelerated development of all transport facilities. The most important tasks in the sphere of transport are: expansion of transport and road construction to meet in full the requirements of the national economy and the population in all types of transport; further modernization of the railways and other transport systems; a considerable increase of the speed of rail, sea, and river traffic; the co-ordinated development of all types of transport as integral parts of a single transport network. The share of pipe transport will increase.

A single deep-water system will link the main inland waterways of the European part of the U.S.S.R.

A ramified network of modern roads will be built

throughout the country. The automobile fleet will increase sufficiently to meet fully freight and passenger traffic requirements; car hire centers will be organized on a large scale. Air transport will become a means of mass passenger traffic extending to all parts of the country.

Up-to-date jet engineering will develop rapidly, above all in air transport, as well as in space exploration.

All means of communication (post, radio, and television, telephone, and telegraph) will be further developed. All regions of the country will have reliable telephone and radio communications and a link-up system of television stations.

Full-scale Communist construction calls for a more rational geographic distribution of the industries in order to save social labor and insure the comprehensive development of areas and the specialization of their industries, do away with the overpopulation of big cities, facilitate the elimination of substantial distinctions between towns and countryside, and further even out the economic levels of different parts of the country.

To gain time, priority will be given to developing easily exploited natural resources that provide the greatest economic effect.

The industry in the areas to the east of the Urals, where there are immense natural riches, raw materials, and power resources, will expand greatly.

The following must be achieved within the next twenty years: in Siberia and Kazakhstan—the creation of new large power bases using deposits of cheap coal or the waterpower resources of the Angara and Yenisei Rivers, the organization of big centers of power-consuming industries and the completion, in Siberia, of the country's third metallurgical base, the development of new rich ore and coal deposits, and the construction of a number of new large machine-building centers; in areas along the Volga, in the Urals, North Caucasus, and Central Asia—the rapid development of the power, oil, gas, and chemical industries and the development of ore deposits. The Soviet people will be able to carry out daring plans to change the courses of some northern rivers and regulate their flow for the purpose of utilizing vast quantities of water for the irrigation of arid areas.

The economy in the European part of the U.S.S.R.,

which contains the bulk of the population and where there are great opportunities for increased industrial output, will make further substantial progress.

The maximum acceleration of scientific and engineering progress is a major national task which calls for daily effort to reduce the time spent on designing new machinery and introducing it in industry. It is necessary to promote in every way the initiative of economic councils, enterprises, social organizations, scientists, engineers, designers, workers, and collective farmers in creating and applying technical improvements. Of utmost importance is the material and moral stimulation of the mass invention and rationalization movements, of enterprises, shops, teams, and innovators who master the production of new machinery and utilize it skillfully.

The Party will do everything to enhance the role of science in the building of Communist society, it will encourage research to discover new possibilities for the development of the productive forces, and the rapid and extensive application of the latest scientific and technical achievements, a decisive advancement in experimental work, including research directly at enterprises, and the efficient organization of scientific and technical information and of the whole system of studying and disseminating progressive Soviet and foreign methods. Science will itself in full measure become a productive force.

The constant improvement in the technology of all industries and production branches is a requisite for industrial development. Technological progress will facilitate the substantial intensification and acceleration of production operations without putting undue strain on the worker, and will achieve the highest degree of precision, the standardization of mass-produced items, and the maximum use of production lines. Machinery will be supplemented and, when necessary, replaced by chemical methods, the technological use of electricity, electrochemistry, electric heat treatment, etc.; radioelectronics, semiconductors, and ultra-sound will occupy a more important place in production techniques. The construction of new, technically up-to-date enterprises will proceed side by side with the reconstruction of those now in existence and the replacement and modernization of their equipment.

The development of the specialization and co-operation of enterprises is a most important condition for technical progress and the rational organization of social labor. Articles of similar type should be manufactured mainly at large specialized plants.

New techniques and the reduction of the working day call for better organization of work. Technical progress and better production organization must be fully utilized to increase labor productivity and reduce production costs at every enterprise. This implies a higher rate of increase in labor productivity as compared with remuneration, better rate-fixing, prevention of loss of working time, and operation on a profitable basis at all stages of production.

Most important will be the task of systematically improving the qualifications of those working in industry and other branches of the economy in connection with technical progress. The planned training, instruction, and rational employment of those released from various jobs and transferred to other jobs due to mechanization and automation are essential.

Existing enterprises will be improved and developed into enterprises of Communist society. Typical of this process will be new machinery, high standards of production organization and efficiency through increased automation of production operations and the introduction of automation into control, an improvement of the cultural and technical standards of the workers, the increasing fusion of physical and mental labor and the growing proportion of engineers and technicians in every industrial enterprise, the expansion of research, and closer links between enterprises and research institutes, promotion of the emulation movement, the application of achievements of science and the best forms of labor organization and best methods of raising labor productivity, the extensive participation of workers' collectives in the management of enterprises, and the spreading of Communist forms of labor.

(2) Development of Agriculture and Social Relations in the Countryside.

Along with a powerful industry, a flourishing, versatile, and highly productive agriculture is an imperative condition for the building of communism. The Party is organizing a great development of productive forces in agriculture, which will enable it to accomplish two basic, closely related tasks: (a) To build up an abundance of high-quality food products for the population and of raw materials for industry, and (b) to effect the gradual transition of social relations in the Soviet countryside to Communist relations and eliminate, in the main, the distinctions between town and country.

The chief means of achieving progress in agriculture and satisfying the growing needs of the country in farm produce are comprehensive mechanization and consistent intensification: high efficiency of crop farming and stock-breeding based on science and progressive experience in all kolkhozes (collectives) and state farms, a steep rise in the yielding capacity of all crops and greater output per hectare with the utmost economy of labor and funds. On this basis, it is necessary to achieve an unintermittent growth of agricultural production in keeping with the needs of society. Agriculture will approach the level of industry in technical equipment and the organization of production, farm labor will turn into a variety of industrial labor, and the dependence of agriculture upon the elements will decrease considerably, and ultimately drop to a minimum.

The development of virgin and fallow land and establishment of new large-scale state farms, the reorganization of the machine-and-tractor stations, the sale of implements of production to the collective farms, and the enhancement of material incentives for agricultural workers—all constitute an important stage in the development of agriculture.

The further advance of the countryside to communism will proceed through the development and improvement of the two forms of Socialist farming—the kolkhozes and state farms.

The kolkhoz system is an integral part of Soviet Socialist society. It is a way charted by V. I. Lenin for the gradual transition of the peasantry to communism; it has stood the test of history and conforms to the distinctive features of the peasantry.

Kolkhoz farming accords in full with the level and needs of the development of modern productive forces in the countryside, and makes possible effective use of new machinery and the achievements of science, and rational employment of manpower. The kolkhoz blends the personal interests of the peasants with common, nation-wide interests, blends individual with collective interest in the results of production, and offers extensive opportunities for raising the incomes and the well-being of peasants on the basis of growing labor productivity. It is essential to make the most of the possibilities and advantages of the kolkhoz system. By virtue of its organizational structure and its democratic groundwork, which will develop more and more, the kolkhoz is a social economic form which insures that production is run by the kolkhoz members themselves, that their creative initiative is enhanced and that they are educated in the Communist spirit. The kolkhoz is a school of communism for the peasantry.

Economic advancement of the kolkhoz system creates conditions for the gradual rapprochement and, in the long run, also for the merging of kolkhoz property and the property of the whole people into one Communist property.

The state farms, which are the leading Socialist agricultural enterprises, play an ever increasing role in the development of agriculture. The state farms must serve the kolkhozes as a model of progressive, scientifically managed, economically profitable social production, of high efficiency and labor productivity.

The C.P.S.U. proceeds from the fact that the further consolidation of the unbreakable alliance of the working class and the kolkhoz peasantry is of crucial political and socio-economic importance for the building of communism in the U.S.S.R.

A. Building Up an Abundance of Agricultural Produce.

In order fully to satisfy the requirements of the entire population and of the national economy in agricultural produce, the task is to increase the aggregate volume of agricultural production in ten years by about 150 per cent, and in twenty years by 250 per cent. Agricultural output must keep ahead of the growing demand. In the first decade the Soviet Union will outstrip the United

States in output of the key agricultural products per head of population.

Accelerated growth of grain production is the chief link in the further development of all agriculture and a basis for the rapid growth of stock-breeding. The aggregate grain crops will more than double in twenty years, and their yielding capacity will double. The output of wheat, corn, cereal, and leguminous crops will increase substantially.

Livestock breeding will develop at a rapid rate. The output of animal products will rise: meat about threefold in the first ten years and nearly fourfold in twenty years, and milk more than double in the first decade and nearly threefold in twenty years. The planned increase in the output of animal products will be achieved by increasing the cattle and poultry population, improving stock and productivity, and building up reliable fodder resources, chiefly corn, sugar-beet, fodder beans, and other crops.

Productivity of labor in agriculture will rise not less than 150 per cent in ten years, and five-to-six-fold in twenty years. The rapid rise of the productivity of farm labor—at a higher rate than in industry—will serve to eliminate the lag of agriculture behind industry and will turn it into a highly developed branch of economy of Communist society.

The further mechanization of agriculture, introduction of comprehensive mechanization and use of automated devices and highly efficient and economical machinery adapted to the conditions of each zone, will be the basis for the growth of productivity of farm labor. The Party considers rapid electrification of agriculture one of the most important tasks. All state farms and kolkhozes will be supplied electric power for production and domestic purposes from the state power grid, and also from power stations built in the countryside.

The technical re-equipment of agriculture must combine with the most progressive forms and methods of the organization of labor and production and the maximum improvement of the cultural and technical education of farm workers. Qualified workers with special agricultural training and proficient in the use of new machinery will increasingly predominate in the kolkhozes and state farms.

To insure high, stable, steadily increasing harvests, to deliver agriculture from the baneful effects of the elements, especially droughts, to steeply raise land fertility, and to rapidly advance livestock breeding, it is necessary:

To introduce in all parts of the country scientific systems of land cultivation and animal husbandry in keeping with local conditions and the specialization of each farm, insuring the most effective use of the land and the most economically expedient combination of branches, the best structure of crop acreage with the substitution of high-yielding and valuable crops for crops of little value and those giving low yields, to insure that every kolkhoz and state farm masters the most advanced methods of crop farming with the application of efficient crop rotation and the sowing of high-grade seeds only, to build up reliable fodder resources in all districts and to introduce the foremost stock-breeding techniques in kolkhozes and state farms;

To effect a scientifically expedient disposition of agriculture by natural economic zones and districts, and a more thorough and stable specialization of agriculture with priority given to the type of farm product where the best conditions for it exist and the greatest saving in outlay is achieved;

To effect a consistent introduction of chemicals in all branches of agriculture, to meet all its needs in mineral fertilizers and chemical means of combating weeds, blights, diseases, and plant and animal pests, and to insure the best of local fertilizers in all kolkhozes;

To apply broadly biological achievements and microbiology, which is assuming ever greater importance to improve soil fertility, to carry through a far-flung irrigation program, to irrigate and water millions of hectares of land in the arid areas and improve existing irrigated farming, to expand field-protective afforestation, building of water reservoirs, irrigation of pastures and melioration of overmoist land, and to combat, systematically, the water and wind erosion of soil.

The Party will promote the development of agricultural science, focus the creative efforts of scientists on the key problems of agricultural progress, and work for the practical application and extensive introduction of the achievements of science and progressive production experience in crop farming and stock-breeding. Research institutions and experimental stations must become important links in agricultural management, and scientists and specialists must become the direct organizers of farm production. Each region or group of regions of the same zonal type should have agricultural research centers, with their own large-scale farms and up-to-date material, and technical resources, to work out recommendations for state farms and kolkhozes applicable to the given district. Agricultural research and educational establishments must be chiefly located in rural areas and be directly associated with farm production, so that students may learn while working and work while learning.

B. *The Kolkhozes and State Farms on the Road to Communism; Remolding Social Relations in the Countryside.*

The economic basis for the development of kolkhozes and state farms lies in the continuous growth and best use of their productive forces, improvement of the organization of production and methods of management, steady rise of labor productivity and strict observance of the principle: higher payment for good work, for better results. On this basis the kolkhozes and state farms will become to an increasing degree enterprises of the Communist type by virtue of their production relations, character of labor, and the living and cultural standard of their personnel.

The policy of the Socialist state in relation to the kolkhozes is based on blending country-wide interests with the material interest of the kolkhozes and their members in the results of their labor. The state will promote the growth of the productive forces of the kolkhoz system and the economic advancement of all kolkhozes. Concurrently, the kolkhoz peasantry must also contribute more widely to the building of Communist society.

The state will insure the full satisfaction of the needs of the kolkhozes in modern machinery, chemicals, and other means of production, will train new hundreds of thousands of skilled farm workers, and will considerably increase capital investments in the countryside, in addition to the greater investments by the kolkhozes themselves. The amount of manufactured goods made available to the kolkhoz villages will increase greatly.

Strict observance of their contracted commitments to the state by the kolkhozes and their members is an irrevocable principle of their participation in the development of the national economy.

The system of state purchasing must be concentrated on increasing the amount and improving the quality of the agricultural products bought on the basis of an all-round advancement of kolkhoz farming. It is essential to co-ordinate the planning of state purchases and the production plans of the kolkhozes, with utmost consideration for the interests of agricultural production, its correct disposition and specialization.

The policy in the sphere of the state purchasing prices of agricultural produce and selling prices of means of production for the countryside must take account of the interests of extended reproduction in both industry and agriculture and of the need to accumulate funds in the kolkhozes. It is essential that the level of state purchasing prices encourage the kolkhozes to raise labor productivity and reduce production expenses, since greater farm output and lower production costs are the basis of greater incomes for the kolkhozes.

The proper ratio of accumulation and consumption in the distribution of incomes is a prerequisite of successful kolkhoz development. The kolkhozes cannot develop without continuously extending their commonly owned assets for production, insurance, cultural and community needs. At the same time, it must be a standing rule for every kolkhoz to raise its members' incomes from collective farming and to enhance their living standard as labor productivity rises.

Great importance attaches to improved methods of rate setting and labor remuneration at kolkhozes, supplementary forms of payment for labor, and other incentives to obtain better production figures. Increasingly equal economic conditions must be provided that will improve the incomes of kolkhozes existing under unequal natural-economic conditions in different zones, and also within the zones, in order to put into effect more consistently the principle of equal pay for equal work on a scale embracing the entire kolkhoz system. Farming on all kolkhozes must be conducted in accordance with a strict principle of profitability.

In its organizational work and economic policy, the Party will strive to overcome the lag of the economically weak kolkhozes and to turn all kolkhozes into economically strong, high-income farms in the course of the next few years. The Party sets the task of continuously improving and educating kolkhoz personnel, of insuring the further extension of kolkhoz democracy and promoting the principle of collectivism in management.

As the kolkhozes develop, their basic production assets will expand, and modern technical means will become dominant.

The economic advancement of the kolkhozes will make it possible to perfect kolkhoz internal relations; to raise the degree to which production is socialized, to bring the rate setting, organization, and payment of labor closer to the level and the forms employed at state enterprises and effect a transition to a guaranteed monthly wage, to develop community services more broadly (public catering, kindergartens and nurseries, and other services, etc.).

At a certain point the collective production at kolkhozes will achieve a level at which it will fully satisfy members' requirements. On this basis supplementary individual farming will gradually become economically unnecessary. When collective production at the kolkhozes is able to replace in full that of the supplementary individual plot of the kolkhoz members, when the collective farmers see for themselves that their supplementary individual farming is unprofitable, they will give it up of their own accord.

As the productive forces increase, inter-kolkhoz production ties will develop and the socialization of production will transcend the limits of individual kolkhozes. The building, jointly by several kolkhozes, of enterprises and cultural and other welfare institutions, state-kolkholz power stations and enterprises for the primary processing, storage, and transportation of farm products, for various types of building, the manufacture of building materials, etc., should be encouraged. As the commonly owned assets increase, the kolkhozes will participate more and more in establishing enterprises and cultural and other welfare institutions for general public use, boarding schools, clubs, hospitals, and holiday homes. All these developments which must proceed on a voluntary basis and when the necessary economic conditions are available, will gradually impart to kolkhoz-co-operative property the nature of public property.

The state farms have a long way to travel in their development—to attain high rates of growth of labor productivity, to steadily reduce production costs and raise farm efficiency. This calls for the economically expedient specialization of state farms. Their role in supplying food to the urban population will grow. They must become mechanized and well-organized first-class factories of grain, cotton, meat, milk, wool, vegetables, fruit, and other products, and must develop seed farming and pure-strain animal husbandry to the utmost.

The material and technical basis of the state farms will be extended and improved, and the living and cultural conditions at the state farms will approach those in towns. State farm management should follow a more and more democratic pattern which will allot a greater role to the personnel, and to general meetings and production conferences in deciding production, cultural, and other community issues.

As the kolkhozes and state farms develop, their production ties with each other and with local industrial enterprises will grow stronger. The practice of jointly organizing various enterprises will expand. This will insure a fuller and more balanced use of manpower and production resources throughout the year, raise the productivity of social labor, and enhance the living and cultural standards of the population. Agrarian-industrial associations will gradually emerge wherever economically expedient, in which, given appropriate specialization and co-operation of agricultural and industrial enterprises, agriculture will combine organically with the industrial processing of its produce.

As production in kolkhozes and state farms develops and social relations within them advance, agriculture rises to a higher level, affording the possibility of transition to Communist forms of production and distribution. The kolkhozes will draw level in economic conditions with the nationally owned agricultural enterprises. They will turn into highly developed mechanized farms. By virtue of high labor productivity all kolkhozes will become economically powerful. Kolkhoz members will be adequately provided and their requirements fully satisfied out of collective-farm production. They will have the services of catering establishments, bakeries, laundries, kindergartens and nurseries, clubs, libraries, and sports grounds. The payment of labor will be the same as at nationally owned enterprises and they will be provided with all forms of social security (pensions, holidays, etc.) out of kolkhoz and state funds.

Gradually, the kolkhoz villages will grow into amalgamated urban communities with modern housing facilities, public amenities and services, and cultural and medical institutions. The rural population will ultimately draw level with the urban population in cultural and living conditions.

Elimination of socio-economic and cultural distinctions between town and country and differences in their living conditions will be one of the greatest gains of Communist construction.

(3) Management of the National Economy and Planning.

The building of the material and technical basis of communism calls for a continuous improvement in economic management. Chief emphasis at all levels of planning and economic management must be laid on the most rational and effective use of the material, labor, and financial resources and natural wealth and on the elimination of excessive expenditures. The immutable law of economic development is to achieve in the interests of society the highest results at the lowest cost.

Planning must at all levels concentrate on the rapid development and introduction of new techniques. It is essential that progressive, scientifically expedient standards for the use of means of production be strictly observed in all sectors of the national economy.

The Party attaches prime importance to the more effective investment of capital, the choice of the most profitable and economical trends in capital construction, achievement everywhere of the maximum growth of output per invested ruble, and reduction of the time lapse between investment and return. It is necessary continuously to improve the structure of capital investments and to expand that portion of them which is spent on equipment, machinery, and machine tools.

Continuous improvement of the quality of output is an imperative factor of economic development. The quality of goods produced by Soviet enterprises must be considerably higher than that of the best capitalist enterprises. For this purpose, it is necessary to apply a broad set of measures, including public control, and to enhance the role of quality indexes in planning, in the assessment of the work of enterprises, and in Socialist emulation.

Communist construction presupposes the maximum development of democratic principles of management coupled with a strengthening and improvement of centralized economic management by the state. The economic independence and the rights of local organs and enterprises will continue to expand within the framework of the single national economic plan. Plans and recommendations made at lower levels, beginning with enterprises, must play an increasing role in planning.

Centralized planning should chiefly concentrate on working out and insuring the fulfillment of the key targets of the economic plans with the greatest consideration paid to recommendations made at lower levels; on co-ordinating and dovetailing plans drawn up locally; on spreading scientific and technical achievements and advanced production experience; on enforcing a single state policy in the spheres of technical progress, capital investment, distribution of production, payment of labor, prices, and finance, and a unified system of accounting and statistics.

It is essential that the national economy develop on a strictly proportionate basis, that economic disproportions are prevented in good time, ensuring sufficient economic reserves as a condition for stable high rates of economic development, uninterrupted operation of enterprises, and continuous improvement of the people's well-being.

The growing scale of the national economy, the rapid development of science and technology call for an improvement of the scientific level of planning, accounting, statistics, and industrial designing. A better scientific, technical, and economic basis for the plans will insure their greater stability, which also presupposes timely correction and amendment of plans in the course of their fulfillment. Planning must be continuous, and the annual and long-term plans must be organically integrated.

Firm and consistent discipline, day-to-day control, and determined elimination of elements of parochialism and of a narrow departmental approach in economic affairs are necessary conditions for successful Communist construction.

There must be a further expansion of the role and responsibility of local bodies in economic management. The transfer of a number of functions of economic management by the all-union bodies to those of the republics, by republican bodies to those of the regions, and by regional bodies to those of the districts should be continued. It is necessary to improve the work of the economic councils as the most viable form of management in industry and building that conforms to the present level of the productive forces. The improvement of the work of economic councils within the economic administration areas will also be accompanied by greater coordination of the work of other economic bodies, in order better to organize the planned comprehensive economic development of such major economic areas as the Urals, the Volga area, Siberia, Transcaucasia, the Baltic area, Central Asia, etc.

Extension of operative independence and of the initiative of enterprise on the basis of the state-plan targets is essential in order to mobilize untapped resources and make more effective use of capital investments, production facilities, and finances. It is necessary for the enterprise to play a substantially greater part in introducing the latest machinery.

The selection, training, and promotion of people to head enterprises and kolkhozes, those who organize and manage production, are of decisive importance in economic management. The sphere of material production is the main sphere in the life of society; the most capable people must, therefore, be given leading posts in the sphere of production.

The direct and most active participation of trade unions in elaborating and realizing economic plans, in matters concerning the labor of factory and office workers, in setting up organs of economic administration and of management of enterprises, must be extended more and more at the top level and locally. The role of the collectives of factory and office workers in matters concerning the work of enterprises must be enhanced.

In the process of Communist construction economic management will make use of material and moral incentives for high production figures. Proper combination of material and moral labor incentives is a great creative factor in the struggle for communism. In the course of the advance to communism the importance of moral labor incentives, public recognition of achieved results, and the sense of responsibility of each for the common cause will become continuously greater.

The entire system of planning and assessing the work of central and local organizations, enterprises, and collective farms must stimulate their interest in higher plan targets and the maximum dissemination of progressive production experience. Initiative and successes in finding and using new ways of improving the quantitative and qualitative indexes of production should be specially encouraged.

There must be a continuous improvement in rate setting, the system of labor payments and bonuses, in the financial control over the quantity and quality of work, in the elimination of leveling and the stimulation of collective forms of incentives raising the interest of each employee in the high efficiency of the enterprise as a whole.

It is necessary in Communist construction to make full use of commodity-money relations in keeping with their new substance in the Socialist period. In this, such instruments of economic development as cost accounting, money, price, production cost, profit, trade, credit, and finance play a big part. When the transition to one Communist form of people's property and the Communist system of distribution is completed, commodity-money relations will become economically outdated and will wither away.

The important role of the budget in distributing the social product and national income will prevail throughout the period of full-scale Communist construction. There will be a further strengthening of the monetary and credit system, a consolidation of Soviet currency, a steady rise of the rate of exchange of the ruble by virtue of its growing purchasing power, and a strengthening of the role of the ruble in the international arena.

It is necessary to promote profitable operation of enterprises, to work for lower production costs and higher profitability. The price system should be continuously improved in conformity with the tasks of Communist construction, technical progress, growth of production and consumption, and the reduction of production expenditures. Prices must, to a growing extent, reflect the socially necessary outlays of labor, insure return of production and circulation expenditures, and a certain profit for each normally operating enterprise. Systematic, economically justified price reductions, based on growth of labor productivity and reduction of production costs, are the main trend of the price policy in the period of Communist construction.

Soviet society possesses immense national assets. For this reason, the role of accounting and control over the maintenance and proper use of the national wealth increases. Thrift, good use of every ruble belonging to the people, competent utilization of funds, the continuous improvement of planning and methods of management, improvement of organization and conscious discipline, and development of the initiative of the people are powerful means of accelerating the advance of Soviet society to communism.

II. THE TASKS OF THE PARTY IN IMPROVING THE LIVING STANDARD OF THE PEOPLE

The heroic labor of the Soviet people has produced a powerful and versatile economy. There is now every possibility to improve rapidly the living standard of the entire population—the workers, peasants, and intellectuals. The C.P.S.U. sets the historically important task of achieving in the Soviet Union a living standard higher than that of any of the capitalist countries.

This task will be effected by: (A) Raising the individual payment of employees according to the quality and quantity of work, coupled with reduction of retail prices and abolition of taxes paid by the population. (B) Increase of the public funds distributed among members of society irrespective of the quantity and quality of their labor, that is, free of charge (education, medical treatment, pensions, maintenance of children at children's institutions, transition to cost-free use of public amenities, etc.).

The rise of the real incomes of the population will be outstripped by rapid increase in the amount of commodities and services, and by far-flung construction of dwellings and cultural and service buildings.

Soviet people will be more prosperous than people in the developed capitalist countries even if average incomes will be equal, because in the Soviet Union the national income is distributed fairly among the members of society and there are no parasitical classes as in the bourgeois countries who appropriate and squander immense wealth plundered from millions of working people.

The Party acts upon Lenin's thesis that Communist construction must be based upon the principle of material incentive. In the coming twenty years payment according to one's work will remain the principal source for satisfying the material and cultural needs of the working people.

The disparity between high and comparatively low incomes must gradually shrink. Increasingly greater numbers of unskilled personnel will become skilled, and the diminishing difference in proficiency and labor productivity will be accompanied by a steady reduction of disparities in the level of pay. As the living standard of the entire population rises, low-income levels will approach the higher, and the disparity between the incomes of peasants and workers, low-paid and high-paid personnel, and the populations of different parts of the country will gradually shrink.

At the same time, as the country advances toward communism, personal needs will be increasingly met out of public consumption funds, whose rate of growth will exceed the rate of growth of payments for labor. The transition to Communist distribution will be completed after the principle of distribution according to one's work will exhaust itself, that is, when there will be an abundance of material and cultural wealth and labor will become life's prime necessity for all members of society.

A. Provision of a High Level of Income and Consumption for the Whole Population.

The national income of the U.S.S.R. in the next ten years will increase nearly 150 per cent, and about 400 per cent in twenty years. The real income per head of population will increase by more than 250 per cent in twenty years.

In the course of the coming ten years the real incomes of factory and office workers (including public funds) per employed person will, on the average, be almost doubled, and in twenty years will increase by approximately 200 to 250 per cent. The increase in the real incomes of factory, office, and professional workers paid relatively lower wages will be brought to a level at which low-paid brackets throughout the country will be eliminated within ten years. The real incomes of factory and office workers receiving the minimum wages will be approximately trebled (including what they get from public funds) over this period.

By virtue of higher rates of growth of the labor productivity of collective farmers their real incomes will grow more rapidly than the incomes of factory workers, and will, on an average per employed person, more than double in the next ten years and increase more than fourfold in twenty years.

The wages of such numerically large sections of the Soviet intelligentsia as engineers and technicians, agronomists and stock-breeding experts, teachers, medical and cultural workers, will rise considerably.

As the incomes of the population grow, the general level of popular consumption will rise rapidly. The entire population will be able to satisfy to the full its need in high-quality and varied foodstuffs. The share of animal products (meat, fats, dairy produce), fruit, and high-grade vegetables in popular consumption will rise substantially in the near future. The demand of all sections of the population for high-quality consumer goods: attractive clothes, footwear, and goods improving and adorning the daily life of Soviet people, such as comfortable modern furniture, up-to-date domestic goods, a wide range of goods for cultural purposes, etc., will be amply satisfied.

Production of motorcars for the population will be considerably extended.

Output of consumer goods must meet the growing consumer demand in full, and must conform to its changes. Timely output of goods in accordance with the varied demand of the population, with consideration for local, national, and climatic conditions, is an imperative requirement for the consumer industries. Good shopping facilities will be arranged throughout the country, this being a necessary and important condition for the satisfaction of the growing requirements of the population.

The second decade will see an abundance of material and cultural benefits for the whole population, and material prerequisites will be created to complete the transition to the Communist principle of distribution according to need in the period to follow.

B. *Solution of the Housing Problem and Improvement of Living Conditions.*

The C.P.S.U. undertakes the task of solving the most acute problem in the improvement of the well-being of the Soviet people—the housing problem. As a result, in the second decade, every family, including newlyweds, will have a comfortable flat conforming to the requirements of hygiene and cultured living. Peasant houses of the old type will, in the main, give place to new modern dwellings or—wherever possible—they will be rebuilt and appropriately improved. In the course of the second decade housing will be gradually provided to all citizens rent free.

An extensive program of public-services construction and of improvements in all towns and workers' estates will be carried out in the coming period, which will involve completion of their electrification, the necessary gasification, provision of public-transport facilities and waterworks, and measures for the further improvement of sanitary conditions in towns and other populated localities, including tree planting, pond building, and effective measures to combat air, soil, and water pollution. Well-appointed small and middle-sized towns will be increasingly developed, making for better and healthier living conditions.

Public-transport facilities (tramways, buses, trolley buses, and subways) will become free in the course of the second decade, and at the end of it such amenities as water, gas, and heating will also be free.

C. *Reduction of Working Hours and the Further Improvement of Working Conditions.*

In the coming ten years the country will go over to a six-hour working day with one day off a week, or a thirty-four-to-thirty-six-hour working week with two days off, and in underground and harmful jobs to a five-hour working day or a thirty-hour, five-day working week.

By virtue of a corresponding rise in labor productivity, transition to a still shorter working week will be begun in the second decade.

The Soviet Union will thus have the world's shortest and, concurrently, the most productive and highest-paid working day. Working people will have much more leisure time, and this will add to their opportunities of improving their culture and technical level.

The length of the annual paid holidays of working people will be increased together with the reduction of the working day. Gradually the minimum length of leave for all industrial, professional, and office workers will increase to three weeks and subsequently to one month. Paid holidays will be gradually extended to kolkhoz members.

All-round measures to make working conditions healthier and lighter constitute an important task in improving the well-being of the people. Modern means of labor safety and hygiene designed to prevent occupational injuries and diseases will be introduced at all enterprises. Night shifts will be gradually abolished at enterprises, save those where round-the-clock operation is required by the production process or the need to service the population.

D. *Health Services and Measures for Increased Longevity.*

The Socialist state is the only state which undertakes to protect and continuously improve the health of the whole population. This is provided for by a system of socio-economic and medical measures. There will be an extensive program designed to prevent and sharply reduce diseases, wipe out mass infectious diseases, and further increase longevity. The needs of the urban and rural population in all forms of highly qualified medical services will be met in full. This calls for the extensive building of medical institutions, including hospitals and sanatoria, the equipment of all medical institutions with modern appliances, and regular medical check-ups for the entire population. Special emphasis must be laid on extending in town and country the network of mother-and-child health institutions (maternity homes, medical consultation centers, children's health homes and hospitals, forest schools, etc.).

In addition to the existing free medical services, accommodation of sick persons at sanatoria and the dispensing of medicines will become gratuitous. In order to afford the population an opportunity to rest in an out-of-town environment, holiday homes, boardinghouses, country hotels, and tourist camps will be built, where working people will be accommodated at a reasonable charge or by way of a bonus, as well as at a discount or gratis.

The Party considers it a most important task to ensure the education from early childhood of a sound young generation harmoniously developed physically and spiritually. This calls for utmost encouragement of all forms of mass sport and physical training, specifically at schools, and for drawing greater and greater sections of the population, particularly the youth, into sports.

E. Improvement of Family Conditions and of the Position of Women. Maintenance of Children and Incapacitated People at Public Expense.

The remnants of the unequal position of women in domestic life must be totally eliminated. Social and living conditions must be provided to enable women to combine happy motherhood with increasingly active and creative participation in social labor and social activities, and in scientific and artistic pursuits. Women must be given relatively lighter and yet sufficiently well-paid jobs. Leave of absence from work during confinement will be of longer duration.

It is essential to provide conditions to reduce and lighten the domestic work of women, and later to make possible the replacement of domestic work by public forms of satisfying the daily needs of the family. Up-to-date inexpensive domestic machinery, appliances, and electrical devices will be made extensively available for this purpose; the needs of the population in service establishments will be fully met in the next few years.

The extension of public catering, including canteens at enterprises, institutions, and in big dwelling houses, until it meets the demands of the population, calls for special attention. The service at catering establishments and the quality of catering must be radically improved, so that meals at public catering establishments should be tasty and nourishing and should cost the family less than meals cooked at home. Price reductions in public catering will keep ahead of price reductions for foodstuffs in the shops. By virtue of this, public catering will be able to take precedence over home cooking within ten to fifteen years.

The transition of free public catering (midday meals) at enterprises and institutions, and for collective farmers at work will begin in the second decade.

A happy childhood for every child is one of the most important and noble aspects of Communist construction. The development of a ramified network of children's institutions will make it possible for more and more families, and in the second decade for every family to keep children and adolescents free of charge at children's establishments if they so desire. State and community children's institutions will be able to accommodate the bulk of children under school age within the next few years.

In town and country there will be full and cost-free satisfaction of the need in kindergartens, playgrounds, nurseries, and young pioneer camps, the provision of mass boarding schools with free maintenance of children, free hot meals at all schools, introduction of extended school hours with free dinners for schoolchildren, and free issue of school uniforms and educational aids.

In keeping with the growth of the national income, the state, the trade unions, and the kolkhozes will in the course of the twenty years gradually undertake maintenance of all citizens incapacitated through old age or some disability. Sickness and temporary disability grants and old-age pensions will be extended to kolkhoz members; old-age and disability pensions will be steadily raised. The number of comfortable homes for old people and invalids providing free accommodations for all applicants will be greatly increased in town and country.

By fulfilling the tasks set by the Party for the improvement of the well-being of the people, the Soviet Union will make considerable headway toward the practical realization of the Communist principle of distribution according to need.

At the end of twenty years public consumption funds will total about half of the aggregate real income of the population. This will make it possible to provide at public expense:

Free maintenance of children at children's institutions and boarding schools (if parents wish);

Maintenance of disabled people;

Free education at all educational establishments;

Free medical services for all citizens, including the supply of medicines and the treatment of sick persons at sanatoria;

Rent-free housing and, later, free public services, free public transport facilities;

Free use of some types of communal services;

Steady reduction of charges for and, partially, free use of holiday homes, boardinghouses, and tourist camps;

Increasingly broad provision of the population with benefits, privileges, and scholarships (grants to unmarried mothers, scholarships for students);

Gradual introduction of free public catering (midday meals) at enterprises and institutions, and for kolkhoz farmers at work.

The Soviet state will thus demonstrate to the world a truly full satisfaction of all the growing material and cultural requirements of man. The living standard of Soviet people will improve all the faster, the faster the productive forces of the country develop and labor productivity grows, and the more broadly the creative energy of the Soviet people comes into play.

The set program can be fulfilled with success under conditions of peace. Complications in the international situation and the resultant necessity of increasing defense expenditures may hold up the fulfillment of the plans for raising the living standard of the people. An enduring normalization of international relations, reduction of military expenditures, and, in particular, the realization of general and complete disarmament under an appropriate agreement between countries, would make it possible greatly to surpass the plans for raising the people's living standard.

The fulfillment of the grand program of improving the living standard of the Soviet people will have world-wide historic impact. The Party calls on the Soviet people to work perseveringly, with inspiration. Every one of the working people of the Soviet Union must do his duty in the building of a Communist society and in the struggle to fulfill the program for the improvement of the people's living standard.

III. The Tasks of the Party in the Spheres of State Development and the Further Promotion of Socialist Democracy

The dictatorship of the proletariat, born of the Socialist revolution, has played an epoch-making role by insuring the victory of socialism in the U.S.S.R. In the course of Socialist construction, however, it underwent changes. After the exploiting classes had been abolished, the state function of suppressing their resistance ceased to exist. The chief functions of the Socialist state—organization of the economy, culture, and education—have developed in full measure. The Socialist state has entered a new phase.

The state has begun to grow over into a nation-wide organization of the working people of Socialist society. Proletarian democracy is becoming more and more a Socialist democracy of the people as a whole. The working class is the only class in history that does not aim to perpetuate its power. Having brought about a complete and final victory of socialism—the first phase of communism—and the transition of society to the full-scale construction of communism, the dictatorship of the proletariat has fulfilled its historic mission and has ceased to be indispensable in the U.S.S.R. from the point of view of the tasks of internal development.

The state, which arose as a state of the dictatorship of the proletariat, has become a state of the entire people, an organ expressing the interests and will of the people as a whole. Since the working class is the foremost and best-organized force of Soviet society, it plays a leading role also in the period of the full-scale construction of communism. The working class will have completed its function of leader of society after communism is built and classes disappear.

The Party holds that the dictatorship of the working class will cease to be necessary before the state withers away. The state as an organization embracing the entire people will survive until the complete victory of communism.

Expressing the will of the people, it must organize the building up of the material and technical basis of communism, and the transformation of Socialist relations into Communist relations, must exercise control over the measure of work and rate of consumption, promote welfare, protect the rights and freedom of Soviet citizens, Socialist law and order and Socialist property, instill in the people conscious discipline and a Communist attitude to labor, guarantee the defense and security of the country, promote fraternal co-operation with the Socialist countries, uphold world peace and maintain normal relations with all countries.

Vigorous extension and perfection of Socialist democracy, active participation of all citizens in the administration of the state, in the management of economic and cultural development, improvement of the government apparatus, and increased control over its activity by the people constitute the main direction in which Socialist statehood develops in the period of the building of communism.

As Socialist democracy develops, the organs of state power will gradually be transformed into organs of public self-government. The Leninist principle of democratic centralism, which insures the proper combination of centralized leadership with the maximum encouragement of local initiative, the extension of the rights of the union republics and greater creative activity of the masses, will be promoted. It is essential to strengthen discipline, control the activities of all the elements of the administrative apparatus, check the execution of the decisions and laws of the Soviet state, and heighten the responsibility of every official for the strict and timely implementation of these laws.

(1) The Soviets and Promotion of the Democratic Principles of Government.

The role of the Soviets, which have become an all-inclusive organization of the people embodying their unity, will grow as Communist construction progresses. The Soviets, which combine the features of a government body and a social organization, operate more and more like social organizations, with the masses participating in their work extensively and directly.

The Party considers it essential to perfect the forms of popular representation and promote the democratic principles of the Soviet electoral system.

In nominating candidates for election to the Soviets, it is necessary to guarantee the widest and fullest discussion of the personal and professional qualities of the candidates at meetings and in the press to insure the election of the worthiest and most authoritative of them.

To improve the work of the Soviets and bring fresh forces into them, it is desirable that at least one-third of the total number of deputies to a Soviet should be elected anew each time so that more hundreds of thousands and millions of working people may learn to govern the state.

The Party considers systematic renewal of the leading bodies necessary to bring a wider range of able persons into them and rule out abuses of authority by individual government officials. It is advisable to introduce the principle that the leading officials of the union, republican, and local bodies should be elected to their offices, as a rule, for not more than three consecutive terms. In those cases when the personal gifts of the official in question are generally believed to make his further activity within a leading body useful and necessary, his re-election may be allowed. His election shall be considered valid, not if he wins with a simple majority, but if not less than three-quarters of the votes are cast in his favor.

The Party regards the perfection of the principles of Socialist democracy and their rigid observance as a most important task. It is necessary to develop more and more fully regular accountability of Soviets and deputies to their constituents and the right of the electorate to recall ahead of term deputies who have not justified confidence placed in them, publicity and the free and full discussion of all the important questions of government and of economic and cultural development at the meetings of Soviets, regular accountability of executive government bodies to meetings of Soviets—from top to bottom, checking the work of these bodies and control over their activity, systematic discussion by the Soviets of questions raised by deputies, criticism of shortcomings in the work of government, economic, and other organizations.

Every deputy to a Soviet must take an active part in government affairs and carry on definite work. The role of the standing committees of the Soviets will become greater. The standing committees of the Supreme Soviets must systematically control the activities of ministries, departments, and economic councils. They must actively contribute to the implementation of the decisions adopted by the respective Supreme Soviets. To improve the work of the legislative bodies and increase control over the executive bodies, deputies shall be periodically released from their official duties for full-time committee work.

An increasing number of questions which now come under the jurisdiction of the departments and sections of executive bodies must be gradually referred to the standing committee of the local Soviets for decision.

The rights of the local Soviets of Working People's Deputies (local self-government) will be extended. Local Soviets will make final decisions on all questions of local significance.

Special attention should be paid to the strengthening of the district bodies. As kolkhoz-co-operative and public property draws closer together, a single democratic body administering all enterprises, organizations, and institutions at district level will gradually take shape.

The participation of social organizations and associations of the people in the legislative activity of the representative bodies of the Soviet state will be extended. The trade unions, the Komsomol (Y.C.L.), and other mass organizations as represented by their all-union and republican bodies must be given the right to take legislative initiative, that is, to propose draft laws.

Discussion by the people of draft laws and other decisions of both national and local significance must become the rule. The most important draft laws should be put to a nation-wide referendum.

The C.P.S.U. attaches great importance to improving the work of the government apparatus, which is largely responsible for the proper utilization of all the resources of the country and the timely settlement of all questions relating to the cultural and everyday needs of the people. The Soviet government apparatus must be simple, qualified, inexpensive, efficient, and free of bureaucracy, formalism, and red tape.

Constant state and public control is an important means of accomplishing this task. In keeping with Lenin's directions, permanent control bodies must function to combine state control with public inspection at the center and in the localities. The Party regards inspection by people's control bodies as an effective means of drawing large sections of the people into the management of state affairs, and control over the strict observance of legality as a means of perfecting the government apparatus, eradicating bureaucracy, and promptly realizing proposals made by the people.

The government apparatus of the Socialist state serves the people and is accountable to them. Negligence and abuse of power by an official must be resolutely combated and the official concerned must be severely punished regardless of the position he holds. It is the duty of Soviet people to see to it that legality and law and order are rigidly enforced. They must not tolerate any abuses, and must combat them.

The Party holds that democratic principles in administration must be developed further. The principle of electivity and accountability to representative bodies and to the electorate will be gradually extended to all the leading officials of state bodies.

An effort should be made to insure that the salaried government staffs are reduced, that ever larger sections of the people learn to take part in administration, and that work on government staffs eventually ceases to constitute a profession.

While every executive must be held strictly and personally responsible for the job entrusted to him, it is necessary consistently to exercise the principle of collective leadership at all levels of the government and economic apparatus.

The broadest democracy must go hand in hand with strict observance of comradely discipline by the working people, which it must promote through control from above and from below. The important thing in the activity of all government bodies is organizational work among the masses, proper selection, testing, and appraisal of officials on the strength of their practical work, and control over the actual fulfillment of the assignments and decisions of the leading bodies.

The further promotion of Socialist law and order and the improvement of legal rules governing economic, organizational, cultural, and educational work and contributing to the accomplishment of the tasks of Communist construction and to the all-round development of the individual are very important.

The transition to communism means the fullest extension of personal freedom and the rights of Soviet citizens. Socialism has granted the working people the broadest guaranteed rights and freedoms. Communism will bring the working people further great rights and opportunities.

The Party calls for enforcing strict observance of Socialist legality, to eradicate all violations of law and order, abolish crime, and remove all the causes of crime.

Justice in the U.S.S.R. is exercised in full conformity with the law. It is based on truly democratic lines: election and accountability of the judges and people's assessors, the right to recall them before expiration of their term, the publicity of court proceedings, and the participation of prosecutors and defenders appointed by social organizations in the work of courts with strict observance of legality and all the rules of judicial procedure. The democratic foundations of justice will be developed and improved.

There should be no room for lawbreakers and criminals

in a society building communism. But as long as there are criminal offenses, it is necessary severely to punish those who commit crimes dangerous to society, violate the rules of the Socialist community, and refuse to live by honest labor. Attention should be focused on crime prevention.

Higher standards of living and culture and greater social consciousness of the people will pave the way to the abolition of crime and the ultimate replacement of judicial punishment by measures of public influence and education. Under socialism, anyone who has strayed from the path of a working man can return to useful activity.

The whole system of government and social organizations educates the people in a spirit of voluntary and conscientious fulfillment of their duties and leads to a natural fusion of rights and duties to form the integral rules of Communist society.

(2) The Further Heightening of the Role of Social Organizations. The State and Communism.

The role of social organizations increases in the period of the full-scale construction of communism. The trade unions acquire particular importance as schools of administration and economic management, as schools of communism. The Party will help the trade unions to take a growing share in economic management and to make the standing production conferences increasingly effective in improving the work of enterprises and exercising control over production. The trade unions shall:

Work constantly to increase the Communist consciousness of the masses, organize an emulation movement for Communist labor, and help the people in learning to manage state and social affairs, take an active part in controlling the measure of labor and rate of consumption;

Encourage the activity of factory and office workers, enlisting their aid in the work for continuous technical progress, for higher productivity of labor, for the fulfillment and overfulfillment of state plans and assignments;

Work steadfastly for the improvement of the skill of factory and office workers and their working and living conditions, protect the material interests and rights of the working people;

Insure that housing and cultural development plans are fulfilled and that public catering, trade, social insurance, and health resort services are improved;

Insure control over the spending of public consumption funds and over the work of all enterprises and institutions serving the people;

Improve cultural services and recreation facilities for the working people, encourage physical training and sports.

The Young Communist League, a voluntary social organization of the youth which helps the Party to educate young people in a Communist spirit, enlist them in the practical job of building the new society, and train a generation of harmoniously developed people who will live, work, and manage public affairs under communism, will play a greater role. The Party regards the youth as a great creative force in the Soviet people's struggle for communism.

The Y.C.L. must display greater initiative in all fields of activity, must encourage the activity and labor heroism of youth. Y.C.L. organizations must concentrate on educating the youth in a spirit of utmost devotion to their country, the people, the Communist Party and the Communist cause, constant preparedness for labor for the good of the country and for overcoming all difficulties and improving the general education and technical knowledge of all young men and women.

It is the sacred duty of the Y.C.L. to prepare young people for the defense of their Socialist country, to educate them as selfless patriots capable of firmly repelling any enemy and also to educate the youth in a spirit of strict adherence to Communist moral principles and standards. Y.C.L. influence in the schools and Young Pioneer organizations must contribute actively to the molding of a buoyant, industrious, and physically and morally sound generation.

A greater role will be played by co-operatives—kolkhozes, consumers', housing, and other co-operative organizations—as a form of drawing the masses into Communist construction, as media of Communist education and schools of public self-government.

Other social associations of the working people—scientific and scientific-technical societies, rationalizers' and inventors' organizations, associations of writers, artists, and journalists, cultural-education organizations, and sports societies will likewise be developed.

The Party regards it as a major task of the social organizations to promote labor emulation in every possible way and to encourage Communist forms of labor to stimulate the activity of working people in building a Communist society, to work for the improvement of the living conditions of the people. Social organizations should be induced to take a greater part in managing cultural and health institutions; within the next few years they should be entrusted with the management of theaters and concert halls, clubs, libraries, and other state-controlled cultural-education establishments; they should be encouraged to play a greater part in promoting public order, particularly through the people's volunteer squads and comradely courts.

To extend the independent activities of members of social organizations, the Party considers it necessary further to reduce their salaried staffs from top to bottom, to renew each public body by roughly as many as one-half of its members at the regular election, and to consider it advisable for the leading functionaries of social organizations not to be elected, as a general rule, for more than two consecutive terms.

As Socialist statehood develops, it will gradually become public Communist self-government which will embrace the Soviets, trade unions, co-operatives, and other mass organizations of the people. This process will represent a still greater development of democracy, ensuring the active participation of all members of society in the management of public affairs.

Public functions similar to those performed by the state today in the sphere of economic and cultural management will be preserved under communism and will be modified and perfected as society develops. But the character of the functions and the ways in which they are carried out will be different from those under socialism. The bodies in charge of planning, accounting, economic management, and cultural advancement, now government bodies, will lose their political character and will become organs of public self-government. Communist society will be a highly organized community of working men. Universally recognized rules of the Communist way of life will be established whose observance will become an organic need and habit with everyone.

Historical development inevitably leads to the withering away of the state. To insure that the state withers away completely, it is necessary to provide both internal conditions—the building of a developed Communist society—and external conditions—the final settlement of the contradictions between capitalism and communism in the world arena in favor of communism.

(3) The Strengthening of the Armed Forces and the Defense Potential of the Soviet Union.

With the wholehearted support of the entire Soviet people, the C.P.S.U. steadfastly upholds and defends the gains of socialism and the cause of world peace, and works tirelessly to deliver mankind for all time from wars of aggression. The Leninist principle of peaceful coexistence has been, and remains, the general principle of the foreign policy of the Soviet state.

The Soviet Union perseveringly seeks to bring about the realization of the proposals for general and complete disarmament under strict international control. But the imperialist countries stubbornly refuse to accept these proposals, and feverishly build up their armed forces. They refuse to reconcile themselves to the existence of the world Socialist system, and openly proclaim their insane plans for the liquidation of the Soviet Union and the other Socialist states through war. This obliges the Communist Party, the armed forces, the state security organs, and all the peoples of the U.S.S.R. to be keenly vigilant with regard to the aggressive intrigues of the enemies of peace, always to protect peaceful labor, and to be constantly prepared to take up arms in defense of their country.

The Party maintains that as long as imperialism survives, the threat of aggressive wars will remain. The C.P.S.U. regards the defense of the Socialist motherland, and the strengthening of the defense potential of the U.S.S.R., of the might of the Soviet armed forces, as a sacred duty of the Party and Soviet people as a whole, as a most important function of the Socialist state. The Soviet Union sees it as its internationalist duty to guarantee, together with the other Socialist countries, the reliable defense and security of the entire Socialist camp.

In terms of internal conditions, the Soviet Union needs no army. But since the danger of war coming from the imperialist camp persists, and since complete and general disarmament has not been achieved, the C.P.S.U. considers it necessary to maintain the defensive power of the Soviet state and the combat preparedness of its armed forces at a level insuring the decisive and complete defeat of any enemy who dares to encroach upon the Soviet Union. The Soviet state will see to it that its armed forces are powerful; that they have the most up-to-date means of defending the country—atomic and thermonuclear weapons, rockets of every range, and that they keep all types of military equipment and all weapons up to standard.

The Party educates the Communists and all Soviet people in the spirit of constant preparedness for the defense of their Socialist country, of love of their armed forces. Defense of the country, and service in the Soviet armed forces, is a lofty and honorable duty of Soviet citizens.

The C.P.S.U. is doing everything to insure that the Soviet armed forces are a well-knit and smoothly operating organism, that they have a high standard of organization and discipline, and carry out in exemplary fashion the tasks assigned them by the Party, the government, and the people, and are prepared at any moment to administer a crushing rebuff to imperialist aggressors. One-man leadership is a major principle of the organization of the Soviet armed forces.

The Party will work indefatigably to train army and navy officers and political personnel fully devoted to the Communist cause and recruited among the finest representatives of the Soviet people. It considers it necessary for the officer corps tirelessly to master Marxist-Leninist theory, to possess a high standard of military-technical training, meet all the requirements of modern military theory and practice, strengthen military discipline. All Soviet soldiers must be educated in the spirit of unqualified loyalty to the people, to the Communist cause, of readiness to spare no effort and, if necessary, to give their lives in the defense of their Socialist country.

Party leadership of the armed forces, and the increasing role and influence of the Party organizations in the army and navy are the bedrock of military development. The Party works unremittingly to increase its organizing and guiding influence on the entire life and activity of the army, air force, and navy, to rally the servicemen round the Communist Party and the Soviet government, to strengthen the unity of the armed forces and the people, and to educate the soldiers in the spirit of courage, bravery, and heroism, or readiness at any moment to take up the defense of their Soviet country, which is building communism.

iv. The Tasks of the Party in the Field of National Relations

Under socialism the nations flourish and their sovereignty grows stronger. The development of nations does not proceed along the lines of strengthening national barriers, national narrow-mindedness and egoism, as it does under capitalism, but along lines of their association, fraternal mutual assistance and friendship. The appearance of new industrial centers, the prospecting and development of mineral deposits, the virgin land development project, and the growth of all modes of transport increase the mobility of the population and promote greater intercourse between the peoples of the Soviet Union.

People of many nationalities live together and work in harmony in the Soviet republics. The boundaries between the constituent republics of the U.S.S.R. are increasingly losing their former significance, since all the nations are equal, their life is based on a common Socialist foundation, the material and spiritual needs of every people are satisfied to the same extent, and they are all united in a single family by common vital interests and are advancing together to the common goal—communism.

Spiritual features deriving from the new type of social relations and embodying the finest traditions of the peoples of the U.S.S.R. have taken shape and are common to Soviet men and women of different nationalities.

Full-scale Communist construction constitutes a new stage in the development of national relations in the U.S.S.R. in which the nations will draw still closer together until complete unity is achieved. The building of the material and technical basis of communism leads to a still greater unity of the Soviet peoples. The exchange of material and cultural wealth between nations becomes more and more intensive, and the contribution of each republic to the common cause of Communist construction increases.

Obliteration of distinctions between classes and the development of Communist social relations make for a greater social homogeneity of nations and contribute to the development of common Communist traits in their culture, morals, and way of living, to a further strengthening of their mutual trust and friendship.

With the victory of communism in the U.S.S.R., the nations will draw still closer together, their economic and ideological unity will increase, and the Communist traits common to their spiritual make-up will develop. However, the effacement of national distinctions, and especially of language distinctions, is a considerably longer process than the effacement of class distinctions.

The Party approaches all questions of national relationships arising in the course of Communist construction from the standpoint of proletarian internationalism and firm pursuance of the Leninist national policy. The Party neither ignores nor overaccentuates national characteristics.

The Party sets the following tasks in the sphere of national relations:

A. To continue the all-round economic and cultural development of all the Soviet nations, insuring their increasingly close fraternal co-operation, mutual aid, unity and affinity in all spheres of life, thus achieving the utmost strengthening of the Union of Soviet Socialist Republics; to make full use of, and advance the forms of, national statehood of the peoples of the U.S.S.R.;

B. In the economic sphere, it is necessary to pursue the line of comprehensive development of the economies of the Soviet republics, effect a rational geographic location of production and a planned working of natural wealth, and promote Socialist division of labor among the republics, unifying and combining their economic efforts, and properly balancing the interests of the state as a whole and those of each Soviet republic.

The extension of the rights of the union republics in economic management having produced substantial positive results, such measures may also be carried out in the future, with due regard to the fact that the creation of the material and technical basis of communism will call for still greater interconnection and mutual assistance between the Soviet republics. The closer the intercourse between the nations and the greater awareness of the country-wide tasks, the more successfully can manifestations of parochialism and national egoism be overcome.

In order to insure the successful accomplishment of the tasks of Communist construction and the co-ordination of economic activities, inter-republican economic organs may be set up in some zones, notably for such matters as irrigation, power grids, transport, etc.

The Party will continue its policy of insuring the actual equality of all nations and nationalities with full consideration for their interests and devoting special attention to those areas of the country which are in need of more rapid development. Benefits accumulating in the course of Communist construction must be fairly distributed among all nations and nationalities;

C. To work for the further all-round development of the Socialist culture of the peoples of the U.S.S.R. The big scale of Communist construction and the new victories of Communist ideology are enriching the cultures of the peoples of the U.S.S.R., which are Socialist in content and national in form. The ideological unity of the nations and nationalities is growing, and there is a rapprochement of their cultures. The historical experience of the development of Socialist nations shows that national forms do not ossify; they change, advance, and draw closer together, shedding all outdated traits that contradict the new living conditions. An international culture common to all the Soviet nations is developing. The cultural treasures of each nation are increasingly augmented by works of international import.

Attaching decisive importance to the development of

the Socialist content of the cultures of the peoples of the U.S.S.R., the Party will promote their further mutual enrichment and rapprochement, the consolidation of their international basis, and thereby the formation of the future single world-wide culture of Communist society. While supporting the progressive traditions of each people, and making them the property of all Soviet people, the Party will in all ways further new revolutionary traditions of the builders of communism common to all nations;

D. To continue promoting the free development of the languages of the peoples of the U.S.S.R. and the complete freedom of every citizen of the U.S.S.R. to speak, and to bring up and educate his children in any language, ruling out all privileges, restrictions, or compulsions in the use of this or that language. By virtue of the fraternal friendship and mutual trust of peoples, national languages are developing on a basis of equality and mutual enrichment.

The voluntary study of Russian in addition to the native language is of positive significance, since it facilitates reciprocal exchanges of experience and access of every nation and nationality to the cultural gains of all the other peoples of the U.S.S.R., and to world culture. The Russian language has, in effect, become the common medium of intercourse and co-operation between all the peoples of the U.S.S.R.;

E. To pursue consistently as heretofore the principles of internationalism in the field of national relations, to strengthen the friendship of peoples as one of the most important gains of socialism, to conduct a relentless struggle against manifestations and survivals of nationalism and chauvinism of all types, against trends of national narrow-mindedness and exclusiveness, idealization of the past and the veiling of social contradictions in the history of peoples, and against obsolete customs and habits. The growing scale of Communist construction calls for the continuous exchange of trained personnel among the nations. Manifestations of national aloofness in the education and employment of workers of different nationalities in the Soviet republics are impermissible. The liquidation of manifestations of nationalism is in the interests of all nations and nationalities of the U.S.S.R.

Every Soviet republic can continue to flourish and strengthen only in the great family of fraternal Socialist nations of the U.S.S.R.

v. The Tasks of the Party in the Spheres of Ideology, Education, Instruction, Science, and Culture

Soviet society has made great progress in the Socialist education of the masses, in the molding of active builders of socialism. But even after the Socialist system has triumphed, there persist in the minds and behavior of people survivals of capitalism, which hamper the progress of society.

In the struggle for the victory of communism, ideological work becomes an increasingly powerful factor. The higher the social consciousness of the members of society, the more fully and broadly their creative activities come into play in the building of the material and technical basis of communism, in the development of Communist forms of labor and new relations between people, and, consequently, the more rapidly and successfully the building of communism proceeds.

The Party considers that the paramount task in the ideological field in the present period is to educate all working people in a spirit of ideological integrity and devotion to communism, and cultivate in them a Communist attitude to labor and the social economy, to eliminate completely the survivals of bourgeois views and morals, to insure the all-round, harmonious development of the individual, to create a truly rich spiritual culture. Special importance is attached by the Party to the molding of the rising generation.

The molding of the new man is effected through his own active participation in Communist construction and the development of Communist principles in the economic and social spheres, under the influence of the educational work carried out by the Party, the state, and various social organizations, work in which the press, radio, cinema, and television play an important part. As Communist forms of social organization are created, devotion to Communist ideas will become stronger in life and work and in human relations, and people will develop the ability to enjoy the benefits of communism in a rational way. Joint planned labor by the members of society, their daily participation in the management of state and public affairs, and the development of Communist relations of comradely co-operation and mutual support recast the minds of people in a spirit of collectivism, industry, and humanism.

Increased Communist consciousness of the people furthers the ideological and political unity of the workers, collective farmers, and intellectuals and promotes their gradual fusion in the single collective of the working people of Communist society.

The Party sets the following tasks:

(1) In the Field of Development of Communist Consciousness.

A. The Shaping of a Scientific World Outlook.

Under socialism and at a time when a Communist society is being built, when spontaneous economic development has given way to the conscious organization of promotion and social life as a whole, and when theory is daily translated into practice, the shaping of a scientific world outlook in all working people is of prime importance. The ideological basis of this world outlook is shaped as Marxism-Leninism, an integral and harmonious system of philosophical, economic, and sociopolitical views. The Party calls for the education of the population as a whole in the spirit of scientific communism and strives to insure that all working people master the ideas of Marxism-Leninism, that they fully understand the course and perspectives of world development, take a correct view of international and domestic events, and consciously build their life on Communist lines. Communist ideas and Communist deeds should blend organically in the behavior of every person and in the activities of all collectives and organizations.

The theoretical elaboration and timely practical solution of new problems raised by life are essential to the successful advance of society to communism. Theory must continue to illuminate the road of practice, and help detect and eliminate difficulties and contradictions hindering successful Communist construction. The Party regards as one of its most important duties to further elaborate Marxist-Leninist theory by studying and generalizing new phenomena in the life of Soviet society and the experience of the world revolutionary working-class and liberation movements, and creatively to combine the theory and the practice of Communist construction.

B. Labor Education.

The Party sees the development of a Communist attitude to labor in all members of society as its chief educational task. Labor for the benefit of society is the sacred duty of all. Any labor for society, whether physical or mental, is honorable and commands respect. Exemplary labor and outstanding management in the social economy should serve to educate all working people.

Everything required for life and human progress is created by labor. Hence everyone must take part in creating the means which are indispensable for his life and work and for the welfare of society. Anyone who received any benefits from society without doing his share of work would be a parasite living at the expense of others.

It is impossible for a man in Communist society not to work, for neither his social consciousness nor public opinion would permit it. Work according to one's ability will become a habit, a prime necessity of life, for every member of society.

C. The Affirmation of Communist Morality.

In the course of transition to communism, the moral principles of society become increasingly important, the sphere of action of the moral factor expands, and the importance of the administrative control of human relations diminishes accordingly. The Party will encourage all forms of conscious civic self-discipline leading to the assertion and promotion of the basic rules of the Communist way of life.

The Communists reject the class morality of the exploiters; in contrast to the perverse, selfish views and morals of the old world, they promote Communist morality, which is the noblest and most just morality, for it expresses the interests and ideals of the whole of working mankind.

Communism makes the elementary standards of morality and justice, which were distorted or shamelessly flouted under the power of the exploiters, into inviolable rules for relations both between individuals and between peoples. Communist morality encompasses the fundamental norms of human morality which the masses of the people evolved in the course of millenniums as they fought against vice and social oppression. The revolutionary morality of the working class is of particular importance to the moral advancement of society. As Socialist and Communist construction progresses, Communist morality is enriched with new principles, a new content.

The Party holds that the moral code of the builder of communism should comprise the following principles:

Devotion to the Communist cause, love of the Socialist motherland and of the other Socialist countries;

Conscientious labor for the good of society—he who does not work, neither shall he eat;

Concern on the part of everyone for the preservation and growth of public wealth;

A high sense of public duty, intolerance of actions harmful to the public interest;

Collectivism and comradely mutual assistance: one for all and all for one;

Humane relations and mutual respect between individuals—man is to man a friend, comrade, and brother;

Honesty and truthfulness, moral purity, modesty and guilelessness in social and private life;

Mutual respect in the family, and concern for the upbringing of children;

An uncompromising attitude to injustice, parasitism, dishonesty, and careerism;

Friendship and brotherhood among all peoples of the U.S.S.R., intolerance of national and racial hatred;

An uncompromising attitude to the enemies of communism, peace, and the freedom of nations;

Fraternal solidarity with the working people of all countries, and with all peoples.

D. The Promotion of Proletarian Internationalism and Socialist Patriotism.

The Party will untiringly educate the Soviet people in the spirit of proletarian internationalism and will vigorously promote the international solidarity of the working people. In fostering the Soviet people's love of their country, the Party maintains that with the emergence of the world Socialist system the patriotism of the members of Socialist society is expressed in devotion and loyalty to their own country and to the entire comity of Socialist countries.

Socialist patriotism and Socialist internationalism necessarily imply proletarian solidarity with the working class and all working people of all countries. The Party will continue perseveringly to combat the reactionary ideology of bourgeois nationalism, racism, and cosmopolitanism.

E. All-Round and Harmonious Development of the Individual.

In the period of transition to communism, there are greater opportunities of educating a new man, who will harmoniously combine spiritual wealth, moral purity, and a perfect physique.

All-round development of the individual has been made possible by historic social gains—freedom from exploitation, unemployment, and poverty, from discrimination on account of sex, origin, nationality, or race. Every member of society is provided with equal opportunities for education and creative labor. Relations of dependence and inequality between people in public affairs and in family life disappear. The personal dignity of each citizen is protected by society. Each is guaranteed an equal and free choice of occupation and profession with due regard to the interests of society.

As less and less time is spent on material production, the individual is afforded ever greater opportunities to develop his abilities, gifts, and talents in the fields of production, science, engineering, literature, and the arts. People will increasingly devote their leisure to public pursuits, cultural intercourse, intellectual and physical development, and artistic endeavor. Physical training and sports will become part and parcel of the everyday life of people.

F. Elimination of the Survivals of Capitalism in the Minds and Behavior of People.

The Party considers it an integral part of its Communist education work to combat manifestations of bourgeois ideology and morality, and the remnants of private-owner psychology, superstitions, and prejudices.

The general public, public opinion, and extensive criticism and self-criticism must play a big role in combating survivals of the past and manifestations of individualism and selfishness.

Comradely censure of anti-social behavior will gradually become the principal means of doing away with manifestations of bourgeois views, customs, and habits. The power of example in public affairs and in private life, in the performance of one's public duty, acquires tremendous educational significance.

The Party uses ideological media to educate people in the spirit of a scientific materialist world conception, to overcome religious prejudices without insulting the sentiments of believers. It is necessary to explain patiently the untenability of religious beliefs, which were engendered in the past when people were overawed by the elemental forces and social oppression and did not know the real causes of natural and social phenomena. This can be done by making use of the achievements of modern science, which steadily solves the mysteries of the universe and extends man's power over nature, leaving no room for religious inventions about supernatural forces.

G. The Exposure of Bourgeois Ideology.

The peaceful coexistence of states with different social systems does not imply discontinuance of the ideological struggle. The Communist Party will go on exposing the anti-popular, reactionary nature of capitalism and all attempts to draw pretty pictures of the capitalist system. The Party will steadfastly propagate the great advantages of socialism and communism over the declining capitalist system.

The Party advances the scientific ideology of communism in contrast to reactionary bourgeois ideology. Communist ideology, which expresses the fundamental interests of the working class and all working people, teaches them to struggle to live and work for the happiness of all. It is the most humane ideology. Its ideals are to establish truly humane relations between individuals and peoples, to deliver mankind from the threat of extermination, and bring about universal peace and a free, happy life for all men on earth.

(2) In the Field of Public Education.

The transition to communism implies training that will make people Communist-minded and highly cultured, thus fitting them for both physical and mental labor, for active work in various social, governmental, scientific, and cultural spheres.

The system of public education is so organized as to insure that the instruction and education of the rising generation are closely bound up with life and productive labor, and that the adult population can combine work in the sphere of production with further training and education in keeping with their vocations and the requirements of society. Public education along these lines will make for the molding of harmoniously developed members of Communist society and for the solution of a cardinal social problem, namely, the elimination of substantial distinctions between mental and physical labor.

The main tasks in the field of instruction and education are:

A. The Introduction of Universal Compulsory Secondary Education.

In the next decade compulsory secondary general and polytechnical eleven-year education is to be introduced for all children of school age, and education of eight grades for young people engaged in the national economy who have not had the appropriate schooling. In the subsequent decade everyone is to receive a complete secondary education. Universal secondary education is guaranteed by the development of general and polytechnical education along with the participation of schoolchildren in socially useful labor to the extent of their physical capacity, as well as by a considerable expansion of the network of evening schools, which provide a secondary education in off-work hours.

Secondary education must furnish a solid knowledge of the fundamentals of the basic sciences, an understanding of the principles of the Communist outlook, and a labor and polytechnical training in accordance with the rising level of science and engineering, with due regard to the needs of society and to the abilities and inclinations of the students, as well as the moral, aesthetic, and physical education of a healthy rising generation.

In view of the rapid progress of science and engineering, the system of industrial and vocational training should be improved continuously, so that the production skills of those engaged in production may go hand in hand with their better general education in the social and natural sciences and with the acquisition of specialized knowledge of engineering, agronomy, medicine, and other fields.

B. *The Public Upbringing of Children of Preschool and School Age.*

The Communist system of public education is based on the public upbringing of children. The educational influence which the family exerts on children must be brought into ever greater harmony with their public upbringing.

The growing number of preschool institutions and boarding schools of different types will fully meet the requirements of all working people who wish to give their children of preschool and school age a public upbringing.

The importance of the school, which is to cultivate love of labor and of knowledge in children and to raise the younger generation in the spirit of Communist consciousness and morality, will increase. An honorable and responsible role in this respect falls to teachers.

C. The Creation of Conditions for High-Standard Instruction and Education of the Rising Generation.

The Party plans to carry out an extensive program for the construction of schools and cultural-education establishments to meet fully the needs of education and instruction. All schools will be housed in good buildings and will go over to a one-shift timetable. They will all have study workshops and chemical, physical, and other laboratories; rural schools will also have their own farming plots; large factories will have production training shops for schoolchildren. The largest facilities—cinema, radio, and television—will be widely used in schools.

For physical training and aesthetic education, all schools and extra-scholastic establishments will have gymnasiums, sports grounds, and facilities for the creative endeavor of children in music, painting, sculpture, etc. The network of sports schools, sports grounds, tourist camps, skiing centers, aquatic stations, swimming pools, and other sports facilities will be expanded in town and countryside.

D. Higher and Secondary Specialized Education.

In step with scientific and technical progress, higher and secondary specialized education, which must train highly skilled specialists with a broad theoretical and political background, will be expanded.

Shorter working hours and a considerable improvement in the standards of living of the entire population will provide everyone with an opportunity to receive a higher or secondary specialized education if he so desires. The number of higher and secondary specialized schools, evening and correspondence schools in particular, as well as higher schools at factories, agricultural institutes on large state farms, people's universities, studios, conservatories, etc., must be increased in all areas of the country, with support from the factories and from the trade unions and other social organizations. The plan is to considerably increase every year the number of students at higher and secondary specialized schools. Specialized education will be afforded to tens of millions of people.

(3) In the Field of Science.

Under the Socialist system of economy, scientific and technical progress enables man to employ the riches and forces of nature most effectively in the interest of the people, to discover new types of energy and to create new materials, to develop means of weather control, and to master outer space. Application of science in production becomes a decisive factor of rapid growth of the productive forces of society. Scientific progress and the introduction of scientific achievements into the economy will remain an object of special concern to the Party.

Most important are the following tasks:

A. Development of Theoretical Investigations.

The further perspectives of scientific and technical progress depend in the present period primarily on the achievements of the key branches of natural science. A high level of development in mathematics, physics, chemistry, and biology is a necessary condition for the advancement of the effectiveness of technical, medical, agricultural, and other sciences.

Theoretical investigations will be promoted to the utmost, primarily in such decisive fields of technical progress as electrification of the whole country, comprehensive mechanization and automation of production, the application of chemistry to the leading branches of the national economy, industrial uses of atomic energy, transport and communications. This applies to:

Studying the power and fuel balance of the country, finding the best ways and means of utilizing the natural sources of power, working out the scientific fundamentals of a single power grid, discovering new power sources and developing methods of direct conversion of thermal, nuclear, solar, and chemical energy into electric power, and solving problems related to control of thermonuclear reactions;

Working out the theory and principles of designing new machines, automatic and telemechanical systems, intensively developing machines, automatic and telemechanical systems, intensively developing radioelectronics, elaborating the theoretical foundations of computing, control, and information machines, and improving them technically;

Investigating chemical processes, working out new, more efficient technologies and creating inexpensive high-quality artificial and synthetic materials for all branches of the national economy; mechanical engineering, building, the manufacture of domestic goods and mineral fertilizers, and creating new preparations for use in medicine and agriculture;

Improving existing methods and devising new, more effective methods of prospecting minerals and making comprehensive use of natural wealth.

Big advances are to be made in the development of all the biological sciences in order successfully to solve medical problems and achieve further progress in agriculture. The main tasks to be solved by these sciences in the interests of mankind are: ascertainment of the nature of the phenomena of life, study and control of the vital processes, in particular, metabolism and heredity. Medicine must concentrate on discovering means of preventing and conquering cancer, virulent cardio-vascular and other dangerous diseases.

It is important to study and extensively use microorganisms in the economy and public health, among other things for the production of foods and fodder, vitamins, antibiotics and enzymes, and for the development of new agricultural techniques.

Artificial earth satellites and spaceships have, by enabling man to penetrate into outer space, provided great opportunities of discovering new natural phenomena and laws, and investigating the planets and the sun.

In the age of rapid scientific progress, the elaboration of the philosophical problems of modern natural science on the basis of dialectical materialism, the only scientific world outlook and method of cognition, becomes still more urgent.

There must be intensive development of research work in the social sciences, which constitute the scientific basis for the guidance of the development of society. Most important in this field is the study and theoretical generalization of the experience gained in Communist construction, investigation of the key objective laws governing the economic, political, and cultural progress of socialism and its development into communism, and elaboration of the problems of Communist education.

The task of economic science is to theoretically generalize new phenomena in the economic life of society, and to work out the national economic problems whose solution promotes successful Communist construction. Economists must concentrate on findng the most effective ways of utilizing material and labor resources in the economy, the best methods of planning and organizing industrial and agricultural production, and elaborating the principles of a rational distribution of the productive forces and of the technical and economic problems of Communist construction.

The investigation of the problems of world history and contemporary world development must disclose the law-governed process of mankind's advance toward communism, the change in the balance of forces in favor of socialism, the aggravation of the general crisis of capitalism, the break-up of the colonial system of imperialism and its consequences, and the upsurge of the national-liberation movement of the peoples.

It is important to study the historical experience of the Communist Party and the Soviet people, the objective laws of development of the world Socialist system and the world Communist and working-class movement.

The social sciences must continue to struggle with determination against bourgeois ideology, against right Socialist theory and practice, and against revisionism and dogmatism. They must uphold the purity of the principles of Marxism-Leninism.

B. *Ties between Science and Production.*

Close ties with the creative labor of the people and practical Communist construction are an earnest of a fruitful development of science.

In conformity with the demands of economic and cultural development, it is essential to extend and improve the network of research institutions, including those attached to the central bodies directing economic development and those attached to the economic councils, and the network of research laboratories and institutes at the major industrial plants and in farming areas, to develop research at higher educational establishments, to improve the geographical distribution of research institutions and higher educational establishments, and to insure the further development of science in all the union republics and major economic areas.

The research institutions must plan and co-ordinate their work in the most important trends of research in accordance with the plans of economic and cultural development. The role of the collective opinion of scientists in directing scientific work will increase. Free comradely discussions promoting the creative solution of pressing problems are an essential condition of scientific development.

The Party will adopt measures to extend and improve the material basis of science and to enlist the most capable creative forces in scientific pursuits.

It is a point of honor for Soviet scientists to consolidate the advanced positions which Soviet science has won in major branches of knowledge and to take a leading place in world science in all the key fields.

(4) In the Field of Cultural Development, Literature, and Art.

Cultural development during the full-scale construction of Communist society will constitute the closing stage of a great cultural revolution. At this stage, all the necessary ideological and cultural conditions will be created for the victory of communism.

The growth of the productive forces, progress in engineering and in the organization of production, increased social activity of the working people, development of the democratic principles of self-government, and a Communist reorganization of everyday life depend in very large measure on the cultural advancement of the population.

Communist culture, which will have absorbed and will develop all the best that has been created by world culture, will be a new, higher state in the cultural progress of mankind. It will embody the versatility and richness of the spiritual life of society, and the lofty ideals and humanism of the new world. It will be the culture of a classless society, a culture of the entire people, of all mankind.

A. All-Round Advancement of the Cultural Life of Society.

In the period of transition to communism, creative effort in all fields of culture becomes particularly fruitful, becomes accessible to all members of society. Soviet literature, music, painting, cinema and theater, and all the other arts, will attain higher standards in their ideological make-up and artistry. People's theaters, mass amateur art, technical invention, and other forms of creative endeavor by the people will become widespread. The amateurs will produce new gifted writers, artists, musicians, and actors. The development and enrichment of the arts are based on a combination of mass amateur endeavor and professional art.

The Party will work unremittingly to insure that literature, art, and culture flourish, that every individual is given full scope to apply his abilities, that the people are educated aesthetically and develop a fine artistic taste and cultural habits.

To provide the material basis for cultural development on a grand scale:

Book publishing and the press will be vigorously developed, and the printing and paper industries will be expanded accordingly;

There will be more libraries, lecture halls and reading rooms, theaters, clubs, houses of culture, and cinemas;

The country-wide radio diffusion network will be completed, television stations covering all industrial and agricultural areas will be built;

People's universities, people's theatrical companies, and other amateur cultural organizations will be widely developed.

A large network of scientific and technical laboratories and of art and cinema studios will be provided for the use of all who have the inclination and ability.

The Party considers it necessary to distribute cultural institutions evenly throughout the country in order gradually to bring the cultural standard of the countryside level with that of the town and achieve rapid cultural progress in all the newly developed areas.

High standards in urban development, in the architectural treatment and planning of towns and rural communities, industrial, cultural, and service premises and dwellings acquire great importance. Art will inspire labor, adorn life, and ennoble man.

B. *Enhancement of the Educational Role of Literature and Art.*

Soviet literature and art, imbued with optimism and dynamic Communist ideas, are great factors in ideological education and cultivate in Soviet people the qualities of builders of a new world. They must be a source of happiness and inspiration to millions of people, must express their will, their sentiments and ideas, must enrich them ideologically and educate them morally.

The highroad of literature and arts lies through the strengthening of links with the life of the people, through faithful and highly artistic depiction of the richness and versatility of Socialist reality, inspired and vivid portrayal of all that is new and genuinely Communist, and exposure of all that hinders the progress of society.

In the art of Socialist realism, which is based on the principles of partisanship and kinship with the people, bold pioneering in the artistic depiction of life goes hand in hand with the cultivation and development of the progressive traditions of world culture. Writers, artists, musicians, theatrical workers, and film makers will have better opportunities of displaying creative initiative and skill, using manifold forms, styles, and genres.

The Communist Party shows solicitude for the proper development of literature and art and their ideological and artistic standards, helps social organizations and literary and art associations in their activities.

C. *The Expansion of International Cultural Relations.*

The Party considers it necessary to expand the Soviet Union's cultural relations with the countries of the Socialist system and with all other countries for the purpose of pooling scientific and cultural achievements and of bringing about mutual understanding and friendship among the peoples.

VI. COMMUNIST CONSTRUCTION IN THE U.S.S.R. AND CO-OPERATION OF THE SOCIALIST COUNTRIES

The C.P.S.U. regards Communist construction in the Soviet Union as a component of the building of Communist society by the peoples of the entire world Socialist system.

The fact that Socialist revolutions took place at different times and that the economic and cultural levels of the countries concerned are dissimilar, predetermines the non-simultaneous completion of Socialist construction in those countries and their non-simultaneous entry into the period of the full-scale construction of communism. Nevertheless, the fact that the Socialist countries are developing as members of a single world Socialist system and utilizing the objective laws and advantages of this system enables them to reduce the time necessary for the construction of socialism and offers them the prospect of effecting the transition to communism more or less simultaneously, within one and the same historical epoch.

The first country to advance to communism facilitates and accelerates the advance of the entire world Socialist system to communism. In building communism, the peoples of the Soviet Union are breaking new roads for mankind, testing their correctness by their own experience, bringing out difficulties, finding ways and means of overcoming them, and selecting the best forms and methods of Communist construction.

Since the social forces—the working class, the co-operative peasantry, and the people's intelligentsia—and the social forms of economy (enterprises based on the two forms of Socialist property) in the Soviet Union and in the other Socialist countries are of one type, there will be common basic objective laws for Communist construction in the U.S.S.R. and in those countries, with due allowance made for the historical and national peculiarities of each country.

The construction of communism in the U.S.S.R. promotes the interests of every country of the Socialist community, for it increases the economic might and defense potential of the world Socialist camp and provides progressively favorable opportunities for the U.S.S.R. to expand its economic and cultural co-operation with the other Socialist countries and increase the assistance and support it renders them.

The C.P.S.U. maintains that the existing forms of economic relations between the Socialist countries—foreign trade, co-ordination of economic plans, and specialization and combination of production—will be developed and perfected more and more.

The Socialist system makes possible the abolition of the economic and cultural gap between countries inherited from capitalism, the more rapid development of the countries whose economy lagged behind under capitalism, the steady promotion of their economy and culture with the purpose of evening up the general level of development of the Socialist countries. This is insured by the advantages of the Socialist economic system and by equality in economic relations, by mutual assistance and the sharing of experience, specifically, by reciprocal exchanges of scientific and technological achievements and by co-ordinated research, by the joint construction of industrial projects and by co-operation in the development of natural resources. All-round fraternal co-operation benefits every Socialist country and the world Socialist system as a whole.

It is in the best interest of Socialist and Communist construction that each Socialist country combine the effort to strengthen and develop its national economy with the effort to expand economic co-operation of the Socialist camp as a whole. The development and leveling of the economy of the Socialist countries must be achieved primarily by every country fully using its internal resources and by improving the forms and methods of economic leadership, steadily applying the Leninist principles and methods of Socialist economic management, and making effective use of the advantages of the world Socialist system.

Material prerequisites for the construction of communism are created by the labor of the people of the country concerned and by its steadily growing contribution to the common cause—the consolidation of the Socialist system. This purpose is served by the application in Socialist construction of the law of planned, proportionate development; encouragement of the creative initiative and labor activity of the masses, continuous perfection of the system of the international division of labor through the co-ordination of national economic plans, specialization and combination of production within the world Socialist system on the basis of voluntary participation, mutual benefit and an over-all improvement of the level of science and engineering, the study of collective experience, the promotion of co-operation and fraternal mutual assistance, strict adherence to the principles of material incentive and the all-round promotion of moral stimuli to work for the good of society, control over the measure of labor and rate of consumption.

Socialism brings peoples and countries together. In the course of extensive co-operation in all economic, socio-political, and cultural fields, the common economic basis of world socialism will be consolidated.

The objective laws of the world Socialist system, the growth of the productive forces of Socialist society, and the vital interests of the people of the Socialist countries predetermine an increasing affinity of the various national economies. As Lenin foresaw, tendencies develop toward the future creation of a world Communist economy regulated by the victorious working people according to one single plan.

The C.P.S.U. and the Communist Parties of the other Socialist countries consider their tasks to be:

In the political field, the utmost strengthening of the world Socialist system, promotion of fraternal relations with all the Socialist countries on lines of complete equality and voluntary co-operation, political consolidation of the countries of the Socialist community in a joint struggle for universal peace and for the complete triumph of communism;

In the economic field, expansion of trade between the Socialist countries, development of the Socialist international division of labor, increasing co-ordination of long-range economic plans among the Socialist countries envisaging a maximum saving of social labor and an accelerated development of the world Socialist economy and the promotion of scientific and technical co-operation;

In the cultural field, steady development of all forms of cultural co-operation and intercourse between the peoples of the Socialist countries, exchanges of cultural achievements, encouragement of joint creative effort by scientists, writers, and artists, extensive measures to insure the mutual enrichment of national cultures and bringing the mode of life and the spiritual cast of the Socialist nations closer together.

The C.P.S.U. and the Soviet people will do everything in their power to support all the peoples of the Socialist community in the construction of socialism and communism.

VII. THE PARTY IN THE PERIOD OF FULL-SCALE COMMUNIST CONSTRUCTION

As a result of the victory of socialism in the U.S.S.R. and the consolidation of the unity of Soviet society the Communist Party of the working class has become the vanguard of the Soviet people, a Party of the entire people, and has extended its guiding influence to all spheres of social life. The Party is the brain, the honor, and the conscience of our epoch, of the Soviet people, which is effecting great revolutionary transformations. It looks keenly into the future and shows the people scientifically motivated roads along which to advance, arouses titanic energy in the masses, and leads them to the accomplishment of great tasks.

The period of full-scale Communist construction is characterized by a further enhancement of the role and importance of the Communist Party as the leading and guiding force of Soviet society.

Unlike all the preceding socio-economic formations, Communist society does not develop sporadically, but as a result of conscious and purposeful efforts of the masses led by the Marxist-Leninist Party. The Communist Party, which unites the foremost representatives of the working people and is closely connected with the masses, which enjoys unbounded authority among the people and understands the laws of social development, provides proper leadership in Communist construction as a whole, giving it an organized, planned, and scientifically based character.

The enhancement of the role of the Party in the life

of Soviet society in the new stage of its development derives from:

The growing scope and complexity of the tasks of Communist construction, which call for a higher level of political and organizational leadership;

The growth of the creative activity of the masses and the participation of fresh millions of working people in the administration of state affairs and of production;

The further development of Socialist democracy, the enhancement of the role of social organizations, the extension of the rights of the union republics and local organizations;

The growing importance of the theory of scientific communism, of its creative development and propaganda, the necessity for improving the Communist education of the working people and for the struggle to overcome the survivals of the past in the minds of people.

There must be a new, higher stage in the development of the Party itself and of its political, ideological, and organizational work that is in conformity with the full-scale building of communism. The Party will continuously improve the forms and methods of its work, so that its leadership of the masses, of the building of the material and technical basis of communism, of the development of society's spiritual life will keep pace with the growing requirements of the epoch of Communist construction.

Being the vanguard of the people building a Communist society, the Party must also be in the van in internal Party organization and serve as an example and model in developing the most advanced forms of public Communist self-government.

Undeviating observance of the Leninist standards of Party life and the principle of collective leadership, enhancement of the responsibility of Party organs and their personnel to the Party rank and file, promotion of the activity and initiative of all Communists and of their participation in elaborating and realizing the policy of the Party, and the development of criticism and self-criticism are a law of Party life.

This is an imperative condition of the ideological and organizational strength of the Party itself, of the greater unity and solidarity of Party ranks, of an all-round development of inner-Party democracy and the activization on this basis of all Party forces, and of the strengthening of ties with the masses.

The cult of the individual and the violations of collectivism in leadership, of inner-party democracy and Socialist legality arising out of it are incompatible with the Leninist principles of Party life. The cult of the individual belittles the role of the Party and the masses and hampers the development of the ideological life of the Party and the creative activity of the working people.

In order to effect the Leninist principle of collective leadership consistently, to insure a greater influx of fresh Party forces into the leading Party organs, to properly combine old and young cadres, and to rule out the possibility of an excessive concentration of power in the hands of individual officials and prevent cases of their getting beyond the control of the collective, the Party considers it necessary to carry out the following measures:

A. To introduce in practice a regular renewal, in certain proportions, of the members of all elected Party bodies—from primary organizations to the Central Committee, at the same time preserving continuity of leadership.

At all regular elections, not less than one-quarter of the members of the Central Committee of the C.P.S.U. and its Presidium shall be renewed. Presidium members shall, as a rule, be elected for not more than three successive terms. Particular Party workers may, by virtue of their generally recognized authority and high political, organizational, and other abilities be successively elected to the leading bodies for a longer period. In that case, the respective candidate is considered elected, provided not less than three-quarters of the votes are cast for him by secret ballot.

Members of the Central Committee of the Communist Parties of union republics, of territorial and regional committees shall be renewed by not less than one-third at each regular election, and those of area, city, and district committees, and the committees and bureaus of primary Party organizations shall be renewed by one-half. Furthermore, members of the leading Party bodies may be elected consecutively for not more than three terms, and secretaries of the primary Party organizations for not more than two consecutive terms.

A Party organization may, in consideration of the political and professional qualities of a person, elect him to a leading body for a longer period. In that case a candidate is considered elected if not less than three-quarters of the Communists attending vote for him.

Party members not re-elected to a leading Party body on the expiration of their term may be re-elected at subsequent elections.

A decision on removal from the Central Committee of the C.P.S.U. and other leading organs shall be adopted solely by secret ballot, and is valid when not less than two-thirds of the total membership of the body concerned vote in favor of the decision.

B. To extend the application of the elective principle and that of accountability in Party organizations at all levels, including Party organizations working under special conditions (army, navy).

C. To enhance the role of Party meetings, conferences, congresses, and plenary meetings of Party committees and other collective bodies. To provide favorable conditions for a free and businesslike discussion within the Party of questions concerning its policy and practical activities, for comradely discussions of controversial or insufficiently clear matters.

D. To reduce steadily the salaried Party staffs, enlisting Communists more extensively as non-salaried workers doing volunteer work.

E. To develop criticism and self-criticism to the utmost as a tried and tested method of work and a means of disclosing and rectifying errors and shortcomings and the proper education of cadres.

In the period of full-scale Communist construction the role and responsibility of every Party member will steadily increase. It is the duty of a Communist, in production, in social and personal life, to be a model in the struggle for the development and consolidation of Communist relations, and to observe the principles and norms of Communist morality. The C.P.S.U. will reinforce its ranks with the most politically conscious and active working people and keep pure and hold high the name of Communist.

The development of inner-Party democracy must insure greater activity among Communists and enhance their responsibility for the realization of the noble Communist ideals. It will promote the cultivation in them of an inner, organic need to behave and act in all matters in full accordance with the principles of the Party and its lofty aims.

The Party will continue to strengthen the unity and solidarity of its ranks, and to maintain the purity of Marxism-Leninism. The Party preserves such organizational guarantees as are provided by the rules of the C.P.S.U. against all manifestations of factionalism and group activity incompatible with Marxist-Leninist Party principles. The unshakable ideological and organizational unity of the Party is the most important source of its invincibility, a guarantee for the successful solution of the great tasks of Communist construction.

The people are the decisive force in the building of communism. The Party exists for the people, and it is in serving the people that it sees the purpose of its activity. To further extend and deepen the ties between the Party and the people is an imperative condition of success in the struggle for communism. The Party considers it its duty always to consult the working people on the major questions of home and foreign policy, to make these questions an object of nation-wide discussion, and to attract the more extensive participation of non-members in all its work. The more Socialist democracy develops, the broader and more versatile the work of the Party among the working people must be, and the stronger will be its influence among the masses.

The Party will in every way promote the extension and improvement of the work of the Soviets, the trade unions, the Y.C.L. and other mass organizations of working people, the development of the creative energy and initiative of the masses, and strengthen the unity and friendship of all the peoples of the U.S.S.R.

The C.P.S.U. is an integral part of the international Communist and working-class movement. The tried and tested Marxist-Leninist principles of proletarian internationalism will continue to be inviolable principles which the Party will follow undeviatingly.

The Communist Party of the Soviet Union will continue to strengthen the unity of the international Communist movement, to develop fraternal ties with all the Communist and workers' parties, and to co-ordinate its actions with the efforts of all the contingents of the world Communist movement, in the joint struggle against the danger of a new world war, for the interests of the working people, for peace, democracy, and socialism.

*　　*　　*

Such is the program of work for Communist construction which the Communist Party of the Soviet Union has mapped out.

The achievement of communism in the U.S.S.R. will be the greatest victory mankind has ever won throughout its long history. Every new step made toward the bright peaks of communism inspires the working masses in all countries, renders immense moral support to the struggle for the liberation of all peoples from social and national oppression, and brings closer the triumph of Marxism-Leninism on a world-wide scale.

When the Soviet people will enjoy the blessings of communism, new hundreds of millions of people on earth will say: "We are for communism." It is not through war with other countries, but by the example of a more perfect organization of society, by rapid progress in developing the productive forces, the creation of all conditions for the happiness and well-being of man, that the ideas of communism win the minds and hearts of the masses.

The forces of social progress will inevitably grow in all countries, and this will assist the builders of communism.

The Party proceeds from the Marxist-Leninist proposition: the people are the makers of history, and communism is a creation of the people, of its energy and intelligence. The victory of communism depends on the people, and communism is built for the people. Every Soviet man brings the triumph of communism nearer by his labor. The successes of Communist construction spell abundance and a happy life for all, and enhance the might, prestige, and glory of the Soviet Union.

The Party is confident that the Soviet people will accept the new program of the C.P.S.U. as their own vital cause, as the greatest purpose of their life, and as a banner of nation-wide struggle for the building of communism. The Party calls on all Communists, on the entire Soviet people—all workingmen and women, kolkhoz farmers and workers by brain—to apply their energies to the successful fulfillment of the historic tasks set forth in this program.

Under the tried and tested leadership of the Communist Party, under the banner of Marxism-Leninism, the Soviet people have built socialism.

Under the leadership of the Party, under the banner of Marxism-Leninism, the Soviet people will build Communist society.

The Party solemnly proclaims: the present generation of Soviet people shall live under communism!

INDEX

DUTTON PAPERBACKS